ANNUAL EGYPTOLOGICAL BIBLIOGRAPHY
BIBLIOGRAPHIE ÉGYPTOLOGIQUE ANNUELLE

INTERNATIONAL ASSOCIATION OF EGYPTOLOGISTS
ASSOCIATION INTERNATIONALE DES ÉGYPTOLOGUES

ANNUAL EGYPTOLOGICAL BIBLIOGRAPHY

BIBLIOGRAPHIE ÉGYPTOLOGIQUE ANNUELLE

1968

COMPILED BY/COMPOSÉE PAR

JAC. J. JANSSEN

LEIDEN
E. J. BRILL
1973

The editor acknowledges the financial contributions for collecting the material for this volume kindly given by the following institutions:

Brown University, Providence, R.I.,
Deutsches Archäologisches Institut, Berlin-Cairo,
Durham University, Durham,
Egypt Exploration Society, London,
Göttinger Akademie der Wissenschaften, Göttingen,
Heidelberger Akademie der Wissenschaften, Heidelberg,
The Metropolitan Museum of Art, New York,
Museum of Fine Arts, Boston, Mass.,
Oosters Genootschap in Nederland, Leiden,
The Oriental Institute, The University of Chicago, Chicago, Ill.,
Schweizerisches Institut für Ägyptische Bauforschung und Altertumskunde, Cairo,
University of Liverpool, Liverpool,
The University Museum, The University of Pennsylvania, Philadelphia, Pa.

Adres van de redacteur / Address of the editor
Addresse du rédacteur / Anschrift des Schriftleiters:

Dr. Jac. J. JANSSEN

Nederlands Instituut voor het Nabije Oosten
Noordeindsplein 4-6
LEIDEN

ISBN 90 04 03649 0

Copyright 1973 by E. J. Brill, Leiden, Netherlands

All rights reserved. No part of this book may be reproduced or translated in any form, by print, photoprint, microfilm, microfiche or any other means without written permission from the publisher

PRINTED IN THE NETHERLANDS

TABLE OF CONTENTS

List of abbreviations VII
Alphabetical list of authors and titles. I
Necrologies 198

LIST OF ABBREVIATIONS

1) *periodicals*, Festschriften *and serials*:

Aegyptus: Aegyptus. Rivista Italiana di Egittologia e di Papirologia, Milano 48 (1968) = Raccolta di scritti in onore di Aristide Calderini.
Address: Largo A. Gemelli 1-20123 Milano, Italia.

AfO: Archiv für Orientforschung. Internationale Zeitschrift für die Wissenschaft vom Vorderen Orient, Graz.
Address: Ernst Weidner, Goethestraße 43, (A-8010) Graz, Österreich.

AJA: American Journal of Archaeology, [New York] 72 (1968).
Address: General Secretary, Archaeological Institute of America, 260 West Broadway, New York, N.Y. 10013, U.S.A.

Antiquity: Antiquity. A Quarterly Review of Archaeology, [Cambridge] 42 (1968).
Address: W. Heffer & Sons Ltd., 104 Hills Road, Cambridge, CB2 1LW, Great Britain.

Archaeology: Archaeology. A Magazine Dealing with the Antiquity of the World, [New York] 21 (1968).
Address: Archaeological Institute of America, 260 West Broadway, New York, N.Y. 10013, U.S.A.

ASAE: Annales du Service des Antiquités de l'Égypte, Le Caire 60 (1968).
Address: Service des Antiquités, Musée Égyptien, Le Caire, Égypte (R.A.U.).

BIE: Bulletin de l'Institut d'Égypte, [Le Caire] 45 (session 1963-1964), 1968.
Address: Les Éditions Universitaires d'Égypte, Alaa Eddin El Shiaty and Co., 41, Sherif Pasha Street, Cairo, Egypt (U.A.R.).

BIFAO: Bulletin de l'Institut français d'Archéologie orientale, Le Caire 66 (1968).
Address: Imprimerie de l'Institut français d'Archéologie orientale, 37 Rue El-Cheikh Aly Youssef (ex-rue Mounira), Le Caire, Égypte (R.A.U.).

BiOr: Bibliotheca Orientalis, Leiden.
Address: Noordeindsplein 4-6, Leiden, Nederland.

Booklist: Booklist [of] the Society for Old Testament Study, 1968.
Address: D. R. Ap-Thomas, Esq., Llansadwrn, Menai Bridge, Anglesey, Great Britain.

BSFE: Bulletin de la Société française d'égyptologie, [Paris], N° 51 (Mars 1968), N° 52 (Juillet 1968).
Address: Mme F. Le Corsu, Cabinet d'Égyptologie, Collège de France, 11, place Marcelin-Berthelot, Paris 5e, France.

CdE: Chronique d'Égypte. Bulletin périodique de la Fondation égyptologique Reine Élisabeth, Bruxelles XLIII, N⁰ 85-86 (1968); rev. *Sefarad* 29 (1969), 161-164 ([B.] Ce[lada]).
Address: Fondation égyptologique "Reine Élisabeth", Musées Royaux d'Art et d'Histoire, Parc du Cinquantenaire, B 1040-Bruxelles, Belgique.

Études et Travaux II: Études et Travaux II, Warszawa, PWN-Éditions scientifiques de Pologne, 1968 = Travaux du centre d'archéologie méditerranéenne de l'académie polonaise des sciences sous la direction de K. Michałowski. Tome 6/ Studia i Prace II, Warszawa, PWN-Państwowe wydawnistwo naukowe, 1968 = Prace zakładu archeologii śródziemnomorskiej polskiej akademii nauk. Redaktor K. Michałowski. Tom 6 (19.7 × 24.7 cm; 323 p., numerous ill., fig., plans); rev. *Orientalia* 38 (1969), 595.

Festschrift Schott: Festschrift für Siegfried Schott zu seinem 70. Geburtstag am 20. August 1967. Herausgegeben von Wolfgang Helck, Wiesbaden, Otto Harrassowitz, 1968(17.9 × 24.9 cm; [VII +] 131 p., 2 loose p. with corrections, 15 fig., 4 pl., frontispiece); rev. *BiOr* 26 (1969), 188-189 (H. de Meulenaere); *Mundus* 6 (1970), 112-114 (Hellmut Brunner); *RdE* 21 (1969), 164-165 (Yvan Koenig); *ZDMG* 120 (1970), 1971, 317-322 (Dietrich Wildung). Pr. DM 38.—

Forschungen und Berichte: Forschungen und Berichte. Archäologische Beiträge, Berlin 10 (1968); at head of title: Staatliche Museen zu Berlin.
Address: Akademie-Verlag GmbH, Leipzigerstraße 3-4, 108 Berlin.

JAOS: Journal of the American Oriental Society, New Haven, Connecticut 88 (1968).
Address: American Oriental Society, 329 Sterling Memorial Library, Yale Station, New Haven, Connecticut 06520, U.S.A.

JARCE: Journal of the American Research Center in Egypt, Princeton, New Jersey 7 (1968); rev. *BiOr* 28 (1971), 36-37 (Luc Limme).
Address: J. J. Augustin Publisher, Locust Valley, New York 11560, U.S.A.

JEA: The Journal of Egyptian Archaeology, London 54 (1968); rev. *Sefarad* 29 (1969), 138-141 ([B.] Ce[lada]).
Address: Honorary Treasurer of the Egypt Exploration Society, 2-3 Doughty Mews, London, WC1N 2PG, Great Britain.

JEOL: Jaarbericht van het Vooraziatisch-Egyptisch Genootschap Ex Oriente Lux, Leiden [VII], N⁰ 20 (1967-1968), 1968; rev. *Sefarad* 29 (1969), 129 ([B.] Ce [lada]).
Address: Noordeindsplein 4-6, Leiden, Nederland.

JNES: Journal of Near Eastern Studies, Chicago, Illinois 27 (1968); rev. *Sefarad* 29 (1969), 142-143 ([B.] Ce[lada]) (nr. 1); *ZAW* 81 (1969), 112-113 (H. W. Hoffmann).
Address: University of Chicago Press, 5801 Ellis Avenue, Chicago, Illinois 60637, U.S.A.

Kêmi: Kêmi. Revue de philologie et d'archéologie égyptiennes et coptes, Paris 18 (1968).
Address: Librairie Orientaliste Paul Geuthner, 12 rue Vavin, Paris 6ᵉ, France.

MDAIK: Mitteilungen des Deutschen Archäologischen Instituts Abteilung Kairo, Wiesbaden 23 (1968).
Address: Verlag Philipp von Zabern, Mainz/Rhein, Bundesrepublik Deutschland.

MIO: Mitteilungen des Instituts für Orientforschung, Berlin 14 (1968).
Address: Akademie-Verlag GmbH, Leipzigerstraße 3-4, 108 Berlin.

Mundus: Mundus. A Quarterly Review of German Research Contributions on Asia, Africa and Latin America. Arts and Science, Stuttgart.
Address: Wissenschaftliche Verlagsgesellschaft mbH, Postfach 40, 7000 Stuttgart 1, Bundesrepublik Deutschland.

Muséon. Le Muséon. Revue d'études orientales. Tijdschrift voor Oriëntalisme, Louvain/ Leuven 81 (1968).
Address: Le Muséon. "Imprimerie Orientaliste", B.P. 41, 3000 Louvain, Belgique.

OLZ: Orientalistische Literaturzeitung, Berlin.
Address: Akademie-Verlag GmbH, Leipzigerstraße 3-4, 108 Berlin.

OMRO: Oudheidkundige Mededelingen uit het Rijksmuseum van Oudheden te Leiden (Nuntii ex museo antiquario Leidensi), Leiden 49 (1968).
Address: Rijksmuseum van Oudheden, Rapenburg 28, Leiden, Nederland.

Oriens Antiquus: Oriens Antiquus. Rivista del Centro per le Antichità e la Storia dell'Arte del Vicino Oriente, Roma 7 (1968).
Address: Via Caroncini 19, Roma, Italia.

Orientalia: Orientalia. Commentarii trimestres a facultate studiorum orientis antiqui pontificii instituti biblici in lucem editi in urbe, [Roma], Nova Series 37 (1968); rev. *ZAW* 81 (1969), 115 (H. W. Hoffmann).
Address: Pontificium Institutum Biblicum, Piazza del Pilotta 35, I-00187 Roma, Italia.

Probleme: Probleme der koptischen Literatur. Herausgegeben vom Institut für Byzantinistik der Martin-Luther-Universität Halle-Wittenberg. Bearbeitet von Peter Nagel [Tagungsmaterialien der II. Koptologischen Arbeitskonferenz des Institutes für Byzantinistik 12. und 13. Dezember 1966. Wiss. Redaktion Peter Nagel, Halle, Martin-Luther-Universität Halle-Wittenberg, 1968] (16.7 × 24.2 cm; 238 p., 6 ill.) = Wissenschaftliche Beiträge der Martin-Luther-Universität Halle-Wittenberg. 1968/1 (K 2); rev. *Mundus* 5 (1969), 313-314 (Hellmut Brunner).

Proceedings: Proceedings of the Twenty-Sixth International Congress of Orientalists. New Delhi. 4-10th January, 1964, Volume II, New Delhi, Organising Committee XXVI International Congress of Orientalists, 1968 (22.3 × 28.5 cm; [VIII +] 254 p., 2 ill., 1 map, 18 pl.); rev. *Archiv Orientální* 39 (1971), 360 (O. Klíma); *Orientalia* 39 (1970), 205-206 (R. Caplice).

RdE: Revue d'Égyptologie, Paris 20 (1968).
Address: Librairie C. Klincksieck, 11, rue de Lille, Paris 7ᵉ, France.

Rivista: Rivista degli Studi Orientali, Roma 43 (1968).
Address: Dott. Giovanni Bardi editore, Salita de crescenzi 16, Roma, Italia.

The Role of the Phoenicians: The Role of the Phoenicians in the Interaction of Mediterranean Civilisations. Papers Presented to the Archaeological Symposium at the American University of Beirut; March, 1967. Edited by William A. Ward, [Beirut, The American University of Beirut, 1968] (19.6 × 28.4 cm; [X +] 152 p., 9 maps, 4 plans, 4 ill., 5 fig. and 40 pl.); series: Centennial Publications; rev. *Berytus* 18 (1969), 169-172 (K. A. Kitchen); *BiOr* 26 (1969), 149 (anonymous); *Orientalia* 40 (1971), 109-115 (Brian Peckham); *The Palestine Exploration Quarterly* 101 (1969), 125 (F.F. B[ruce]). Pr. casebound $ 8, paperbound $ 7.

Sefarad: Sefarad. Revista del Instituto Arias Montano de Estudios Hebraicos y Oriente Proximo, Madrid-Barcelona.

IV Сессия по Древнему Востоку: IV Сессия по Древнему Востоку. 5-10 Февраля 1968 г. Тезисы докладов, Москва, Издательство восточной литературы, 1968 (14.5 × 21.5 cm; 106 p.). At head of title: Академия Наук СССР. Ленинградское отделение Института Народов Азии.

The Joseph Smith Egyptian Papyri: The Joseph Smith Egyptian Papyri. Translations and Interpretations = *Dialogue. A Journal of Mormon Thought*, Dialogue Foundation, Stanford, California, Vol. 3 No. 3 (Autumn 1968), 67-105.

ВДИ: Вестник Древней Истории, Москва 1 (103)- 4 (106), 1968.
Address: Москва В-36, ул. Дмитрия Ульянова. Д. 19, Комн. 237, Институт всеобщей Истории, АН СССР.

ZÄS: Zeitschrift für ägyptische Sprache und Altertumskunde, Berlin 95,1 1968.
Address: Akademie-Verlag GmbH, Leipzigerstraße 3-4, 108 Berlin.

ZAW: Zeitschrift für die alttestamentliche Wissenschaft, Berlin.
Address: Walter de Gruyter & Co., Berlin 30.

ZDMG: Zeitschrift der Deutschen Morgenländischen Gesellschaft, Wiesbaden 118 (1968), 1968; rev. *ZAW* 81 (1969), 122 ([G. Fohrer]).
Address: Franz Steiner Verlag GMBH, Bahnhofstrasse 39, Postfach 743, 62 Wiesbaden, Bundesrepublik Deutschland.

2) *other abbreviations*:

AEB:	*Annual Egyptological Bibliography/Bibliographie égyptologique annuelle.*	m:	metre(s).
		p.:	page(s)
		pl.:	plate(s).
		publ.:	publication(s).
cfr:	*confer*, compare	pr.:	price.
cm:	centimetre(s)	rev.:	review *or* summary.
col.:	column	⌐⌐:	above a numeral, this hieroglyph indicates a monograph.
etc.:	*et cetera.*		
fig.:	figure(s).		
ill.:	illustration(s).		
km:	kilometre(s).		

ALPHABETICAL LIST OF AUTHORS AND TITLES

68001 ABD EL-RAZIK, Mahmud, Study on Nectanebo Ist in Luxor Temple and Karnak, *MDAIK* 23 (1968), 156-159, with 8 pl.

On the construction activities of this king. The author discusses the lion sphinx allée (bordered by walls and planted with trees and flowers), a pylon and a stela.
M. Heerma van Voss

ABDEL-HAMID, Fouad, see our number 68021.

68002 ABOU GHAZI, Dia', Bewailing the King in the Pyramid Texts, *BIFAO* 66 (1968), 157-164.

The author lists, and partly translates, several passages from the *Pyramid Texts* that deal with the various stages of bewailing the dead king, and points out that they represent glorification as well as simple mourning. *Dieter Mueller*

68003 ABOU-GHAZI, Dia', Alexandre Piankoff (1897-1966), *CdE* XLIII, N° 85 (1968), 104-110.

Obituary notice with bibliography.
Compare our number 67645.

68004 ABOU GHAZI, Dia', Two New Monuments Inscribed in Hieroglyphics from Ptolemaic Egypt, *BIFAO* 66 (1968), 165-169, with 2 fig. and 1 pl.

The author publishes a stela of Ptolemy VIII discovered at Sakha in 1963, and a lapislazuli tablet with the names of Cleopatra and her son Caesarion that presumably came from a foundation deposit. *Dieter Mueller*

68005 EL-ACHIERY, H., M. ALY et M. DEWACHTER, Le speos d'el-Lessiya. Cahier II. Plans d'architecture. Dessins-index, Le Caire, Centre de documentation et d'études sur l'ancienne Égypte, 1968 (21 × 27 cm; [I +] 11 p., 1 folding table [= p. 10], 43 pl. [3 folding] including 1 folding plan). At head of title: Collection scientifique.

The text gives a list of the drawings, one of the various scenes, and indexes to divinities, royal and geographical names found in the texts, as well as a concordance between part I and the present volume. Plates I-VIII contain drawings of the architecture of the temple, plates IX-XLIII of its reliefs, of which the photographs are published in cahier I (see our number 68167).

68006 el ACHIERY, H., P. BARGUET et M. DEWACHTER, Le temple d'Amada. Cahier I. Architecture, Le Caire, Centre de documentation et d'études sur l'ancienne Égypte, 1967 (21 × 26.8 cm; portefolio, containing IX + 7 + 14 loose p., 9 fig. [including plans] and 48 loose pl. [including maps and plans]). At head of title: Collection scientifique.

The General Introduction by Ahmed Badawi and Ch. Desroches-Noblecourt, in French and Arabic, deals with the plan of the entire publication in 6 volumes.
On p. 1-8 the authors of the present volume briefly discuss the various architectural parts of the building.
The plates contain 3 maps, 2 general plans and 19 plans of details (pl. 20 will be included into part 6); 13 pl. with 41 photographs and 1 drawing, representing the temple as it has been (drawings by Norden, Gau and Monneret de Villard) and in its state previous to the replacement, with several details. The last group of plates, numbered a-m, contain drawings of various sections.
See also our numbers 68021, 68059, 68060 and 68118.

el ACHIERY, H., see also our number 68167.

68007 ADAMS, W. Y., Continuity and Change in Nubian Cultural History, *Sudan Notes and Records*, Khartoum 48 (1967), 1-32, with 4 fig.

The study contains a provisional evaluation of the results of the Nubian archaeological salvage program.
The author sketches the established theory of Nubian cultural history as it was generally accepted previous to the present campaign. He also indicates the points on which these views have now to be altered, referring to a great many recent articles and books. In two diagrams the differences between old and new conceptions are schematized. The most important improvement in our understanding of Nubian history appears to concern relationships between the various cultures; formerly change was mainly explained as the result of immigration of new peoples and races, whereas now continuity appears to be the predominant feature.
The author points out that the main sources of change have been the fluctuation of the Nile level (cfr fig. 4), by which the long hiatus in Lower Nubia during the last millennium B.C. will be explained, and the ever renewed influence of ancient Egypt.
Sources of continuity have been: environment, proximity of Egypt, and particularly the influence of Africa, which appears *e.g.* in the re-emergence again and again of bed burial and hand-made pottery.

For solution of problems still evident in Nubian history the author points to Upper Nubia.

Though the Nubian campaign intends to stop finally at Dal we should go further South, at least to Khartoum.

68008 ADAMS, William Y., Invasion, Diffusion, Evolution?, *Antiquity* 42 (1968), 194-215, with 1 fig.

Important theoretical study about the diffusionist, evolutionist and invasionalist theories of history, and their application to the history of Nubia.

Apart from summarizing the theories the author discusses the various types of evidence which may bear upon the question of continuity or change in the population of Nubia: cultural (pottery and burial customs), linguistic, racial, and indirect evidence (*e.g.* stratigraphy, site distribution, and chronology). In three tables the archaeological evidence discussed is summarized.

The author states as his conclusion: "There is clearly no need to invoke wholesale migration to account for any of the cultural transformations in Nubian history."

Cfr our preceding number.

68009 ADAMS, William Y., Progress Report on Nubian Pottery. I. The Native Wares. II. The Imported Wares, Lexington, Kentucky, [1968] (21 × 27.5 cm; part I: [II +] 66 p., 6 pl. containing diagrams; part II: [II +] 66 p., 3 pl. containing diagrams).

This study in typescript contains two articles intended for publication in *Kush* 15 and 16, constituting the sequel to our numbers 62007 and 64003.

Part I contains a detailed analytical study of Ancient Nubian pottery. After some introductory remarks the categories of classification are discussed. There follows a study of one Meroitic and eight Nubian groups of wheel-made wares, and their general evolutionary tendencies. The last pages are devoted to hand-made ware and its evolution.

Part II deals with the imported wares, which are in general technologically superior but stylistically inferior to indigenous wares. There are distinguished four families: the wares from the Aswân factories, from the Middle and the Lower Egyptian families, and the Mameluke wares, each family being divided into several groups according to the period during which they are made. The author also discusses the relationship between Egyptian and Nubian pottery (p. 24-32), the origin of Meroitic industry (33-38), the origin of the classic Christian style (38-39), the role of the Aswân wares in the later Classic Period and the end of the Nubian wheel-made industry (43-44). At the end reflections of change and causality.

Xerox copies of these studies are obtainable from the author, University of Kentucky, Department of Anthropology, Lexington, Kentucky, 40506, U.S.A.

68010 ADAMS, William Y., Settlement Pattern in Microcosm: The Changing Aspect of a Nubian Village during Twelve Centuries, *in*: K. C. Chang, *Settlement Archaeology*, Palo Alto, California, National Press Books, [1968], 174-207, with 7 plans.

This is an attempt to define the changing relationship of man and environment in ancient Nubia, as evidenced by changes that took place in the village of Meinarti, on an island at the foot of the second cataract, where excavations revealed some 20 occupation levels, from 200 A.D. to the end of the Christian period (cfr our number 65002).

The author gives a survey of the geography and history of Nubia, and of the village itself. There are two constants: the ethnic composition of the population and the location of the village. Its architectural history resolves itself into seven phases, each represented by two or three levels and each exhibiting a distinct development trend, such as the helter-skelter growth of phase 2 and the battle against the rising river in phase 3.

The author discusses the seven phases and studies the influence of the determining factors, natural as well as cultural.

For a review of the article by Gordon R. Willey see the same work, p. 222.

68011 ADRIANI, Achille, Evaristo Breccia, *Studi Etruschi*, Firenze Serie 2, 36 (1968), 517-519.

Obituary notice.

68012 AKURGAL, Ekrem, The Birth of Greek Art. The Mediterranean and The Near East. Translated by Wayne Dynes, London, Methuen, [1968] (17.7 × 22.2 cm; 258 p., map, 171 fig. [including 8 plans], 68 ill. [1 folding, 44 in colour], colour ill. on box) = Art of the World. A Series of Regional Histories of the Visual Arts, 26.

In this book dealing with the connections between Neo-Assyrian, Aramean, Neo-Hittite, Phoenician and Syrian arts and early Greek art, Egypt is sometimes dealt with since it influenced some aspects of Near Eastern art styles, particularly the Phoenician-Syrian (p. 143-154). For direct influence on early Greek art (kouroi) see p. 176.

Index on p. 248-258.
We did not see the American edition and the original German edition (Baden-Baden, 1966). L. M. J. Zonhoven

68013 ALDRED, Cyril, Akhenaten. Pharaoh of Egypt — a new study, London, Thames and Hudson, [1968] (19.4 × 25.3 cm; 272 p., 17 colour ill., 120 ill., 6 fig.); series: New Aspects of Antiquity. Edited by Sir Mortimer Wheeler; rev. *Biblia Revuo* 5 (1969), 119-122 (Donald Broadribb); *CdE* XLIV, N° 88 (1969), 278-280 (Winifred Needler); *JARCE* 8 (1969-1970), 101-102 (Alan R. Schulman); *JEA* 57 (1971), 217-219 (K. A. Kitchen); *The Times Literary Supplement* 68 (1969), 757. Pr. £ 4/4 s.

Although written for the general reader and, therefore without critical footnotes (a few notes on p. 262-264) the study presents in many respects a new picture of the Amarna Period, as the Preface of Sir Mortimer Wheeler indicates.

In the Introduction Aldred relates the history of our knowledge about Akhenaton, followed in Part I by *The Context*. In the first four chapters the author attempts to outline the main features of history and civilisation previous to the Amarna Age, and those of the reign of Amenophis III in particular, while in chapter V the orthodox conceptions concerning the period of Akhnaton are presented.

Part II is devoted to *The Problems*. Chapter VI deals with familial relationships, stressing the importance of the family of Yuya and Tuyu, to which *i.a.* belong queen Tiye and Eye, the later pharaoh and probably the father of Nefertiti and Mutnodjem. As for the family of Akhnaton himself, the author suggests that Nefertiti died about year 12, that both Smenkhkare and Tutankhamon were sons of Amenophis III and Tiye, and that the coregency of the former falls within the reign of Akhnaton.

In chapter VII Aldred indicates various reasons for the assumption of a coregency of 12 years between Amenophis III and Akhnaton (the author did not yet know the study of Redford, our number 67465).

Chapter VIII discusses the pathology of Akhnaton. Though his later statues may exhibit the physical characteristics of a patient suffering from Fröhlich's syndrome, and in that case Amenophis III may have been the actual father of Nefertiti's daughters, the proofs for such a theory are not decisive.

Chapter IX deals with the Valley Tomb No 55, its discovery and its occupants. The mummy there found has now been proved to be that of Smenkhkare; the bulk of the equipment was that of Tiye; both may have been buried in this tomb, together with Akhnaton; the tomb was rifled in the Amarna Period.

Chapter X is devoted to the "heresy" of Akhnaton. Aldred demonstrates that it was not so much a revolution as well a return, gradually developed, to some conceptions of the Old Kingdom. There was not such a thing as a struggle between Church and State, nor any official or unofficial opposition to the king.

The *Amarna Letters* are the subject of chapter XI. The timespan covered by them appears to be about 10 years, which strengthens the supposition of a long coregency between Amenophis III and his son.

Part III, *The Synthesis*, contains in two chapters Aldred's picture of the period and a survey of the Amarna Period aftermath, in which he particularly points to the economic chaos caused by Akhnaton's forced concentration on the Aton cult. In an *Epilogue* the author demonstrates former theories of Akhnaton as a revolutionary to be un-historical. The illustrations, which are accompanied by extensive explanations and which constitute an integral part of the text, show among much that is usual a few less known objects (*e.g.* the block-statue of a certain Ay from the Brooklyn Museum, ill. 66).

A select bibliography to the various topics on p. 265-266, an index on p. 269-272.

We did not see the German version, *Echnaton. Gott und Pharao Ägyptens*, Bergisch Gladbach, 1968 (pr. DM 44), translated by J. Rehork.

68014 ALDRED, Cyril, Old Kingdom Art in Ancient Egypt, London, Alec Tiranti Ltd, 1968 (12.9 × 19 cm; VIII + 40 p., 71 fig. on 64 pl., map); rev. *BiOr* 26 (1969), 193 (Elisabeth Staehelin).   Pr. bound 12 s.

Reprint of our number 713 with a few excisions, some adjustments in the bibliography, and an addition to the preface.

68015 ALDRED, Cyril, Two Monuments of the Reign of Ḥoremḥeb, *JEA* 54 (1968), 100-106, with 5 fig. and 1 pl.

A pink granite block in the Royal Scottish Museum (N° 1965.318) and said to have come from Bubastis has possibly been used as a weight although this was not its original purpose. It probably formed part of a miniature obelisk and is inscribed with the names of Ḥoremḥeb and part of the titulary of Ramses I, thus perhaps suggesting a coregency between the two kings.

The remains of an alabaster statue in the N.E. corner of the forecourt of the temple of Dendera once described as of

Mutemwiya, is probably really a portrait of queen Mutnodjme, wife of Ḥoremḥeb, and the writer suggests that the epithets used on the back pillar point to some relationship with Nefertiti. *E. Uphill*

68016 ALLAM, S., Sind die nichtliterarischen Schriftostraka brouillons?, *JEA* 54 (1968), 121-128.

In this study the author discusses the question as to whether the non-literary written ostraka are draughts intended only to serve as designs for clear writing on papyrus. He cites many examples from Ramesside times, giving particular attention to those from Deir el-Medîneh. *E. Uphill*

ALLIOT, Maurice, see our number 68614.

68017 ALMAGRO BASCH, Martin y Martin ALMAGRO GORBEA, Estudios de Arte Rupestre Nubio. I. Yacimientos situados en la orilla oriental del Nilo, entre Nag Kolorodna y Kars (sic!) Ibrim (Nubia egipcia), Madrid, Ministerio de Asuntos Exteriores, Direccion de Relaciones Culturales, Ministerio de Educacion Nacional, Direccion General de Bellas Artes, [1968] (21 × 26.5 cm; 327 p., 2 maps, 285 fig., 121 ill. on 50 pl.) = Comite Español de Excavaciones Arqueologicas en el Extranjero. Memorias de la Mision Arqueologica en Egipto, 10; rev. *Archiv Orientální* 39 (1971), 84-91 (Fr. Váhala).

Aufgenommen wurden die Felsbilder folgender Gebiete: Nag Kolorodna, Nag Gafur, Khor Zurqan, Khor Agabed Magaqya, Khor Oshiya, Khor Kilobersa, Khor Madik, Khor Warga, Khor Agabed Khiul, Khor Shawashab, Khor Aquiba, Nag Migrab, Khor Ghattas und die Bilder von Qasr Ibrîm-Süd. Es handelt sich zumeist um Menschen- und Tierdarstellungen; bei den Haustier-Abbildungen überwiegt das Rind. Die Elefantendarstellungen heben deutlich die Eigentümlichkeiten der afrikanischen Spezies hervor. Besonders interessant ist vielleicht die eigenartige Darstellung eines Streitwagens (Fig. 16), ein römischer (?) Kriegerkopf mit Helm und Backenbart (Fig. 198) und die Abbildung eines Menschen, der anscheinend die bekannte Hörnerkrone der christlichen Periode trägt (Fig. 263). Zu den ägyptischen Darstellungen und Inschriften vgl. man unsere Nr. 66397. Die Druckfehler in außer-spanischen Eigennamen wirken sehr störend; Kars wird durchgehend statt Kasr (richtiger: Qasr) verwendet. *Inge Hofmann*

ALMAGRO GORBEA, Martin, see our preceding number.

68018 ALTENMÜLLER, Hartwig, Zur Überlieferung des Amduat, *JEOL* VII, 20 (1967-1968), 1968, 27-42.

La version ancienne de l'Amdouat ne comprenait pas de nom royal. Celui-ci fut introduit parfois en pleine phrase: il n'entraîne de changement grammatical qu'en un seul cas. Dans les trois premières Heures, le nom peut s'intercaler, mais le plus souvent il remplace un suffixe verbal. Le décorateur de tombe l'insère en outre aux endroits vides, ceci depuis le temps du vizir User. L'expression *gm wš* ne signale pas forcément des lacunes accidentelles (voir déjà notre n° 61351). Les coupures interviennent souvent au milieu d'un mot, et leur place grammaticale n'a rien de fortuit. La plupart de ces "lacunes" peuvent s'expliquer par un projet d'insertion: l'archétype aurait porté un vide préparé par omission de mots. La meilleure tradition de l'Amdouat illustré apparaît chez U et Th I, dont découlent R VI et R IX; celle de la XIXe dynastie dépendait d'un même modèle. Elles doivent s'être différenciées bien avant Thoutmosis Ier. Par ailleurs, la "Version abrégée" de l'Amdouat présente des passages parallèles plus complets, qui permettent de déceler des omissions dans toute la version illustrée. Il conviendrait de dater du Moyen Empire l'œuvre originelle. *J. Custers*

68019 ALTENMÜLLER, Hartwig, Zwei neue Exemplare des Opfertextes der 5. Dynastie, *MDAIK* 23 (1968), 1-8.

Sequel to our number 67014.
The author deals with two more copies, the former in Pabasa's Theban tomb 279 (Saitic), the latter published by Vandier in our number 68605. *M. Heerma van Voss*

68020 ALTENMÜLLER-KESTING, Brigitte, Reinigungsriten im ägyptischen Kult, Hamburg, 1968 (14.8 × 21.1 cm; [VI +] 228 p., 5 fig., 4 pl.).

Thesis for a doctor's degree in Hamburg, consisting of two parts. In Part A the author studies the purification rites in the cult of the dead: the offering ritual and the ritual of the Opening of the Mouth, while Part B is devoted to the ritual of the temples, divided into the purification of the king and the daily ritual in which the god of the temple is purified. The purification of the offering and the offering table is not taken into consideration since it would require a separate study.
The author concentrates her attention on the question whether one may speak of a "purification ritual" as such, or whether various purification ceremonies originally belonged to certain rituals from which they have been detached in order to be used in other cult situations. At the end of her summary (p. 212-219) she states as the main result of her

research that the first supposition is not correct. She establishes two sources for the purification texts, the offering ritual and an only partly reconstructable revivication ritual, from which the purification spells in the various rituals have been derived, with adaptations to the different situations.

68021 ALY, Mohammed, Fouad ABDEL-HAMID et M. DEWACHTER, Le temple d'Amada. Cahier IV. Dessins. Index. Tables des concordances, Le Caire, Centre de documentation et d'études sur l'ancienne Égypte, 1967 (21 × 26.8 cm; portefolio containing [II +] 37 p. and 83 unnumbered pl. [with drawings]). At head of title: Collection scientifique.

The present volume contains drawings of the scenes, the photographs being published in volume II. There is an index relating the drawings to the photographs, as well as a list of representations mentioning the subject and date of each scene, its Egyptian title (in hieroglyphs), and the gods represented. Further indexes give the various types of royal hairdress, the royal crowns, and the names and epithets of the divinities occurring in the scenes and the texts.
On p. 27-30 some addenda and corrections to vols III and IV; on p. 31-36 a "table de concordance", in which also reference to the numbers of Porter and Moss, *Topographical Bibliography*, vol. VII.
See also our numbers 68006, 68059, 68060 and 68118.

ALY, Mohammed, see also our number 68005.

68022 AMIRAN, Ruth, Note on One Sign in the Narmer Palette, *JARCE* 7 (1968), 127, with 2 pl. and a fig.
A communication on the sign interpreted by Yadin (our number 4334) as a desert kite.
The author concludes that the picture represents the lotus-plant showing two stems. The register under consideration means: "2000 slain (symbolized by the sign and by two lying figures) from a town (depicted as a fortified enclosure)".
M. Heerma van Voss

68023 AMIRAN, Ruth, Two Canaanite Vessels Excavated in Egypt with Egyptian 'Signatures', *Israel Exploration Journal*, Jerusalem 18 (1968), 241-243, with 1 pl.
Study of the representation of a 'bird' on two vessels, one from Tarkhan (Petrie collection, University College N° 17089) and one from Sakkara (Cairo Museum; cfr Emery, *Great Tombs of the First Dynasty*, I [our number 839], p. 121-124). On the former, a Canaanite jug, the representation of a 'bird', probably a Horus-falcon, has been scratched into

the surface of the fired vessel, and the same addition is found on the other vessel, though here in paint. The author suggests that the additions mean that the vessels after transport had been received and 'recorded' in a royal warehouse.

68024 Ancient Egypt, for two thousand years the world's most magnificent civilization. Text by Tom Prideaux. Photographed by Brian Brake, *Life*, Chicago, Illinois 60611, Vol. 64 (1968), [see below], with many ill. (numerous in colour).
Pr. of separate copy $ 0.35
This fine series was published in several parts.
   I. *Grant Pleasure Daily to my Heart*, No. 14 (April 5, 1968), 42-59.
   II. *Divine Order from Kings and Gods*, No. 15 (April 12, 1968), 58-72B.
   III. *A Miracle of Strength and Grace*, No. 16 (April 19, 1968), 62-76 (Old Kingdom — Middle Kingdom).
   IV. *The Sudden Thrust of Empire*, No. 22 (May 22/May 31, 1968), 34-48 (Middle Kingdom — New Kingdom).
   V. *Magic Passage to Eternity*, No. 23 (June 7, 1968), 66-79 (New Kingdom).
   VI. *The Great Search beneath the Sands*, No. 24 (June 14, 1968), 55-72 (archaeological work *in situ*).
M. Heerma van Voss

ANDERSON, J. E., see our number 68630.

68025 Anonymous, Chronologies in Old World Archaeology. Archaeological Seminar at Columbia University 1966-1967, *AJA* 72 (1968), 302-320.
On p. 302-303 J. F. R. von Beckerath discusses the dates of the 3rd millennium B.C. in Egypt, given by Hayes in *CAH* Volume I, Chapter VI (our number 62259).
Though there is a general agreement concerning the dates from the IIIrd Dynasty onwards those of the earlier period are still uncertain. Proceeding from an average reign of 20 years — slightly more than that of the later dynasties — for 13 kings of the Ist and IInd Dynasty the author suggests for the beginning of Egyptian history the century between 3000 and 2900 B.C.

68026 Anonymous, Death in the Desert circa 3000 B.C., *View*, London, Number 22 (December 1968), 22-24, with 5 fig. (3 in colour) and 2 colour pl. (on cover).
On mummification, burial and radiography. The present periodical is "the Kodak view of the photographic scene".
M. Heerma van Voss

68027 Anonymous, Department of Egyptian Antiquities. Acquisitions, January to July 1967, *The British Museum Quarterly*, London 32 (1967-1968), 152.

The acquisitions are: a stela from Serabit el-Khadim (= Gardiner-Peet-Černý, *The Inscriptions of Sinai*, N° 295), and two relief-fragments from tombs from Dendera (= Petrie, *Dendereh*, pl. VII a, left, and pl. IXb-X).

68028 Anonymous, Department of Egyptian Antiquities. Acquisitions, July to December 1966, *The British Museum Quarterly*, London 32 (1967-1968), 56.

Four acquisitions are mentioned: A Saite stela, two marbles with royal names from the Ist Dynasty, and a Ptolemaic amulet.

68029 Anonymous, Exposition pour une donation, *Connaissance des Arts*, Paris N° 201 (novembre 1968), 13-15, with 1 ill.

Announcement of an exhibition of objects given by Henry de Boisgelin to the Louvre Museum, which include some Egyptian antiquities.

68030 Anonymous, К 70-летию В.И. Авдиева, *ВДИ* 4 (106), 1968, 191-192.

"The Seventieth Birtday of V.V. Avdiev".

68031 Anonymous, Musée d'art et d'histoire. Acquisitions de l'année 1967, *Genava*, Genève 16 (1968), 317-331, with 1 ill.

Mentions three Egyptian acquisitions, among which 2 scarabs.

68032 Anonymous, Le Musée des Beaux-Arts en 1966, *Bulletin du Musée Hongrois des Beaux-Arts*, Budapest 31 (1968), 87-93, with 6 ill.

Mention of the acquisition of 3 Egyptian objects, among which the lid of a sarcophagus from the Roman Period (see fig. 50).

68033 Anonymous, The nodding falcon of the Guennol Collection at the Brooklyn Museum, *The Brooklyn Museum Annual* 9 (1967-1968), 69-87, with 19 ill.

Publication of a granite falcon statue in the Guennol collection, now lent to the Brooklyn Museum (Reg. no. L. 65.2) and formerly belonging to the collection of the sculptor Epstein.
The only parallel known is the bird statue from Koptos in the Ashmolean Museum (1894.105a), which is of uncertain date. The falcon is modeled in such a way as to make it nod

by a slight touch under the tail, which the author suggests to have been done in answer to oracles. In connection the author discusses later nodding falcons.

Comparing the Guennol falcon with other animal statues, e.g. the Berlin baboon (no 22607) and the lion in the Metropolitan Museum of Art (no 66.99.2) they appear to form a group closely related in style, characterized by their compact and unbroken lines; they all three may date from the beginning of the Ist dynasty according to the inscription of the name of Narmer on the Berlin baboon. The Berlin lion (no 24440) and the Koptos lion in the Ashmolean Museum (no 1894.105b) with their more naturalistic details may date from the time of king Djer.

68034 Anonymous, The Triumph of Abu Simbel, *The Illustrated London News*, London Volume 253, No 6740 (October 5, 1968), 28-29, with 4 ill.

Mention of the inauguration of the Abu Simbel temple on its new site (September 22).

68035 ANTHES, Rudolf, Bemerkungen zu einigen Problemen der ägyptischen Grammatik, *JEA* 54 (1968), 31-39.

This article deals with the moving object *iri n* as used in the *Pyramid Texts* and during the Old Kingdom. Many examples showing its use are quoted.   *E. Uphill*

68036 ANTHES, Rudolf, Orion, Fuss und Zehe, *Festschrift Schott* 1-6.

The author raises the question whether the $s3ḥ$-star in the *Pyr. Texts* is Orion or not. Proceeding from the remark of Briggs (cfr our number 2475, vol. IV, Excursus 7) that individual life or personification was only ascribed to stars and not to constellations the author studies the occurrences of $s3ḥ$ and has to conclude that the result, which points indeed to Orion, leads to a contradiction. Since, however, $s3ḥ$ means 'toe', it may be that the star Rigel (arab. *rigl* = foot) from the constellation Orion was meant.

In the Berlin planetarium the author saw that in Egypt in *c*. 3000 B.C. Rigel rose on the same spot in the horizon $1\frac{1}{2}$ hours before Sirius, which explains the connection between these stars in the *Pyr. Texts*. Therefore $s3ḥ$ will have been Rigel.

68037 ARNOLD, Dieter, Bemerkungen zu den Königsgräbern der frühen 11. Dynastie von El-Târif, *MDAIK* 23 (1968), 26-37, with 4 plans (3 on folding p.) and 9 pl.

Beschreibung der drei Intef-Gräber, Besprechung ihrer Architektur und zeitlichen Abfolge.
Es ist sehr unwahrscheinlich, dass zu ihrer Anlage je eine Pyramide gehört hat. *M. Heerma van Voss*

68038 ARNOLD, Dieter und Jürgen SETTGAST, mit einem Beitrag von Jan ASSMANN, Vierter Vorbericht über die vom Deutschen Archäologischen Institut Kairo im Asasif unternommenen Arbeiten (5. und 6. Kampagne), *MDAIK* 23 (1968), 9-25, with 2 ill. (including a plan), 2 tables and 8 pl.

Sequel to our number 67034.
Assmann contributed *Arbeiten im Grab des B3s3* (p. 20-25).
M. Heerma van Voss

68039 ARNOLD, Dorothea, Keramikbeispiele aus den Gräbern der frühen 11. Dynastie von *El-Târif*, *MDAIK* 23 (1968), 38-67, with 9 ill. (comprising numerous drawings).

Die Verfasserin veröffentlicht Biespiele der ersten Stufe der Keramikentwicklung während der 11. Dynastie in Theben. Sie zeigt und beschreibt eine Auswahl der Scherben. Dabei unterscheidet sie vier verschiedene Tonarten und Überzüge.
M. Heerma van Voss

68040 Artefact. 150 jaar Rijksmuseum van Oudheden. 1818-1968. Een keuze uit de verzamelingen, [Leiden, Rijksmuseum van Oudheden, 1968] (25.5 × 25.7 cm; 82 p., 150 pl. [6 in colour]).

The introduction to this Festschrift of the Leiden Museum of Antiquities relates the history of the collections.
There follow chapters on the various departments, the Egyptian collection being described by A. Klasens (p. 27-41). Altogether 70 objects from all periods of the Egyptian history are dealt with, from prehistoric vessels to a Coptic tissue, each of them accompanied with the pertinent data such as museum number, provenience, materials, measures, and publications. In short descriptions the place of the objects within the Egyptian civilisation is sketched.
Each of the objects described is represented by one or more splendid photographs (pl. 24-82) made by F. G. van Veen.

68041 ARTZI, Pinḥas, Some Unrecognized Syrian Amarna Letters (EA 260, 317, 318), *JNES* 27 (1968), 163-169.

The author quotes Gelb's view that these three letters which form a group cannot be used effectively when set among the S. Palestinian Amarna letters. Knudtzon gave no clear reason for placing the origin of these Dagan-takala letters in south west Palestine. Using material from a Hebrew edition of the Amarna correspondence now in preparation, the geographical location of the despatch point appears to be a border station of the Egyptian empire in Syria and far to the north east of the previously suggested area as it was on the fringe of the desert. *E. Uphill*

ASSMANN, Jan, see our number 68038.

68042 AYAD, Boulos Ayad, The Topography of Elephantine according to the Aramaic Papyri, Cairo, [no publisher], 1967 (15.4 × 23.3 cm; 18 p., 5 plans). At head of title: Publications of the Institute of Coptic Studies. Department of Semitic Studies.

From the study of the contract-texts of houses from Elephantine the author concludes that "above" here means the Southern side and "below" the Northern side. Accordingly plans of the houses are drawn.
Compare our number 68138.

68043 BACON, Edward, Computers to Akhenaten's Rescue, *The Illustrated London News*, London Volume 253, No 6747 (1968), 25, with 3 ill.

Note about the Akhenaten Temple Project.

BADAWI, Ahmad, see our numbers 68006, 68059, 68060 and 68169.

68044 BADAWY, Alexander, The Excavation of the Fortress at Askur by the University of California: First Season (1962-63), *Proceedings* 20.

Summary of our number 64032.

68045 BADAWY, Alexander, A History of Egyptian Architecture. The Empire (the New Kingdom). From the Eighteenth Dynasty to the End of the Twentieth Dynasty. 1580-1085 B.C., Berkeley and Los Angeles, University of California Press, 1968 (18.3 × 26 cm; XXXIX + 548 p., 261 fig., 67 pl. in colour [including frontispiece]); rev. *BiOr* 27 (1970), 199-203 (Peter Munro); *JARCE* 8 (1969-1970), 100-101 (Alan R. Schulman); *Orientalia* 39 (1970), 204-205 (R. North).

Sequel to our numbers 3192 and 66034.
After an introductory chapter on the geographical, cultural and political background there follow three main chapters, each introduced by a discussion of the evidence from texts and from representations in reliefs and paintings.
Chapter II, on domestic architecture, contains sections on the town house, the palaces, the cities (planning and housing), and the granaries and magazines, while an important section

(p. 75-127) is devoted to the study of the domestic buildings of Amarna.

Chapter III, on religious architecture, first describes the typical cult temple, its wall scenes and its orientation, followed by a description of several examples, from the Delta to Southern Nubia, particularly the Karnak temples (232-266). Then the author discusses other types, the peripetal temple, the rock-cut temple, and the mortuary temples and mortuary chapels for private people.

Chapter IV deals with the tombs, royal as well as private, those of Thebes, of Deir el-Medîneh, of Amarna, and of provincial cemeteries.

Chapter V, on military architecture, discusses various types and describes some actual fortified structures.

Chapter VI deals with architectural statuary, chapter VII with garden architecture, and chapter VIII contains a survey of the achievement of monumental architecture in the Empire.

There follow notes (511-523), a list of architectural terms (an addition to that mentioned in our abstract 66034), a short bibliography and indexes (531-548).

68046 Badisches Landesmuseum. Bildkatalog. Eine Auswahl aus den Sammlungen, Karlsruhe, 1968 (21×21 cm; 400 [unnumbered] p., 13 + 304 ill.).

A brief introduction to the Egyptian collection by Jürgen Thimme on p. 27. A view of the Egyptian room in the basement on p. 26.

Illustrations 11-15 represent Egyptian objects. Technical details are given in the catalogue at the end of the book.

68047 BAER, Klaus, The Breathing Permit of Hôr. A Translation of the Apparent Source of the Book of Abraham, *Dialogue. A Journal of Mormon Thought*, Stanford, California 3, No. 3 (Autumn 1968), 109-134, with 3 pl.

The description and identification of the corpus of funerary papyri once in the possession of Joseph Smith, founder of the Mormon Church, and recently rediscovered in the Metropolitan Museum, is followed by an up-to-date translation of the "Breathing Permit" of Hôr, the source for the Book of Abraham. *Dieter Mueller*

68048 BAKIR, Abd-El-Mohsen, The Middle-Kingdom Cairo Letter. A Reconsideration (Papyrus 91061 = CGC No. 58045), *JEA* 54 (1968), 57-59, with 2 pl.

This is another translation of a document originally published by T.G.H. James in the Hekanakhte Papers. It is written by the scribe Nakhte to another scribe *Sww*. A grammatical commentary which differs in some respects from the readings suggested by James is appended.   *E. Uphill*

68049 BAKRY, H. S. K., Aṣfûnul-Matâ'neh Sondages, *ASAE* 60 (1968), 37-53, with 83 pl., including 1 map and 4 plans.

Between Dec. 1963 and Febr. 1966, several sondages were made in a land-reclamation area N.W. of Esna, where a considerable number of tombs was found. Some bodies were buried in rectangular pits oriented from E to W, while others had been put into anthropoid pottery coffins. Only one mud-brick building containing human bones and skulls came to light, but an adjacent Coptic cemetery yielded tombs with vaulted roofs or brick tombstones, some of which were painted.   *Dieter Mueller*

68050 BAKRY, H. S. K., A Family from Saïs, *MDAIK* 23 (1968), 69-74, with 5 fig. (1 and 2 comprising 6 plans) and 1 pl.

The Kawâdy mound, about 2 km to the North-East of Sais' main mound, was excavated in 1965.

A vast late cemetery was found. Among the objects, there is a fine porphyry block statue from the Late Period. The author publishes the piece and establishes the genealogy of Tefnakht, the owner.   *M. Heerma van Voss*

68051 BAKRY, H. S. K., A Fragment of a Sphinx Found in the Mortuary Temple of Amenōphis III, *MDAIK* 23 (1968), 68, with 1 pl.

Irrigation activities in the Western part of Amenophis III's funerary temple produced a fragment of an alabaster sphinx ursurped by the king.

The right side of the base represents four African lands; cfr our number 66181.   *M. Heerma van Voss*

68052 BAKRY, H. S. K., A Late-Period Statuette, *ASAE* 60 (1968), 1-6, with 4 pl.

The author publishes the upper part of a naophore statue, now in private possession, that presumably comes from the early XXVIIth Dyn. The fragmentary inscription on its back mentions Neith, Lady of Sais, and Osiris in the House of the Bee.   *Dieter Mueller*

68053 BAKRY, H. S. K., A Ptolemaic Stela from Lower Nubia, *ASAE* 60 (1968), 27-35, with 3 pl.

A translation with commentary of a funerary stela that belonged to a priest from Philae and was found by G. A. Reisner on El-Heiseh, an island south of Aswan, in 1907/08 (Aswan Inv. No. 1037).   *Dieter Mueller*

68054 BAKRY, H. S. K., Reconstruction of the Third Pylon at Karnak, *ASAE* 60 (1968), 7-14, with 30 pl. and 4 p. of hieroglyphic text (= p. 7-14).

A report on the work carried out at the Third Pylon between 1960 and 1963, richly documented with photos of the various stages and accompanied by copies of the inscriptions on the pylon. *Dieter Mueller*

68055 BAKRY, H. S. K., A Statue of Pedeamūn-Nebnesuttaui, *ASAE* 60 (1968), 15-25, with 8 pl.

In 1958, a steatite statue was discovered near an Islamic cemetery 25 miles N.E. of Tanta (Cairo J.d'E. 89618). It is 14.4. in. high and represents a certain *P3-dy-imn nb nswt-t3wy*, scribe of the God's books in the House of Amun and superintendent of the priests of Sakhmet (*sš md3. t-ntr pr 'Imn mr w'b.w Shm.t*). The statue belongs to the early XXVIth Dyn. and is crowned with the two feathers worn by this class of priests during ceremonies. *Dieter Mueller*

68056 BANK, A., I. DIAKONOV, B. PIOTROVSKI, М. 3. Матье (1899-1966), Сообщения Государственного Эрмитажа, Ленинград 29 (1968), 83-84, with portrait.

"M. E. Matthieu (1899-1966)".
Obituary article. Compare our number 66650.

68057 BANU, Ion, Sensuri universale și diferențe specifice în filozofia Orientului antic. Vol. I. Mesopotamia, Egipt, China, București, Ed. Stiințifică, 1967 (456 p.); rev. *Bibliotheca Classica Orientalis* 14 (1969), 61-63 (anonymous); *Studia et acta orientalia* 7 (1968), 305-308 (Constantin Daniel).

"Sens universels et differences specifiques dans la philosophie de l'Orient ancien". Not seen.

68058 BARGUET, Paul, Le pharaon Aménophis IV Akhénaton et l'exaltation du pouvoir royal, *Cahiers d'Histoire*. Publiés par les Universités de Clermont-Lyon-Grenoble, Grenoble 13 (1968) (= *Mélanges d'Histoire André Fugier*), 27-30.

The author explains the resistance of Amon's clergy against the religious revolution of Akhenaton by pointing at the "consubstantiation" between Aton and the Pharaoh, the latter thus being a genuine god, the source of life like the Nile, *etc.*, which shocked the priests.

68059 BARGUET, P. et M. DEWACHTER, Le Temple d'Amada. Cahier II. Description archéologique. Planches, Le Caire, Centre de documentation et d'études sur l'ancienne Égypte, 1967 (21 × 26.8 cm; portefolio, containing [II+] 29 loose p.

and 109 loose pl., including two plans). At head of title: Collection scientifique.

After a preface by Ahmed Badawi and Christiane Desroches-Noblecourt there follows an archaeological description of the temple (p. 1-17), discussing its history and mentioning all decorations of its various building elements. As for the style of the representations Barguet stresses its unity, whether the scenes date from the coregency of Tuthmosis III and Amenophis II or from the reign of Tuthmosis IV.

The plates represent all wall decorations, scenes and texts, in photograph.

See also the following number and our numbers 68006, 68021 and 68118.

68060 BARGUET, P., A. Abdel Hamid YOUSSEF et M. DE-WACHTER, Le temple d'Amada. Cahier III. Textes, Le Caire, Centre de documentation et d'études sur l'ancienne Égypte, 1967 (21×26.8 cm; portefolio containing [II+] 59 loose p. and 1 loose plan). At head of title: Collection scientifique.

Apart from a preface by Ahmed Badawi and Christiane Desroches-Noblecourt this volume contains copies of all hieroglyphic texts of the temple, drawn by the second author and checked by the first one.

See also the preceding number and our numbers 68006, 68021, and 68118.

68061 BARNS, John, A New Wisdom Text from a Writing-board in Oxford, *JEA* 54 (1968), 71-76, with 4 pl.

This plaster-covered writing-board (Ashm. Mus. 1964, 489a, b) was bequeathed to the Ashmolean Museum by Sir Alan Gardiner. The wood has gone but the plaster with hieratic writing on it remains, the surviving pieces measuring 26× 10 cm and 23×13 cm. Gardiner noted its Hyksos "curly writing" and thought it probably came from Lord Carnarvon's five years' excavations at Thebes. The subject of the text is both moral and patriotic but the meaning often obscure and cannot as yet be duplicated elsewhere. The author gives a translation and commentary.   *E. Uphill*

68062 BARTA, Winfried, Aufbau und Bedeutung der altägyptischen Opferformel, Glückstadt, Verlag J. J. Augustin, 1968 (21.2×29.7 cm; XIV + 365 p.) = Ägyptologische Forschungen begründet von Alexander Scharff † herausgegeben von Hans-Wolfgang Müller, Universität München. Heft 24; rev. *CdE* XLVI, N° 91 (1971), 97-100 (Herman de Meulenaere).

The extensive study of the offering formula consists of two parts. In Part I the author discusses form and structure of the formula. In order to enable a discussion he distinguishes between the *ḥtp-di-nsw*-formula (Königsformel), the mention of a god or gods (Gotterformel) and the petitions (Bitten). He draws up a catalogue of the formula, the occurrences reaching from the IVth Dynasty until the Roman Period (p. 3-221). There follows a discussion of the criteria for dating the texts (222-252); the places where the formula occurs, tombs, sarcophagi, *etc.*; the way they are written; and the 314 different petitions (234-246).

Part II contains the interpretation of the formula in its three constituent phrases. The author *i.a.* states that the word *ḥtp* here is always a substantive; the preposition *n* in the god's formula introduces a dative; omission of parts of the formula or even complete phrases is abbreviation; the sense is the same throughout all periods.

The author further establishes the existence of three types of the *ḥtp-di-nsw* ritual:

Type A: in the royal cult the king gives an offering to his predecessors in order to emphasize his connections with them and to oblige his successors to the same service;

Type B/1: in the divine cult the king offers to the gods and receives as substitute of mankind the divine boons;

Type B/2: in the enlarged cult of the gods the king gives an offering to the gods in order to obtain a divine boon for a private person.

In the second half of Part II (296-332) the various kinds of boons are discussed and summarized in several categories. Indexes to names, words and petitions on p. 338-365.

68063 BARTA, Winfried, Das Götterkultbild als Mittelpunkt bei Prozessionsfesten, *MDAIK* 23 (1968), 75-78, with 3 ill.

Das Kultbild ist in seinem Schrein verborgen bei Barkenprozessionen mitgeführt worden.

68064 BARTA, Winfried, Zum scheinbaren Bedeutungswandel des Seth in den Pyramidentexten, *JEOL* VII, 20 (1967-1968), 1968, 43-49.

L'auteur propose de voir en Seth l'énergie vitale mâle personnifiée. Le rôle de porte-soleil et l'aspect négatif du dieu s'expliqueraient par sa nature même. Westendorf a reconnu en lui la force physique du roi, qui peut s'affaiblir, mais engendre le jeune Horus et subsiste donc. Pour comprendre l'évolution de Seth dans les *Textes des Pyramides*, il convient de comparer la version d'Ounas à celles de la VIe dynastie prises en bloc. Le nom de Seth est noté chez Ounas par l'image de l'animal; la VIe dynastie l'écrira par les signes phonétiques *stš*. Mais les conceptions restent au fond assez proches. Les textes montrent *a*) le roi identifié à Seth, ou à Horus et Seth; *b*) Seth, H. et S. ou encore l'Ennéade favorables au roi; *c*) Seth ennemi du roi, d'Horus et du roi, ou enfin d'Osiris. Le pourcentage des différentes formules permet de noter une croissance des éléments défavorables. Ce n'est qu'un déplacement d'accent dans une personnalité complexe. Le monarque concentre en lui-même deux types éternels de vigueur, l'une statique: Seth, l'autre subordonnée et toujours renaissante: Horus. *J. Custers*

68065 BASTA, M., Excavations in the Desert Road at Dahshur, *ASAE* 60 (1968), 57-63, with 10 pl.

Sondages along the road leading from the pyramid of Pepy II into the Western Desert yielded fragments of four more stelae from the reign of Psammetichus I. This road, which was discovered in 1887 by Sir Flinders Petrie, ends on an elevation more than 18 km west of Pepy's pyramid. It is covered with broken pottery, but excavations carried out there failed to unearth any trace of the barracks supposed to have been located in this area. *Dieter Mueller*

BAUER, Eddy, see our number 68307.

68066 BAUMGARTEL, Elise J., About some Ivory Statuettes from the "Main Deposit" at Hierakonpolis, *JARCE* 7 (1968), 7-14, with 22 ill. on 11 pl.

The two groups of ivories found by Quibell and Green and discussed by the author, are not all early dynastic.
Some (boys and others) are earlier than the end of the Old Kingdom.
The women in a coat belong to the XIIth Dynasty. A small number is later (?). *M. Heerma van Voss*

68067 BAUMGARTEL, Elise J., Merimda, *Proceedings* 3-5.

Study of the material from the site of Merimda so far as it is known to be at present in various museums, the present whereabouts of the bulk of the finds being unknown. The author points at the close relationship with the Nubian A-Group and rejects the theory of an early West Delta Kingdom as the nucleus of a Lower Egyptian Kingdom.

68068 BAUMGARTEL, Elisabeth J., The Predynastic Cemetery at Naqada, *ZÄS* 95, 1 (1968), 72.

The author is preparing a tomb register of Petrie's 1895 excavations at Naqada, and asks for information on material now in private possession, or in museums not yet covered by her search.

Compare now Elise J. Baumgartel, *Petrie's Naqada Excavation. A Supplement*, London, Bernard Quaritch Ltd, 1970. *Dieter Mueller*

68069 v. BECKERATH, Jürgen, Ein neues Monddatum der ägyptischen Geschichte?, *ZDMG* 118 (1968), 18-21.

The author criticizes Hornung's conclusion (our number 67278) concerning the lunar date in the Pap. Ermitage no. 1116A, suggesting that it may point either to year 1416 or to year 1420 B.C. as being year 19 of Amenophis II.
See now also Richard A. Parker, Once again the Coregency of Thutmose III and Amenhotep II, *in*: *Studies Wilson* 75-82.

68070 von BECKERATH, Jürgen, Die "Stele der Verbannten" im Museum des Louvre, *RdE* 20 (1968), 7-36 (including 2 p. with hieroglyphic text), with 1 pl.

Depuis que Brugsch (*Reise nach dem Grossen Oase El Khargeh*, pl. 22) a publié cette stèle en 1878, en dehors d'une copie de Breasted faite pour le *Wörterbuch* en 1901 restée inédite mais qui servit de base à la traduction donnée dans *BAR* IV, § 650-61, aucune étude systématique de cet important document n'a été entreprise. Beckerath lui consacre ici une étude complète, comprenant une édition du texte en facsimilé, une traduction et deux commentaires. Le premier est textuel et se préoccupe essentiellement de questions d'établissement du texte, de grammaire et de vocabulaire, tandis que le second, d'ordre général, met au point les problèmes historiques soulevés. La stèle (connue en français sous le nom de "Stèle du bannissement"=Louvre C. 256) apporte en effet un intéressant témoignage sur l'opposition rencontrée à Thèbes par le grand prêtre Menkheperré, qui devait sa fonction à son père le roi tanite Pinedjem I, et ne put se maintenir qu'à la condition de rappeler les ennemis de son pouvoir, que son prédécesseur avait bannis à Khargeh.
Une des découvertes les plus intéressantes de la nouvelle étude de ce document est celle d'un hymne à Amon jusqu'ici méconnu et inconnu, occupant les lignes 12 à 15 de la stèle, dont l'auteur donne une transcription métrique selon les principes élaborés par Fecht. *Ph. Derchain*

von BECKERATH, Jürgen, see also our number 68025.

68071 BELL, Lanny, The Work of the University Museum at Thebes, *Expedition*, Philadelphia 10, Number 2 (Winter 1968), 38-47, with 2 maps, a plan, 3 fig. and 4 ill.

The results of Clarence I. Fisher's excavations at Draʿ

Abû el-Naga' in 1921-1923 have never been published. In order to prepare a publication of the Ramesside tombs in this area the author has worked a season at Thebes, copying texts from the tombs 35, 157 and 283, which belong to three High-Priests of Amon.

68072 BENGSTON, Hermann, Annibale Evaristo Breccia. 18.7.1876-28.7.1967, in: *Jahrbuch Bayerische Akademie der Wissenschaften*, München 1968, 185-187, with a portrait.

Obituary notice.

BENGTSON, Hermann, see also our number 68098.

68073 BERGMAN, Jan, Ich bin Isis. Studien zum memphitischen Hintergrund der griechischen Isis-aretalogien, Uppsala, Almqvist & Wiksell, 1968 (16.5 × 24.7 cm; 349 p.) = Acta Universitatis Upsaliensis, Historia Religionum 3; rev. *Acta Orientalia* 33 (1971), 347-357 (H. Ludin Jansen); *BiOr* 27 (1970), 207-208 (W. Wessetzky); *CdE* XLIV, N° 88 (1969), 285-286 (Constant de Wit); *JEA* 56 (1970), 230-231 (J. Gwyn Griffiths); *Nederlands Theologisch Tijdschrift* 24 (1969), 122-123 (Th. P. v. B[aaren]); *Orientalia* 38 (1969), 376 (É. des Places); *RdE* 22 (1970), 212-214 (Ph. Derchain).
Pr. bound sw. kr. 60

In der aretalogischen Überlieferung spricht die memphitische Isis. Den allgemeinen ägyptischen Nährboden beleuchtet der Verfasser dieses Buches durch eine Konfrontation der griechischen Tradition mit Königs- und Maatideologie.
Ohne Zweifel hat man mit einer priesterlichen Auslegung auch in der Diaspora zu rechnen.
Bergman betont die grosse Lebenskraft der echten ägyptischen Vorstellungen.
Textbeilage 1) enthält die Aretalogie von Kyme-Memphis, 2) eine Proklamation von Esna (Sauneron, Nr. 307, 23 *sqq.*).
Am Ende Literatur-, Sach-, Wort- und Stellenverzeichnisse.
M. Heerma van Voss

68074 BERNARD, Claude, A la découverte du Louvre. Égypte-Orient-Grèce, Paris, Magnard, [1968] (17 × 22 cm; 80 p., 8 pl. [containing 72 ill.], 1 plan, 1 fig., ill. on cover); rev. *Bulletin critique du livre français* 24 (1969), 597.

The first chapter of this guide for the general visitor of the Louvre Museum, called *Les belles histoires de l'archéologie*, mentions *i.a.* the find of the Stone of Rosetta and the discovery of Tutankhamon's tomb (p. 7-9).
There follows a chapter on the Egyptian antiquities (11-30), in which the prominent objects are described in the order in

which they are exhibited. Twenty-two of them are represented, though on a very small scale.

68075 BIETAK, Manfred, Bericht über die erste Grabungskampagne auf Tell ed-Dabʿa im Ostdelta Ägyptens im Sommer 1966, *Bustan*, Wien 9, Heft 1 (1968), 20-33, with 8 pl.

Preliminary report of the Austrian excavations at Tell ed-Dabʿa in 1966.
The site is in the neighbourhood of Khataʿna, 4 km from Qantir, and is probably what remains of an enormous field of ruins. The history of the place may date from the XIIth Dynasty. During the campaign 6 levels have been distinguished, from Ptolemaic to late Middle Kingdom, the most important being level E from the Second Intermediate Period.
It contains non-Egyptian material which belongs to Palestinian M.Br. II b and c, *e.g.* so-called Hocker-burials under the floor of the houses; Syro-Palestinian types of daggers and battle-axes, and Tell el-Yahudieh-ware and other foreign types of pottery. Important are also burials of equides, possibly teams of horses. It appears that the Asiatics here kept their own culture at least until the early New Kingdom.
Tell ed-Dabʿa may thus appear to be the most important centre of the Hyksos, and its excavation may shed new light on the history of the period.

68076 BIETAK, Manfred, Studien zur Chronologie der nubischen C-Gruppe. Ein Beitrag zur Frühgeschichte Unternubiens zwischen 2200 und 1550 v. Chr., Wien, Hermann Böhlaus Nachf., 1968 (21 × 30 cm; 188 p., 48 fig., 19 pl., 1 map) = Österreichische Akademie der Wissenschaften, Philosopisch-Historische Klasse. Denkschriften, 97. Band. Berichte des Österreichischen Nationalkomitees der UNESCO-Aktion für die Rettung der Nubischen Altertümer V; rev. *CdE* XLIV, N° 88 (1969), 292-293 (Inge Hofmann); *JEA* 57 (1971), 224-228 (E. P. Uphill); *Man* 4 (1969), 298-299 (Bruce G. Trigger); *ZDMG* 120 (1970), 1971, 333-335 (J. v. Beckerath). Pr. Ö.S. 240

Die Untersuchung geht auf die Dissertation des Verfassers (Wien 1963) zurück. Im 1. Teil wird eine relative Stufenfolge innerhalb des Fundmaterials der C-Gruppen-Friedhöfe herausgearbeitet, wobei sich drei große Chronologiestufen abgrenzen lassen. Die absolute Chronologie, die im zweiten Hauptteil abgehandelt wird, stützt sich auf ägyptische Siegel, Skarabäen, Skaraboide und importierte Keramik.

Sie umfaßt den Zeitraum von der 6. Dynastie (Stufe I a) bis zur 18. Dynastie (Stufe III). Die Träger der C-Gruppen-Kultur hält der Verf. für Einwanderer aus dem Westen und setzt sie in Beziehung zu den von $Hrḫwf$ erwähnten $Tmḥ.w$.

Inge Hofmann

68077 BIETAK, Manfred, Vorläufiger Bericht über die erste und zweite Kampagne der österreichischen Ausgrabungen auf Tell Ed-Dabʿa im Ostdelta Ägyptens (1966, 1967), *MDAIK* 23 (1968), 79-114, with 9 fig. including 6 plans (1 folding) and 4 pl.

Circa 8 km nördlich vom alten Phakusa fand man eine Siedlung der syrisch-palästinensischen Mittleren Bronzezeit-Kultur II.
Neu ist die Anwendung von Totentempeln mit Nekropolen, die herum konstruiert wurden; cfr aber Tell el-Ajjul.
Die Alabaster- und Fayencegefäße und viele Keramikformen sind vielleicht ägyptisch.
Die vorliegende Stadtkultur wurde die ganze Hyksoszeit hindurch beibehalten. Unter den gefundenen Individuen hat man zahlreiche Nichtmediterranide angetroffen.
Nichts spricht dagegen, Auaris in dieser Gegend zu lokalisieren.

M. Heerma van Voss

68078 BINGEN, Jean, Rapport des Directeurs, *CdE* XLIII, N° 85 (1968), 5-9.

68079 BLEEKER, C. J., Guilt and Purity in Ancient Egypt, *in*: *Proceedings of the XIth International Congress of the International Association for the History of Religions. Volume II. Guilt or Pollution and Rites of Purification*, Leiden, E.J. Brill, 1968, 47.

Summary of a lecture.
For the same subject cfr our number 66062.

68080 BLEEKER, C. J., Religious Tradition and Sacred Books in Ancient Egypt, *in*: *Holy Book and Holy Tradition*. International Colloquium held in the Faculty of Theology, University of Manchester. Edited by F. F. Bruce and E. G. Rupp, [Manchester], Manchester University Press, [1968], 20-35.

The relation between scripture and tradition is a typical Christian problem, which does not exist in ancient Egypt, where religion was primarily a question of cult, without church or theologians who could raise the problem. Coherent descriptions of myths are equally lacking, though mythical conceptions were present, among others the idea of the divine, creative word and the magical, creative power of writing. The Egyptians also have realized the significance of oral tradition, appearing from the half secular, half sacred stories, as well as of a rich, religious written tradition (*e.g.* appearing from the *Book of the Dead*) with a certain measure of codification. None of the various types of sacred books, however, had the character of a holy book.

68081 BLOCH, Raymond [and] Alain HUS, Les conquêtes de l'archéologie, [Paris], Hachette, [1968] (15 × 21.1 cm; 316 p., 96 ill., 10 plans and map); rev. *Latomus. Revue d'études latines* 28 (1969), 806-807 (R. Chevallier).

In this popular introduction to archaeology a chapter is devoted to ancient Egypt (p. 147-223). It is divided into two parts, one dealing with the archaeological research from the early XIXth Dynasty onwards, the other with the history of Egypt. Particular attention is paid to the monuments, while the last sections deal with the main excavation sites.

From the photographs we mention those of objects seldom represented, *e.g.* the colossus in the granite quarries of Aswan (178-179) and the falcon statue with Ramesses II at Es-Sebua (198).

68082 BÖHLIG, Alexander, Mysterion und Wahrheit. Gesammelte Beiträge zur spätantiken Religionsgeschichte, Leiden, E. J. Brill, 1968 (16.5 × 24.3 cm; XII + 266 p.) = Arbeiten zur Geschichte des späteren Judentums und des Urchristentums 6; rev. *BiOr* 26 (1969), 433-434 (Willy Rordorf).

Among other articles in this collection of contributions to the knowledge of the New Testament and Gnosticism:
Zum Martyrium des Jakobus (p. 112-118), in which an emendation and translation is given of Nag-Hammadi Codex V p. 62, 16-63, 29.
Probleme des Manichäischen Lehrvortrages (p. 228-244). On p. 232-233, etymology of the words ⲗⲓϧⲙⲉ and ⲛⲟⲃⲉ (both in the "Kephalaia des Lehrers").
Eine Bemerkung zur Beurteilung der Kephalaia (p. 245-251). On p. 247-249 translation and comparison of some parts of the "Kephalaia des Lehrers". L. F. Kleiterp

68083 BOGOSLOVSKI, E. S., "Послушные призыву" в Египте периода XVIII Династии. Автореферат диссертации на соискание ученой степени кандидата исторических наук. Ленинград, 1968 (14 × 20 cm; 14 p.). At head of title: Ленинградский государственный университет имени А. А. Жданова.

" 'Listeners to the call' in Egypt during the period of the XVIIIth Dynasty".

68084 BOGOSLOVSKI, E. S., "Послушные призыву" в хозяйствах частных лиц Египта (XV-XIV веков до нашей эры), IV Сессия по древнему Востоку, 39-40.

" 'Listeners to the Call' on private estates of Egypt (XVth-XIVth centuries B.C.)".
The *sḏm-ꜥš*-people were overseers of the house, scribes of the estate, butlers (*wbꜣw=wdpw*), followers, gardeners, sailormen, doorkeepers, butchers, poultry breeders, granary workers, *etc.*, both slaves and serfs, but not peasants or priests.

E.S.Bogoslovsky

68085 BOGOSLOVSKI, E. S., Руководители ткачей в Египте. XVI-XV вв. до н.з., *ВДИ* 1 (103), 1968, 87-96, with an English summary on p. 96.

"Weavers' Managers in Egypt of the Sixteenth and Fifteenth Centuries B.C.".
Of 72 known managers of the weavers (*imi-r*, *ḥry* and *sš mrt*) the majority were employed on the estate of Amūn, including the mortuary temples of kings and queens, though managers on private and royal estates are also attested. According to their social standing and actual position they fall into four groups: I magnates; II middle-ranking estate leaders; III actual weavers' managers; IV possible weavers' managers. The first two groups took no part in the actual work, which was directed by the persons included in groups III and IV. They were petty officials on the various estates and managed either whole workshops or specialised departments.
In a table the data concerning 52 of the officials are collected.

E. S. Bogoslovsky

68086 BONGRANI FANFONI, Luisa, Due usciabti del Museo Civico di Reggio Emilia, *Rivista* 43 (1968), 23-25, with 2 pl.

Les oushebtis 251 et 252 du Musée de Reggio Emilia sont au nom de Mehy. L'oushebti semblable C. G. Caire 47241 peut être destiné au même Mehy, et porte lui aussi le titre *ꜥꜣ n mw n pr Wsir*. Le seul parallèle est une statuette de Rifa, où le titre "*ꜥꜣ n mw* du Ramesseum" est mis en rapport avec les jardins: cela incite à comprendre "préposé aux canalisations". Le nom coupe l'énoncé du titre sur les quatre figurines. Elles seraient datables fin XIXe — début XXe dynastie. *Pr Wsir* paraît être un centre d'activité; cela n'exclut pas l'hypothèse que la statuette appartienne au même personnage.
Les notes 1 et 2 énumèrent d'autres objets égyptiens du

musée de Reggio, la planche 2 montre un cône funéraire du w'b et scribe Usirhat. *J. Custers*

BORGER, Riekele, see our number 68219.

68087 BOTHMER, Bernard V., Alexandre Piankoff (1897-1966), *in*: Alexandre Piankoff, *The Pyramid of Unas*, [Princeton, 1968], 117-118.

Obituary notice. See our number 67645.

BOTHMER, Bernard V., see also our number 68503.

BOTTÉRO, Jean, see our number 68186.

68088 BOTTI, Giuseppe. Il Libro del Respirare e un suo nuovo esemplare nel papiro demotico N. 766 del Museo Egizio di Torino, *JEA* 54 (1968), 223-230, with 1 pl.; rev. *Enchoria* 1 (1971), 57 (Heinz-Josef Thissen).

The *Book of Breathings* is closely connected with Thebes. This example is described by the author as 0.309 m high by 0.225 m broad, with thirty lines of vertical column writing in demotic and several horizontal lines to the left on the recto, but only two badly damaged lines on the verso. It is dedicated to the memory of Patermuthis born of Senchonsis. Transliteration, translation and notes are given. *E. Uphill*

68089 du BOURGUET, Pierre, L'art copte, Paris, Éditions Albin Michel, 1968 (18 × 23.5 cm; 240 p., 87 fig., 22 pl., 55 pl. in colour); series: L'art dans le monde. Fondements historiques, sociologiques et religieux [Civilisations non européennes]; rev. *Orientalia* 38 (1969), 496 (H. Quecke); *Revue Biblique* 77 (1970), 302-304 (B.C[ouroyer]).

French edition of our number 67084.

68090 du BOURGUET, P., Les impératifs profonds de l'art pharaonique, *Boletín de la Asociación española de orientalistas*, Madrid 4 (1968), 139-144.

Jede Kunst, so auch die pharaonische, muss gesehen werden in dem geographischen, historischen und sozialen Rahmen, in dem sie entstand. Die altägyptische Kunst ist zudem tiefgehend durch die Religion bestimmt und, hierauf möchte Verfasser einen ganz besonderen Akzent setzen, durch die Person des Pharao, "la source même de l'art". *I. Gamer-Wallert*

du BOURGUET, Pierre, see also our number 68286.

68091 BOYER, Carl B., A History of Mathematics, New York-London-Sidney, John Wiley & Sons, 1968 (15.5 × 23.5 cm; XV + 717 p., 35 ill., numerous fig.). Pr. 97 s.

Chapter II (p. 9-25) is devoted to ancient Egypt. In the paragraphs 3-8 some problems are discussed of the *Rhind Mathematical Papyrus* (c. 1650 B.C.; going back to a text from c. 2000-1800 B.C.). Paragraph 9 deals with the *Golenishev* or *Moscow Papyrus* (c. 1890 B.C.).

On p. 15, line 21, at the end, read $\frac{2}{10}$ instead of $\frac{1}{10}$; on p. 18, line 31, $3\frac{13}{81}$ instead of $3\frac{1}{6}$. The reference to "the Egyptian rule for the circumference of a circle "(p. 18, 19) is unwarranted; none such rule is known. Probably Boyer is rendering here an interpretation of V. V. Struve. *A. J. E. M. Smeur*

68092 BRANDON, S. G. F., The Life-Giving Significance of Lustration in the Osirian Mortuary Ritual and in Primitive Christian Baptism, *in*: *Proceedings of the XIth International Congress of the International Association for the History of Religions. Volume II. Guilt or Pollution and Rites of Purification*, Leiden, E. J. Brill, 1968, 52-53.

Summary of a lecture.
The author establishes a similar pattern of idea and practice in the Osirian cult and the primitive Christianity.

68093 BRANDYS, Henryk, Female Statuette of Prince's Servant named *Nbw-n-ib* from the Collection of the National Museum in Cracow, *Études et Travaux* II 99-106, with 5 ill. and 2 fig.

The author deals with a statuette made in Thebes representing a standing woman. He describes the object with great precision from the archaeological point of view and gives the translation of the inscription consisting of an abbreviated text of an offering formula. *A. Szczudlowska*

68094 BRATTON, F. Gladstone, A History of Egyptian Archaeology, New York, Crowell, 1968 (315 p., 6 fig., 3 plans, 5 maps, 24 pl.); rev. *Journal of Biblical Literature* 88 (1969), 223-224 (John van Seters).

American edition of our number 67088. Not seen.

68095 BRENTJES, Burchard, Altorientalisches zur Geschichte des Handsymbols, *Wissenschaftliche Zeitschrift Martin-Luther-Universität*. Gesellschafts- und sprachwissenschaftliche Reihe, Halle-Wittenberg 17, Heft 6 (1968), 1-7, with 8 ill. and 2 fig.

In ancient Egypt the cut-off hand of an enemy served as a victory trophy (ill. 10). The hand symbol appears first on protodynastic seals and was still used on amulets during the Late Period. *L. M. J. Zonhoven*

68096 BRENTJES, Burchard, Grundeigentum, Staat und Klassengesellschaft im Alten Orient, *Ethnographisch-Archäologische Zeitschrift*, Berlin 9 (1968), 245-266.

Sequel to our next number.
On p. 251-253 the author discusses landed property of the pharaoh and his officials, quoting Helck (our number 58284) and Labib (our number 547) and calling ancient Egypt a class-society on an agricultural foundation.
Bibliography on p. 263-264, followed by a discussion between the author and Rigobert Günther and Heinz Kreißig.

68097 BRENTJES, Burchard, Zur Stellung der Produzenten materieller Güter im orientalischen Altertum, *Ethnographisch-Archäologische Zeitschrift*, Berlin 9 (1968), 45-68.

This study is part of a discussion about prehistory and protohistory and the problems of the division of history into periods.
The author deals with the position of the producers of material goods on the basis of the Marxist philosophy. There are only a few remarks on ancient Egypt. Bibliography on p. 66-68.

68098 BRESCIANI, Edda, Egypt and the Persian Empire, *in*: Hermann Bengtson, *The Greeks and the Persians from the Sixth to the Fourth Centuries*, London, Weidenfeld and Nicolson, [1968], 333-353.

This is a translation in English by John Conway. The original edition was published in German in 1965 by Fischer Bücherei (cfr our number 65085).
The author gives a survey of our present knowledge of the Persian Period in Egypt from Cambyses' conquest until that by Alexander, thus including the native XXVIIIth-XXXth Dynasties, from Amyrtaeus to the Second Conquest in 343. Some pages are devoted to the political organisation of Egypt as a satrapy, to legal documents and to the arts. Notes on p. 425-428.

68099 BRESCIANI, Edda, Missione di scavo a Medinet Madi (Fayum — Egitto). Rapporto preliminare delle campagne di scavo 1966 e 1967, Milano-Varese, Istituto Editoriale Cisalpino, [1968] (24.6 × 33 cm; 170 p., 22 fig., including 1 map and 4 plans, 84 pl. [on p. 79-168] and 4 coloured pl. [on p. 71-77]; at head of title: Istituto di papirologia dell'università degli studi di Milano; rev. *BiOr* 26 (1969), 335-336 (France Le Corsu); *Rivista* 44 (1969), 56-58 (Sergio Donadoni).

Pr. L 20,000

After a note about the site of Medinet Madi Part I describes the campaign of 1966 on the eastern kôm. There follows a catalogue of the finds, stone and bronze objects, coins, *etc.* In a separate chapter the author studies Demotic inscriptions on the socles of the sphinxes of the dromos.

Part II is devoted to the campaign of 1967, describing details of a building of unknown nature, possibly a public *thesauros* from the 1st century A.D. and all objects here found, among which many pots of various shapes.

68100 BRESCIANI, Edda, Tre documenti dall' Egitto, *Studi classici e orientali*, Pisa 17 (1968), 232-236, with 2 pl.

Publication of three Egyptian monuments: a fragment of the base of a Saitic statue inscribed with the titles and name of a certain Hor; a small anepigraph stela with the representations of a man's bust and the figure of a sitting man; and a funerary stela from Husseneiah (Tell Nebesheh) with a Demotic text containing six names (1st century B.C. — 1st century A.D.).

BRESCIANI, Edda, see our number 68462.

68101 B[RUCE], F. F., Alan Rowe, *Palestine Exploration Quarterly*, London 100 (1968), 76-77.

Obituary notice.

68102 BRUNNER, Hellmut, "Eure Rede sei Ja Ja, Nein Nein" im Ägyptischen, *Festschrift Schott* 7-12.

The idea expressed in the words of Mt 5, 37, meaning that one speaks untruthful if heart and tongue do not agree, is also found in Egypt. The author comments on passages from *Amenemope*, *Ptahhotep* and the *Shabaka-stone*, stressing that the tongue is subordinate to the heart.

68103 BRUNNER, Hellmut, Eine wiedergefundene ägyptische Statue, *JEA* 54 (1968), 129-134, with 2 pl.

A description of two newly discovered Egyptian statues located in August 1965 in the grounds of the Villa Melzi, Bellagio, and previously published in an 18th century work. The first is a cube statue 86 cm high in pink granite, bearing the name and titles of the Overseer of the City and Vizier of Per Ramesses, Parahotep. The other statue is a standing figure of a lion-headed goddess also in granite with the lower part of the legs missing, and comparable with those found in the Mut temple of Amenhotep III. *E. Uphill*

68104 BRUNNER, Hellmut, Zur Hundeinschrift des AR, *ZÄS* 95,1 (1968), 72.

The three words *dmi*, *sntr*, and *sft* in ll. 5-7 are not part of the inscription proper, but represent an abbreviated list of funerary equipment. *Dieter Mueller*

68105 BRUNNER, Hellmut, *in*: *Bibel-Lexikon*. Herausgegeben von Prof. Dr. Herbert Haag, [Einsiedeln-Zürich-Köln], Benzinger Verlag, [1968].

Several lemmata written for the first edition by Jozef M. A. Janssen are revised by Brunner, while some new ones have been added and still others have been reprinted unchanged.

68106 BRUNNER-TRAUT, Emma, Ägyptische Mythen im Physiologus (zu Kapitel 26, 25 und 11), *Festschrift Schott* 13-44, with 2 fig. and 2 pl.

The author studies chapters 25 and 26 of the *Physiologus*, the former relating the battle between the enhydros, *i.e.* the otter, and the crocodile, the latter that between the ichneumon and the dragon. She proves them to be two separate stories, both derived from Egyptian myths and both reflecting the battle between light (the sun-eye) and darkness. The otter is here the counterpart in the water of the ichneumon by land.

In this context the author draws up a list of seven representations of an upright otter, all dedicated to Uto and bearing on the head a sun-disk and uraeus (add now the statuette found by Emery at Sakkara, *JEA* 57 [1971], pl. VIII, 6). These late bronzes are usually assumed to represent the ichneumon, the otter being rather rare in ancient Egypt, but they show all characteristics of the latter.

At the end a few lines are devoted to chapter 11 of the *Physiologus*, telling that a naked man repels the serpent, which is connected with the motif of the naked Harpokrates.

68107 BRUNNER-TRAUT, Emma, Altägyptische Tiergeschichte und Fabel. Gestalt und Strahlkraft, Darmstadt, Wissenschaftliche Buchgesellschaft, 1968 (16.9 × 24.6 cm; X + 68 p., 37 fig. on 16 unnumbered p.); rev. *BiOr* 26 (1969), 203 (J. Gwyn Griffiths); *CdE* XLIV, N° 87 (1969), 83-85 (Jan Quaegebeur); *JNES* 30 (1971), 83-86 (Thomas C. Hartman); *Mundus* 5 (1969), 202-204; *OLZ* 66 (1971), 241-242 (W. Beltz); *RdE* 22 (1970), 214-217 (P. Vernus); *ZDMG* 120 (1970), 1971, 332-333 (Erika Feucht). Pr. bound DM 19.30

Reprint of our number 59097, with a few additions to the table of motifs (p. 7-17).

68108 BRUYÈRE, Bernard, Hommage d'un vieil ami, *JEA* 54 (1968), 9-10.

The author pays tribute to Professor J. Černý on the occasion of his 70th birtday and recounts his associations with him beginning 43 years ago with their work at the site of Deir el-Medîneh. *E. Uphill*

BUECHNER, Thomas S., see our number 68503.

68109 BUTZER, Karl W. and Carl L. HANSEN, with contributions by Egbert G. LEIGH, Jr., Madeleine Van CAMPO, and Bruce G. GLADFELTER, Desert and River in Nubia. Geomorphology and Prehistoric Environments at the Aswan Reservoir, Madison, Milwaukee, and London, The University of Wisconsin Press, 1968 (16.5 × 24 cm; XXI + 562 p., 173 fig.); rev. *Antiquity* 44 (1970), 158-160 (William Y. Adams); *CdE* XLIV, N° 87 (1969), 98-100 (P. Vermeersch); *Israel Exploration Journal* 19 (1969), 127-128 (D. Niz). Pr. bound £ 8/7 s.

Zwischen 1962 und 1965 wurde von der Yale Prehistoric Nubia Expedition eine detailierte Studie über pleistozäne Palä-Ökologie durchgeführt. Das vorliegende Werk legt die Ergebnisse der Forschungen von 1962-1963 auf dem Gebiet der geomorphologischen und geologischen Geschichte folgender Gebiete dar: Kom Ombo-Ebene, nubischer Raum Ägyptens, Kurkur-Oase und Küstenregion von Mersa Alam am Roten Meer. Die Seiten 153-195 beschäftigen sich mit der prähistorischen Archäologie des nubischen Raumes; in Kap. 9 wird eine Rekonstruktion der Geschichte des saharanischen Nil versucht. Elf Einzeluntersuchungen schließen das Werk ab. *Inge Hofmann*

68110 [CACHOUX, Michel], Trésors d'hier, *Connaissance des Arts*, Paris N° 199 (septembre 1968), 86-95, with 16 ill. in colour.

Egyptologists may be interested in the ill. on p. 93 representing a Saite bronze cat.

68111 CAMINOS, Ricardo A., A Fragmentary Hieratic School-book in the British Museum (Pap. B.M. 10298), *JEA* 54 (1968), 114-120, with 2 pl.

This papyrus fragment once the property of Anthony Charles Harris and since 1872 in the British Museum, was probably acquired from Thebes about 1854/5. The text is on the recto, literary hieratic and about XXIst Dynasty in date. Much of it is too fragmentary to make sense and appears to have been unconnected sentences designed for school work, but six sentences exhibit interesting variations on a 'theme' sentence arranged in parallel pairs of Middle and Late Egyptian forms. Full commentaries are given.
E. Uphill

68112 CAMINOS, Ricardo A., The Shrines and Rock-Inscriptions of Ibrim, London, Egypt Exploration Society, 1968 (25.5 × 27.3 cm; XII + 114 p., 4 fig., 42 pl.) = Archaeological Survey of Egypt edited by T. G. H. James. Thirty-second Memoir; rev. *BiOr* 28 (1971), 186-188 (Labib Habachi); *OLZ* 65 (1970), 132-134 (W. Helck); *RdE* 20 (1968), 179-180 (J. López). Pr. bound £ 12

An epigraphic expedition of the Egypt Exploration Society was undertaken in 1961 in the district of Qasr Ibrim, the ancient Miam. Members were the author (of Brown University) and two handymen. Compare already our numbers 61366 and 62289.

The underlying volume offers the results of this campaign following a historical and topographical introduction. The bulk of the findings is confined to the New Kingdom. Among the shrines (not funerary in character) four were constructed in the XVIIIth and XIXth Dynasties. The remaining two, contiguous to them, are uninscribed and undatable.

Out of the four incomplete rock-stelae we mention the monument of our numbers 62270 and 66113.

Nine graffiti (Middle Kingdom — New Kingdom) conclude the publication proper preceding elaborate indexes and 42 plates. *M. Heerma van Voss*

van CAMPO, Madeleine, see our number 68109.

CAQUOT, André, see our number 68367.

CASKEL, Werner, see our number 68279.

68113 CASTIGLIONE, László, Diocletianus és a Blemmyes, *Antik Tanulmányok*. Studia Antiqua, Budapest 15 (1968), 203-220, with 12 fig.

"Diocletian und die Blemmyes".

Die Terracotta Inv. Nr. 22.737 der Staatlichen Museen zu Berlin trägt die Bezeichnung: "Bärtiger Gott in römischer Soldatentracht, der ein knieendes, Bes-artig aussehendes Wesen am Schopfe packt". Es is die einzige spätrömische Komposition im Stile eines altägyptischen Bildes. Auf Grund des Porträtstyps lässt sich das Zeitalter der Tetrarchie feststellen. Diocletian hat Ägypten im Jahre 298 besucht. Er hat den Dodekaschoinos aufgegeben, die Gegend mit Nobatai besiedelt, um die Blemmyes fern zu halten. Die Terracottenfigur ist als Demonstration anlässlich des Kaiserbesuches zu betrachten und das "Bes-artige Wesen" kann die erste bekannte Darstellung des Volkes der Blemmyes sein.

Die Siegesdarstellung des Mandulis-Tempels von Kalabscha zeigt die Niederstechung eines Barbaren, in der ebenfalls die Darstellung desselben Barbaren erkennbar ist.
Vilmos Wessetzky

68114 CELADA, Benito, Concepto de Dios en Egipto, *Sefarad* 28 (1968), 237-288.

"The Idea of God in Egypt".
This is a lecture given at the 28th Spanish Biblical Week (Madrid, Sept. 1968), the subject of the week being "The Idea of God in the Bible". The author has supplemented his paper with an impressive bibliography and abundant notes (205) apparently trying to explain in detail his assertions and discussing at the same time the different opinions pro and contra. It is difficult to follow the reasoning of the author through the accumulation of opinions, textual materials and theological considerations. It seems that the central idea of the author is to elucidate the progress and vicissitudes of the transcendence of God in ancient Egypt. Celada follows principally Morenz, *Die Heraufkunft des transzendenten Gottes in Aegypten* (our number 64346) and also Junker and Drioton inasmuch as Morenz agrees with them. The best approximation to what the author intends to prove or explain may be obtained from the subtitles of his paper which are as follows: "Why do we study the Idea of God in Egypt"; "In the Center of Life"; "The principal Enigmae"; "Antiquity of the Idea of God in Egypt. 'God' and 'Strength' "; "Less favourable Connotations of the Word God, 'Maat' "; "The monotheistic Interpretation of Junker and Drioton"; "The Monument of Memphite Theology"; "Was there an initial Phase of Immersion of God in the World?"; "Was God immanent in the Kings of the first Dynasties?"; "Progressive Movement of Transcendence of God and Degradation of the Pharaoh?"; "The God of the official Cult, the personal Piety, the Theologians and Sages"; "Unity, Pluralism and Trinity". *Perla Fuscaldo*

68115 CELADA, Benito, "Menes", fundador de Egipto. Precisión histórica y nuevos datos acerca del género literario de historia primitiva, *Cultura Bíblica*, Madrid 214 (1967), 169-171; rev. *Sefarad* 28 (1968), 166-167 (A[ntonio] P[eral]).

"Menes, founder of Egypt. Historical precision and new data on the literary form of early history".
A short article about Menes The author thinks that he was a fictitious personage, an artificial creation of later times with features both mythological and of the Egyptian history. Celada denies that the word *mn* belonging to the documents

of the dynasty was a personal name. He pretends that *mn* which the priests could show to Greek visitors was really the king N.N. (*mn*) employed in the ritual of the temple. Celada feels himself supported by H. Brunner, *Menes als Schöpfer* (our number 2747) and Ph. Derchain, *Ménès, le roi "Quelqu'un"* (our number 66166). There is no discussion of the evidence concerning the existence or non-existence of Menes. *Perla Fuscaldo*

68116 de CENIVAL, Françoise, Un document inédit relatif à l'exploitation de terres du Fayoum (P. dém. Lille, Inv. Sorb. 1186), *RdE* 20 (1968), 37-50, with 1 pl.; rev. *Enchoria* 1 (1971), 58 (Heinz-Josef Thissen).

Éditon comprenant photographie, fac-similé, transcription phonétique et traduction du document mentionné dans le titre. Il s'agit d'un écrit double (dont un des exemplaires était scellé) relatif à l'attribution de terres et à des redevances dues pour leur exploitation au Fayoum, daté de 248 a.C. Le commentaire très détaillé comprend notamment une longue discussion du terme $ḏr$ (ou $ḏlꜥ / ḏr3$) désignant certains types de terrains situés à proximité des rives du fleuve ou des canaux. *Ph. Derchain*

68117 de CENIVAL, Jean-Louis, Vingt ans d'acquisitions au Département des Antiquités égyptiennes du Musée du Louvre, *BSFE* N° 51 (Mars 1968), 5-16, with 1 ill. and 2 pl.

Une exposition à l'Orangerie a réuni un certain nombre d'objets choisis parmi ceux que le Musée du Louvre a acquis ces vingt dernières années; une soixantaine de pièces égyptiennes y figuraient. La présente causerie donne une idée des acquisitions annuelles en énumérant l'ensemble des acquisitions faites au cours de deux années moyennes: 1948 et 1953, et d'une année fort riche, surtout par la qualité des pièces: 1967. Mentionnons, pour cette dernière année, une harpê de bronze marquée aux cartouches de Ramsès II, une stèle du roi Kahedj (?), qui doit remonter à la IIIe dynastie, et une grande stèle d'époque gréco-romaine, avec scènes de culte en l'honneur des parents, figurés sous forme de statues-cubes. *J. Custers*

de CENIVAL, Jean-Louis, see also our number 68486.

68118 ČERNÝ, J., Le temple d'Amada. Cahier V. Les inscriptions historiques, Le Caire, Centre de documentation et d'études sur l'ancienne Égypte, 1967 (21 × 26.8 cm; portefolio containing [VI +] 11 [unnumbered] p. and 12 pl., including a map and a plan). At head of title: Collection scientifique.

Publication, without transcription, of the two historical texts from the temple of Amada: the stela of Amenophis II in the sanctuary and that of the year 5 of Merenptah on the thickness of the entrance, the latter presented by the vice-roy of Nubia Messuy.

Of each text there is given a handcopy, a facsimile and a photograph. Moreover, for the Merenptah stela there is also a copy of the facsimile made by Breasted, and photographs and facsimiles of its fragmentary parallels in Wadi es-Sebua' and Amara-West.

For the other volumes, see our numbers 68006, 68021, 68059 and 68060.

CHANG, K. C., see our number 68010.

68119 CHASSINAT, Émile, Le mystère d'Osiris au mois de Khoiak (fascicule II), Le Caire, Imprimerie de l'Institut français d'Archéologie orientale, 1968 (25 × 34.8 cm; XVI + 490 p. [numbered 345-834]). At head of title: Publications de l'Institut français d'Archéologie orientale du Caire.

Sequel to our number 66131.

In the preface François Daumas, who took care of the publication twenty years after the death of the author, describes its history and the policy followed in the edition. The foreword, meant for both fascicles, is by Chassinat himself. This fascicle contains text, translation and commentary on columns 40-159, *i.e.* Book V-VII (p. 345-808). There follows a complete translation of all seven Books (809-823). Indexes by Roger Khawam on p. 825-830.

68120 CHATTERJI, Suniti Kumar, India and Ethiopia from the Seventh Century B.C., Calcutta, 1968 (16 × 25 cm; IX + 80 p., 27 ill. on 26 pl.) = The Asiatic Society. Monograph Series 15.

In der vorliegenden Arbeit werden die Beziehungen zwischen dem heutigen Äthiopien, Ägypten und dem Sudan einerseits und Indien andererseits untersucht. Uns interessieren die ersten 5 Kapitel des recht ungeordneten Werkes: die Bevölkerung Nubiens besteht aus "Hamiten" und "Negern", wobei auf die Darstellung roter und schwarzer Krieger im Tempel von Beit el Wali und die Nennung von roten und schwarzen Noba in der 'Ezāna-Inschrift gut 1600 Jahre später hingewiesen wird. Nachdem die Sabäer im heutigen Äthiopien gelandet waren, suchten sie als "Herrenvolk" "Lebensraum" am Nil. So nimmt es nicht Wunder, daß das "Nubische" (gemeint ist das Meroitische) doch eher "a Cushitic speech of the Hamitic family, and not a Negro speech" (p. 3) ist.

Kapitel II gibt einen kurzen Überblick über die Geschichte

der 25. Dynastie in Ägypten, Kapitel III die Beziehungen Ägyptens zu Indien: ein Teil der Seevölker nahmen, nach ihrer Vertreibung aus Ägypten, an einer in der Rig-Veda VII, 18 genannten Schlacht teil, und zwar als Śigru, Yakṣu und Turvaśa (eine Kombination aus Tursha und Washsha). Auch die Pulastyas und die Kapardins der vedischen Texte sind im Westen bekannt, nämlich als Philister und Keftiu (S. 11). Aber es ist beruhigend zu wissen, daß diese Völker "were not properly Hamitic Egyptians, and certainly not Ethiopians" (S. 12).

Zusammen mit den Herrschern von Assyrien und Babylon wird Taharqa (sic!) in einem späten vedischen Text, dem Śatapatha-Brāhmaṇa XIII, 4, 3 unter dem Namen Tārkṣya Vaipaścita, König der Vögel, genannt. Auf eine philologische Erklärung eines Zusammenhanges von Tārkṣya mit *Thrq*, das nach einer neueren Untersuchung möglicherweise *T-d-q* gelesen werden muß, wird verzichtet (S. 15 f.). Im Kapitel V über die Beziehungen Äthiopiens zu Indien wird wieder auf das meroitische Reich eingegangen. Anscheinend war Arkells Artikel "Meroe and India" (unsere Nr. 2180) unbekannt. So wird der Hinweis, mehrköpfige und mehrgliedrige Götter seien in Indien um die Zeitenwende nicht nachweisbar, lediglich wiederholt. Ein indischer Vorwurf für den dreiköpfigen und vierarmigen Apedemak auf der Westwand des Löwentempels von Naqa wird ohne weitere Untersuchung negiert. Der Verf. nimmt irrigerweise an, Apedemak hätte "sometimes three lion-heads" (S. 26), auch übersieht er, daß es in der Kushana-Periode nicht nur vielköpfige, sondern auch mehrgliedrige Götter gab.

Daß das arabische Element "had entirely supplanted the original Cushitic and Negro speeches of ancient Nubia" (S. 27) muß dahingehend richtiggestellt werden, daß die meroitische Sprache bereits in christlicher Zeit durch das Altnubische verdrängt war, bevor die Araber kamen, die dann ihrerseits das Nubische zwar in seiner geographischen Ausdehnung beschränkten, obwohl es als Sprache bis heute besteht.

Der Verf. hielt auf dem 27. Internationalen Orientalistenkongreß in Ann Harbor einen Vortrag über das gleiche Thema: "There was a little discussion, and my point of view created some interest and was generally supported" (S. VIII).
Inge Hofmann

68121 CHEHAB, Maurice, Relations entre l'Égypte et la Phénicie des origines à Oun-Amon, *The Role of the Phoenicians* 1-8, with 7 pl.

The author discusses the relations between Egypt and

Phoenicia from prehistoric times onwards. After referring to a few instances from the earliest period he deals with the Old, Middle and New Kingdom in their relations to Phoenicia, particularly to Byblos. Various Egyptian objects there found are mentioned.

See also our number 68371.

CHMIELEWSKA, Maria, see our number 68630.

CHMIELEWSKI, Waldemar, see our number 68630.

68122 CHRISTENSEN, Erwin O., A Guide to Art Museums in the United States, New York, Dodd, Mead & Company, [1968] (12.2 × 23 cm; XIV + 303 p., 511 ill.).

Basic information about 88 museums in the United States. We mention the Egyptian collections of the Museum of Fine Arts, Boston (p. 9-10); the Worcester Art Museum (25-26); the Metropolitan Museum of Art (49-50); the Brooklyn Museum (96-97). From each of them a few important objects are described. From other collections, *e.g.* the Cleveland Museum of Art (168) and the City Art Museum in St. Louis (199-200) only one Egyptian object is mentioned.

CHRISTOPHE, Louis-A., see our number 68614.

68123 CLÈRE, J. J., The Collection of "Book of the Dead" Papyri in the Brooklyn Museum, *The Brooklyn Museum Annual* 9 (1967-1968), 88-91, with 2 ill.

The Brooklyn Museum possesses at least 15 copies of the *Book of the Dead*, dating from the New Kingdom to the Roman Period; two of them are written on linen, four are more or less complete, the rest fragmentary. Five of them are described in detail, and the problems of preservation discussed.

68124 CLÈRE, J. J., Deux statues 'gardiennes de porte' d'époque ramesside, *JEA* 54 (1968), 135-148, with 2 ill. and 3 pl.

Two statuettes of the period of Ramesses II showing innovations introduced at this time. The first is a cube statuette of black granite 16 cm high in Brighton museum to which it was presented by Mr. James Ashbury in 1878. It was briefly published by Weigall in 1901, and represents the royal scribe Minmose who is of sufficient importance to be attested elsewhere. The second example is in a private collection in Lyons and is of unknown provenance. It is also a cube or 'sistrophore' statue in schist measuring 15.5 cm high and represents Pyiay. Both these men were doorkeepers of temples. *E. Uphill*

68125 CLÈRE, J. J., La légende d'une scène d'oracle, *Festschrift Schott* 45-49.

Study of a passage in the scene representing the procession of the divine bark on Cairo stela JE 43649 (cfr Legrain, *ASAE* 16 [1916], 161-170 and Moret, *Comptes rendus de l'Académie des Inscriptions et Belles-Lettres*. 1917, 157-165). By comparing it with a passage in a hymn to Amenophis I the author is able to read the last words of the sentence as *mḥ ỉb.f ỉm.k*.

68126 CLÈRE, J. J., Un mot pour "mariage" en égyptien de l'epoque ramesside, *RdE* 20 (1968), 171-175.

Plusieurs inscriptions de Deir el Médineh prouvent que le mot *ḥmsy* en néo-égyptien signifie mariage. *grgt* (copte ⲅⲣⲅⲉ) désigne alors la dot. *Ph. Derchain*

68127 CLÈRE, J. J., Nouveaux fragments de scènes du jubilé d'Aménophis IV, *RdE* 20 (1968), 51-54, with 3 fig. and 1 pl.

Publication de deux fragments appartenant à des scènes du jubilé d'Aménophis IV, vus dans une collection privée et depuis acquis par le Louvre (Nos E 26013 et 26014), que l'auteur rapproche de débris analogues trouvés notamment à Médamoud, où le roi, en costume de *ḥb sd*, est suivi d'un chambellan (*imi ḫnt*) profondément incliné. *Ph. Derchain*

68128 CONRAD, Diethelm, Studien zum Altargesetz. Ex. 20: 24-26, Marburg, 1968 (15 × 21 cm; 163 p.); rev. *ZAW* 81 (1969), 127 ([G. Fohrer]).

Thesis for a doctor's degree in Marburg / Lahn.
Study about the altar-law in the Book Exodus. The author also deals with the altars in Egypt (p. 105-108), concluding that the step-altar was conceived to be the throne of a mighty god, usually the sun-god.

68129 COONEY, John D., Amarna Art in the Cleveland Museum, *The Bulletin of the Cleveland Museum of Art*, Cleveland 55 (1968), 2-17, with 17 ill. (one in colour [on cover]).

The following pieces are described and illustrated: 1. rose quartzite head of Amenophis III (61.417), with part of a curious inscription on the back-pillar (*nsw.t bity ḥḳ3 t3 ꜥḥ* [...]), comparable to two earlier portraits (head, granite, Cleveland 52.513 and limestone relief piece, MMA, New York); 2. three *talatats* from the Aten temple at Karnak: an Akhenaten portrait (59.188), a Nefertiti portrait (59.186) and a fragmentary scene of some workers (59.187). The first two are in sunk relief, the latter is in raised relief. 3. a trial piece in limestone, used on both sides by different hands (20.1975), earlier dated by Capart (*Documents*, I, 43; pl. 61) to the XIXth Dynasty. 4. black steatite cosmetic tray

(14.538) in the form of a lotus pool with two bultis. 5. fragment of an alabaster toilet spoon (32.35), found in El Amarna, comparable to similar objects in the MMA at New York and the Kofler Collection (Luzern). 6. two groups of white faience beads, purchased at Aswan. Pieces of one group are inscribed with the cartouche of Amenophis III (19.619); another group (19.618) consists of uninscribed pieces. Other parts of the latter necklace are kept in the Louvre (E. 22687). 7. fragment of a faience inlaid headdress (20.1976). Additional objects listed (not illustrated) are: 8. an inscribed limestone door jamb; 9. a painted pottery jar; 10. cylindrical faience fragment with grooves and ridges. The latter three came from the English excavations at El Amarna.

J. F. Borghouts

68130 COONEY, John D., Gods Bearing Gifts for the King, *The Bulletin of the Cleveland Museum of Art*, Cleveland 54 (1967), 279-289, with 6 ill. (one in colour [= p. 280-1]).

Description of a painted inscribed limestone relief in the Cleveland Museum (no. 61.205) with 3 standing nome gods bearing offerings, dedicated by Amenophis III. Part of one of the cartouches has been deleted in the Amarna-period; but by mistake (?) the hieroglyphs containing the name of Amon were left intact. The well-fed gods belong to the IXth nome of Lower Egypt (left), the IIIrd nome of Upper Egypt (center) and the XVIIth nome of Lower Egypt (right); the combination of Upper and Lower Egyptian nome deities in one row is unique for this sort of representations. Remarkable among the many details of animals and food offerings are the *gerenuk*, an antelope species rather rarely represented in Egyptian art (p. 283; 189, note 3 [additions to L. Keimer, *ASAE* 41 (1942), 161 sqq.]) and some opium poppies, perhaps for a religious purpose. The provenance of the relief is unknown; since it rather comes from a temple than from a royal tomb, the author presumes that it may have come from Amenophis III's Theban funerary temple, since long destroyed. Perhaps it is a *talatat*.

The author compares the nome gods to similarly obese Nile gods and for this purpose adduces another museum piece: an inscribed bronze statue base dedicated to Amon-Re (14.578) of the Late Period (owner: Tefnakhte?) with Harpocrates flanked by two kneeling Nile gods (so far unpublished).

The Cleveland relief is further compared to two similar museum pieces in the Walters Art Gallery in Baltimore (illustrated; nos. 22.100 and 22.93, both published by Steindorff in his *Catalogue* [1946]) showing kneeling gods.

The author traces them back to the Abydos temple of Ramses II at Abydos, whose reliefs have been steadily misused in modern times. To this temple probably also belongs a Brooklyn Museum relief fragment (illustrated; no. 11.670, previously unpublished).
For a correction compare *The Bulletin of the Cleveland Museum*, Cleveland 55 (1968), 303. *J. F. Borghouts*

68131 COONEY, John D., Intaglios, Cameos, and Related Works, *The Bulletin of the Cleveland Museum of Art*, Cleveland 55 (1968), 113-119, with 9 ill.

The author describes a series of cameos now in the Cleveland Museum of Art, two of which—a royal head (66.370) and an actor's mask (64.417), both of glass—come from Egypt and may be dated to the Ptolemaic period. In connection with a carnelian bull (14.568), a feldspar duck (14.569) and a carnelian frog (14.570) of the XVIIIth Dynasty, he discusses the probable date of a lapislazuli dwarf in the University College of London, tentatively assigned by Sir Flinders Petrie to the Roman Period, but more probably belonging to the end of the New Kingdom or shortly after.
Dieter Mueller

68132 COONEY, John D., Siren and Ba, Birds of a Feather, *The Bulletin of the Cleveland Museum of Art*, Cleveland 55 (1968), 262-271, with 13 ill. (one on back cover).

After describing some Greek siren figures the author discusses the probable derivation from the Egyptian *ba*, illustrating his argument by details from the unpublished *Papyrus of Hori* (Cleveland Museum 21.1032) of the XXIst Dynasty. The forms of the siren and the *ba* were identical, every variation in the iconography of the latter also occurring in the former. The late appearance of the siren in Greek art and literature increases the probability of its Egyptian origin. Although the *ba* appears from the 15th century B.C.— the author publishes a late XVIIIth Dynasty bronze fragment of two crossed arms clasping a *ba* bird (Cleveland Museum 14.556) belonging to a head of a lady (cfr our number 65125) —it was only from the XXVIth Dynasty onwards that it was frequently used as an amulet and made as a sculpture. This is also the formation period of the later Greek art.
The author further discusses the methods of patinating bronze (cfr our number 66145), *i.e.* referring to the gold dagger of queen Aahotep with its vertical strips of black bronze. Black bronzes from the Greek art are also mentioned, one of which is an Infant Hercules found in Egypt.

68133 Le CORSU, F., Un oratoire pompéien consacré à Dionysos-Osiris, *BSFE* N° 51 (Mars 1968), 17-31, with 2 ill. and 1 pl.

Deux pièces de la "Casa dei cubiculi floreali", à Pompéi, gardent la figuration d'éléments religieux égyptiens, entourant Dionysos. L'auteur montre par trois exemples: l'Iseum de Pompéi, la Villa des Mystères, le Sérapeum de Memphis, que les cultes d'Isis et de Dionysos sont mêlés, le second concrétisant l'aspect de renaissance d'Osiris, comme Sérapis symbolise la mort. *J. Custers*

68134 Le CORSU, France, Un oratoire pompéien consacré à Dionysos-Osiris, *Revue Archéologique*, Paris 1967, 239-254, with 10 ill.

A more complete version of our preceding number.

68135 Le CORSU, F., Stèles-portes égyptiennes à éléments emboîtés d'époque gréco-romaine, *RdE* 20 (1968), 109-125, with 8 ill. and 3 fig.

Huit monuments du type décrit dans le titre sont ici publiés. Ils ont servi certainement d'opercules à des *loculi* de la nécropole alexandrine. Le décor comprend d'ordinaire un uraeus sortant de la porte de la chapelle, où l'auteur voudrait voir une figure d'Hathor dans sa fonction funéraire. Le signe de la plante 𓇚 qui orne certaines d'entre elles paraît devoir être considéré comme une graphie de *ḏt* "éternité" ou de *mꜣꜥ ḫrw*. *Ph. Derchain*

68136 COTTRELL, Leonard, The Warrior Pharaohs, London, Evans Brothers Limited, [1968] (14.5 × 22 cm; VIII + 137 p., 1 map, 24 pl., frontispiece [in colour]); rev. *BiOr* 27 (1970), 19-20 (I. Pomorska). Pr. 35 s.

Description for the general public of the wars of ancient Egypt from Hor-Aha until Ramses III.

68137 COUROYER, B., Amenemopé, XXIV, 13-18, *Revue Biblique*, Paris 75 (1968), 549-561.

L'auteur propose de traduire:
"L'homme est limon et paille,
Dieu est son modeleur.
C'est lui qui défait et fait chaque jour...".
L'influence sur le *Siracide*, 33, 10-13, lui paraît très probable.
M. Heerma van Voss

68138 COUROYER, B., Le temple de Yaho et l'orientation dans les papyrus araméens d'Éléphantine, *Revue Biblique*, Paris 75 (1968), 80-85.

Referring to his previous article of the same title (our number 61151), the author produces further evidence for his contention that the enumeration of the cardinal points in the Aramaic papyri from Elephantine follows the Egyptian custom of orientation towards the South. He points out that the use of *mwʿh sms* for "orient" and *mʿrb* for "occident" can be traced back to the Amarna letters and the times of Amenophis III, when *wbn* frequently replaces *i3b.t* even in Egyptian texts.

With regard to the term *tmw'anty*, equated with Egyptian *t3 my(.t) ntr* "dromos" in the previous article, the author emphasizes that it is sometimes translated by the Iranian word *hnpn'*, for which W. Eilers has recently suggested the meanings "covered passage, bazaar". It has not been established that the dromos in Elephantine or the market places in Ancient Egypt were covered, but it seems significant that the term *ḥft-ḥr.t* for "dromos tax" also suggests a close connection between the temple and the market place, and that the existence of a "Royal Treasury" (*'wṣr mlk'*) next to the *hnpn'* supports the reading θη[σ(αυρὸς) δ]ρόμου in Pap. Amh. 122, 8.

Compare our number 68042. *Dieter Mueller*

68139 CRAMER, Maria, Zum Aufbau der koptischen Theotokie und des Difnars. Bemerkungen zur Hymnologie, *Probleme* 197-223, with 6 ill. (= p. 217-222).

Observations about the construction and rythm of Coptic hymns. *L. F. Kleiterp*

68140 CROWFOOT PAYNE, Joan, Lapislazuli in Early Egypt, *Iraq*, London 30 (1968), 58-61.

In addition to a study by Georgina Herrman, Lapis Lazuli: The Early Phases of its Trade (*Iraq* 30 [1968], 21-59), which deals with Mesopotamia, the author discusses the early occurrences of the material in Egypt. A list of them is given, divided into three groups: The Gerzean Period, Dynasties O-I, Dynasties IV-VI.

68141 CURTO, Silvio, Di uno scarabeo egizio trovato in Italia, *La Parola del Passato*, Napoli fasc. 119 (1968), 149-152, with 2 fig.

The inscription on an Egyptian scarab found in Calabria in a tomb of the 8th cent. reads either *Wsr mn m3ʿ.t Rʿ stp n Rʿ* (in which case it would go back to the early years of Ramesses II), or *Wsr m3ʿ.t Rʿ stp n 'Imn(-Rʿ)*—a name frequently attested on scarabs from the XXIInd and XXIIIrd Dyn. (893-740 B.C.). *Dieter Mueller*

68142 CURTO, Silvio and M. MANCINI, News of Kha' and Meryt, *JEA* 54 (1968), 77-81, with 4 fig. and 2 pl. (p. 80-81 in Italian).

The restoration of the exhibition room devoted to the objects from the tomb of this couple recently undertaken at Turin, resulted in a number of discoveries. The corners of the sarcophagus of Meryt bear signs intended to help the workmen when re-assembling it after taking it into the tomb in sections. Her coffin is covered with microscopically thin goldleaf and has a white outlined figure of Nut inside. Her face mask is gilded and the eyebrows and eyesockets are inlaid in blue glass, while the eyes are of opaque white and translucent black glass. X-rays of the mummies reveal that they carry fine ornaments such as a gold ring collar, necklace, heart scarab and amulets, gold ear-rings and bracelets, *usekh*-collar and elaborate girdle. The positions of these are also interesting. *E. Uphill*

CURTO, Silvio, see also our number 68182.

68143 CZAPKIEWICZ, Andrzej, Z historii badań nad toponomastyka Egiptu, *Onomastica*, Warszawa 13, 1/2 (1968), 345-352.

"From the History of Studies on the Toponymy of Egypt". The author classifies Arabic and Egyptological works devoted to place names in Egypt. He states that the research works proceeded in the following directions: 1) establishing the reading of a name, 2) establishing the etymology, 3) localization of a place on the basis of name's etymology, 4) analysis of the name's structure. *A. Szczudłowska*

68144 DĄBROWSKA-SMEKTAŁA, Elżbieta, Coffins found in the Area of the Temple of Tuthmosis III at Deir el-Bahari, *BIFAO* 66 (1968), 171-181, with 6 fig. and 13 pl.

Publication of the following objects found by the Polish Mission in the course of the third season (1963-1964).
Intact wooden coffin from the Late Period. Owner: the Overseer of the priests (of Min, Horus, and Wepwawet) *'Ir.ty-rw-t3w* (see our next number). Inventory Number F. 4032.
As before. Owner: the Mistress of the house (?) *Ns-Ḥnsw*. F. 5592.
As before. Owner: the Mistress of the house *W3d-rn.s*. F. 5593.
As before (only bottom left). F. 4033.
Wooden coffin of unknown girl. Roman Period (?). F. 4034.
Two mummies.

Embalming materials. Some of them were arranged in the shape of the (missing) body in the coffin first mentioned above. This dummy was bandaged like a real mummy.

M. Heerma van Voss

68145 DĄBROWSKA-SMEKTAŁA, Elżbieta, Fragment of Hieratic Papyrus of '*Ir.ty rw-t3w*, *BIFAO* 66 (1968), 183-189, with 3 pl.

Publications of fragments of *Book of the Dead* 146 from the Saitic-Persian Period. The manuscript (F. 5594) was found by the Polish Mission working at Deir el-Bahri, April 1964.

M. Heerma van Voss

68146 DABROWSKA-SMEKTALA, Elzbieta, List of Objects Found at Der el-Bahari in the Area of the Tuthmosis III's Temple, *ASAE* 60 (1968), 95-130, with 36 pl.

A brief description of 119 objects discovered in 1962/63 and 1963/64. *Dieter Mueller*

68147 DĄBROWSKA-SMEKTAŁA, Elżbieta, Remarks on the Restoration of the Eastern Wall on the 3rd Terrace of Hatshepsut Temple, *Études et Travaux* II 65-78, with 11 ill., 1 folding pl. and 2 fig.

L'article présente les travaux de reconstruction d'un fragment du mur Nord-Est de la 3e terrace du temple de Hatchepsout à Deir el-Bahari. Le plan joint à l'article présente l'état du mur et des représentations conservées, après la reconstruction effectuée dans la saison 1967/68.

A. Szczudłowska

68148 DĄBROWSKA, E. and GARTKIEWICZ, P. Preliminary Report Concerning the Restoration of the Wall on the 3rd Terrace of the Hatshepsut Temple at Deir el-Bahri During the Season 1965-1966, *ASAE* 60 (1968), 213-219, with 5 folding pl.

Measurements taken in the temple, and newly discovered joints of wall blocks, were instrumental in the temporary restoration of the eastern wall of the hypostyle hall.

Dieter Mueller

68149 DĄBROWSKI, Leszek, Preliminary Report on the Reconstruction Works of Hatshepsut's Temple at Deir el Bahari, *ASAE* 60 (1968), 131-137, with 10 pl., including plans and sections.

While work continued on the front colonnade of the upper terrace and the third terrace court of Hatshepsut's temple, further attempts were made to clear the ground on the S.W.

side where traces of a temple of Thutmosis III had been discovered previously. *Dieter Mueller*

68150 DĄBROWSKI, Leszek, Temple de Hatchepsout à Deir el-Bahari, 3ᵉ terrasse. Projet de la reconstruction du mur ouest de la cour, *Études et Travaux* II 39-45, with 3 ill., 2 pl. [including 2 plans], 6 cross-sections.

A short article discussing the work on the reconstruction of a wall, once erected in the western part of Hatshepsut's temple and destroyed in ancient times by falling rocks. Now 200 blocks of this wall have been recovered.

A. Szczudlowska

68151 DANELIUS, Eva, The Sins of Jeroboam Ben-Nabat, *The Jewish Quarterly Review*, Philadelphia 48 (1967-1968), 93-114 and 204-223.

In dealing with the "sins of Jeroboam ben-Nabat" the author demonstrates that the images installed by the king were no calves but heifers, representations of the cow-goddess such as known from the Hathor shrine in the temple at Deir el-Bahri (p. 109-112). Jeroboam, whose "father's" name the author explains as $nb.t$, The Lady, that is Hathor (p. 212), may have brought her cult from Egypt, where he had been an exile. His promotion of the cult of this goddess may have been the reason why, according to I Kings and Josephus, during Shishak's invasion in the 5th year of Rehoboam Israel's territory remained untouched. If this is correct, Shoshenq's list of captured towns at Karnak is to be dismissed as unhistorical (214-217).

68152 DANIEL, Constantin, Les noms égyptiens de certaines types de vases grecs, *Studia et Acta Orientalia*, Bucarest 5-6 (1967), 379-387.

Continuing the investigations of P. V. Jernstedt (see our number 3387, 4635, 46336 and 58337) the author attempts to demonstrate the Egyptian origin of some Greek names of vases. He suggests the following derivations: βῆσσα $< bꜥ$ ($= bd3$?); δέπας $< t3b$; λέβης $< rb$; μάνης $< mn$; χόννος $< hnw$. The Aegeo-cretan and the Phoenician languages may have been the links between the Egyptian and the Greek.

68153 DANIEL, Constantin, La prohibition du fer dans l'Égypte ancienne, *Studia et acta orientalia*, Bucarest 7 (1968), 3-21.

The author raises the question why the Egyptians did not use the iron on any large scale previous to the Roman Period, though the ore was available in Egypt and lack of fuel

did not prevent the development of the copper industry, nor of the iron smelting-works in the kingdom of Meroe. The reason may be that in the Late Period the use of the metal was prohibited for religious reasons, iron being a Sethian metal—except for meteoric iron, which was in fact used for sacred objects.
The main sources for our knowledge are Greek authors, since also the word for iron seems to have been avoided.
As an additional reason for the prohibition of iron the author suggests the wish of the later rulers to prevent their subjects from being adequately armed, for fear of revolts; thus they made use of the religious tabu.

68154 DANIEL, Glyn, The First Civilisations. The Archaeology of Their Origins, London, Thames and Hudson, [1968] (16 × 24 cm; 208 p., 2 fig., 14 maps, 79 ill. on 48 pl.); rev. *Antiquity* 43 (1969), 161-162 (Gordon R. Willey).

The book, which is not meant for the specialist (p. 13), deals with the origins of early civilisations.
Egypt is discussed in chapter 4 (p. 83-93), particularly the question whether its civilisation has been dependent on Sumer or not. The author suggests that, though there have been early contacts, the development of Egypt was only stimulated by them, not caused.

68155 DAUMAS, François, Fouilles et travaux de l'Institut français d'Archéologie orientale durant l'année 1967-1968, *Comptes rendus de l'Académie des Inscriptions et Belles-Lettres*. 1968, Paris, 395-408, with 14 ill.

Report on the activities of the French Institute at The Kellia, Karnak and Dendera.
At The Kellia an extensive monastery at Qasr el Waheida was excavated. At Karnak work in the temple of Montu has been resumed, while at Dendera mainly the sanatorium was studied.
There follow short notes on the campaign at Esne, and an expedition to "the cells" 30 km west of Wâdi Natrûn published by Prince Umar Tussūn (*Société royale d'archéologie d'Alexandrie. Mémoires*. Tome 7, 1935).

68156 DAUMAS, François, Les propylées du temple d'Hathor à Philae et le culte de la déesse, *ZÄS* 95, 1 (1968), 1-17, with 6 pl. and a plan.

Publication et traduction (avec commentaire) d'inscriptions du temple remontant au moins à Ptolémée VI Philométor. Les planches montrent en outre les représentations des colonnes.

Le rapprochement des données de Philae, d'Edfou, de Dendara, de Médamoud et de la biographie d'Ounnofré (notre n° 3481, p. 194-196) permet à l'auteur de conclure à de véritables mystères d'Hathor. *M. Heerma van Voss*

68157 DAUMAS, François, La vie dans l'Égypte ancienne, Paris, Presses Universitaires de France, 1968 (11.6 × 17.7 cm; 128 p., 27 fig.) = "Que sais-je ?" Le point des connaissances actuelles. N° 1302; rev. *BiOr* 26 (1969), 328-329 (Claudia Dolzani); *Bulletin critique du livre français* 24 (1969), 695; *CdE* XLIV, N° 88 (1969), 265-266 (R. Dusoir); *OLZ* 66 (1971), 241 (E. Staehelin); *Revue de l'histoire des religions* 177 (1970), 207-209 (A. Barucq); *Rivista* 44 (1969), 51-54 (Claudio Barocas).

This volume of the popular series "Que sais-je ?" is devoted to daily life in ancient Egypt.
The main chapters, together containing half the book, deal with country-life (I) and town-life and crafts (III), while each is followed by a shorter chapter, printed in smaller type: one about hunting and fishing (II) and one about costume and ornaments (IV). There follow four short chapters about food and games (V), the army (VI), the intellectual circles (VII) and religious life (VIII), the latter called "piety and popular festivals, death and burial".
A short annotated bibliography on p. 126-127.

DAUMAS, François, see also our number 68119.

68158 EL-DAWAKHLY, Zeinab, On the Relation between *Imni*, Physician of the Middle Empire, and *Kkw*, Scribe of the House of Life, *BIE* 45 (session 1964-1965), 1968, 95-99, with 3 fig. and 1 pl.

La stèle du Caire Cat. 20023, provenant d'Abydos, montre au revers 14 personnes accompagnées de leurs noms et qualités. Il faut y corriger en *s3*, "fils", un signe lu erronément *wr*, et ne pas séparer deux lignes du texte. Quant à l'ordre de filiation, malgré l'usage des XIIe et XIIIe dynasties, c'est bien "le scribe du *pr-ꜥnḫ* Kekou, fils du médecin Imeni" qu'il faut comprendre. La disposition des figures sur le reste du monument le confirme, comme d'autre part une citation de la statue d'Oudjahorresné, parlant du recrutement des membres du *pr-ꜥnḫ* dans l'élite intellectuelle.
J. Custers

68159 DAWSON, Warren R. and P. H. K. GRAY, Catalogue of Egyptian Antiquities in the British Museum. I. Mummies and Human Remains, London, The Trustees of the British Museum, 1968 (28 × 34.8 cm; XIII + 44 p., frontispiece,

37 pl.); rev. *BiOr* 26 (1969), 189-192 (Suzanne Ratié);
CdE XLIV, N° 88 (1969), 289-290 (Herman de Meulenaere);
JARCE 8 (1969-1970), 99-100 (Alan R. Schulman); *JEA* 56
(1970), 224-226 (Peter A. Clayton); *RdE* 21 (1969), 161-164
(M. A. Dollfus). Pr. bound £6

After a historical introduction by Dawson, the catalogue proper follows. Among other data it presents the results of a radiographic examination. The general medical and anatomical conclusions are offered in an appendix by Gray.
This is the first volume in a new series dealing with objects which bear no inscriptions or would not be classified primarily as written documents.
Preface by I. E. S. Edwards. *M. Heerma van Voss*

68160 DAYTON, John, The Last Elephants of Arabia, *Antiquity* 42 (1968), 42-45, with 1 pl.

The author mentions the discovery of a rock-drawing in Egyptian style near the ruins of Dedan in the Wadi Kura (Saudi Arabia), representing an elephant and a human fore-arm and open hand. Discussing the period to which it may be ascribed he stresses that the drawing was unfinished and that it exhibits the characteristics of the Syrian elephant. He suggests the XIXth Dynasty to be the most likely date of the drawing.

68161 DELCOR, M., Réflections sur l'inscription phénicienne de Nora en Sardaigne, *Syria*, Paris 45 (1968), 323-352, with 6 ill.

Study of the famous Phoenician inscription of Nora. The author suggests to read in line 3 בשרדן, "on Sardinia", discussing in this connection the data and theories about the Shardana in Egyptian sources (p. 339-344).

68162 Demotische und Koptische Texte, Köln und Opladen, Westdeutscher Verlag, 1968 (16.5 × 24 cm; 92 p., 1 plan, 1 table, 5 folding pl., 5 pl.) = Wissenschaftliche Abhandlungen der Arbeitsgemeinschaft für Forschung des Landes Nordrhein-Westfalen. Sonderreihe Papyrologica Coloniensia Vol. 2; rev. *BiOr* 27 (1970), 210-216 (E. A. E. Reymond); *CdE* XLV, N° 89 (1970), 80-84 (Jan Quaegebeur); *Enchoria* 1 (1971), 61 (Heinz-Josef Thissen); *JARCE* 8 (1969-1970), 92-93 (Richard A. Parker); *OLZ* 66 (1971), 243-245 (I. Grumach); *Orientalia* 38 (1969), 497-498 (H. Quecke); *RdE* 21 (1969), 171-173 (F. de Cenival). Pr. DM 39.50

In dieser Abhandlung hat Erich Lüddeckens die demotischen *Papyri Köln 2411* und *2412* herausgegeben. Die Abstands-(138/7 v. Chr.) und die Eheurkunde (107 v. Chr.) werden in Transkription, in Übersetzung, mit Beschreibung, Anmerkungen, und Wörterverzeichnis, und auf photographischen und gezeichneten Tafeln vorgelegt.

Angelicus Kropp, Alfred Hermann † und Manfred Weber verdankt man ein Märchen im Bibelstil (Schreibübung), eine sahidische Predigt und einen Ölsegen.

Diese koptischen Mss *Köln 3287, 3286* und *1471* (5.-6. Jahrhundert) werden beschrieben und übersetzt (mit Kommentar). Die Texte sind in Druck und photographisch reproduziert worden.
M. Heerma van Voss

68163 DERCHAIN, Philippe, Religions dans l'Égypte tardive. Colloque tenu à Strasbourg du 16 au 18 mai 1967, *Kêmi* 18 (1968), 99-101.

Le quinzaine de savants participants, appartenant à plusieurs disciplines, ont été surpris de l'abondance des échanges et des emprunts entre les civilisations et les religions égyptienne, grecque et juive.

Pour la publication du colloque, voir maintenant *Religions en Égypte hellénistique et romaine*. Colloque de Strasbourg 16-18 mai 1967, Paris, Presses Universitaires de France, 1969.
J. Custers

68164 DESANGES, J., Les Romains à Premis (Kasr Ibrim) au IIIème siècle après J.C.?, *Meroitic Newsletter. Bulletin d'Informations Méroitiques*, Paris 1 (Oct. 1968), 19.

Ein Präfekt hat einen Brief von actum prem(is), d.h. von Premis (Kasr Ibrim) an einen tabularius und seinen proximus der Finanzverwaltung in Ägypten geschrieben. Da auf dem verso des Papyrus das Jahr 247 n. Chr. angegeben ist, scheint erwiesen zu sein, daß zwischen der Regierung Caracallas und derjenigen Diokletians Premis wenigstens vorübergehend von römischen Truppen besetzt war.
Inge Hofmann

68165 DESANGES, Jehan, Vues grecques sur quelques aspects de la monarchie méroïtique, *BIFAO* 66 (1968), 89-104.

L'interprétation des témoignages grecs conduit l'auteur à évoquer une image aux contours incertains du pouvoir royal méroïtique.

Dans un P.S., il s'occupe de nos numéros 67600 et 66342.
M. Heerma van Voss

68166 DESROCHES-NOBLECOURT, Ch., La cueillette du raisin à la fin de l'époque amarnienne. Toutankhamon fut-il portraituré sous l'aspect d'un petit prince?, *JEA* 54 (1968), 82-88, with 2 fig., 2 ill. and one pl.

The Louvre museum possesses a small ivory plaque (N° E.

14374) showing a young prince holding a bouquet of lotus flowers and bending down to pick a bunch of grapes from under a vine, worked in the Amarna style. The writer compares it to the well-known ivory box of Tutankhamun and suggests the style is that of the period immediately after Akhenaten, the figure shown may well be the young king himself and the scene a poetical reference to rebirth.

E. Uphill

68167 DESROCHES-NOBLECOURT, Ch., S. DONADONI, Gamal MOUKHTAR, avec la collaboration de H. el-ACHIERY et M. DEWACHTER, Le speos d'El-Lessiya. Cahier I. Description archéologique. Planches, Le Caire, Centre de documentation et d'études sur l'ancienne Égypte, 1968 (21 × 27 cm; VII + 27 p., 3 maps [2 folding], 51 ill. [1 in colour] on 42 pl. [8 folding]). At head of title: Collection scientifique.

The preface mentions previous studies of the temple and the work for the present publication. The temple is described in its general outlay, and all reliefs in detail. The photographs illustrate both. Though the reliefs are rather faint the pictures are clear, while two inscriptions, hardly legible from the photograph, are also given in line-drawing. For line-drawings of the scenes, compare our number 68005.

The present volume does not contain the royal stelae at both sides of the entrance nor the graffiti on the rock, which will be published in a third volume.

68168 DESROCHES-NOBLECOURT, Chr. [and] Georg GERSTER, Die Welt rettet Abu Simbel, Wien-Berlin, Verlag A. F. Koska, [1968] (23.2 × 29.9 cm; 244 p., 144 pl. [51 in colour], 30 fig., 3 maps); rev. *CdE* XLIV, N° 89 (1970), 113-114 (Herman de Meulenaere). Pr. bound DM 67

Der erste Teil des Buches wurde von Frau Desroches-Noblecourt geschrieben und von Dr Hans Rieben unter Mitarbeit von Ruth Antelma übersetzt. Er beschäftigt sich mit Entwicklung, Geschichte, gemeinsamen Zügen, Stilen und archäologischen Einzelheiten der beiden Tempel und mit dem Kult. Vor allem bestätigt der grosse Tempel das Männliche, der Kleine das Weibliche.

Den zweiten Teil (über die Rettung der Heiligtümer) und achtundzwanzig der Bilder verdankt man Dr Gerster.
Vorwort von Dr Franz Zeit.
Man vergleiche unsere Nummer 65317.

M. Heerma van Voss

68169 DESROCHES-NOBLECOURT, Chr. [and] Ch. KUENTZ,

Le petit temple d'Abou Simbel. "Nofretari pour qui se lève le dieu-soleil". I. Étude archéologique et épigraphique. Essai d'interpretation [and] II. Planches, Le Caire, 1968 ([Texte]: 27 × 35 cm; XIX + 243 p., colour ill. on cover, frontispiece in colour, 2 ill. on endpapers, 33 fig. including 1 plan, 1 unnumbered pl. facing p. 50; Planches: 32 × 43 cm; X p., colour ill. on cover, 2 ill. on endpapers, 1 map, 127 pl. including 5 in colour, 1 plan [= pl.3], 1 folding colour plan [= pl. 127], numerous drawings facing the pl.) = Ministère de la Culture. Centre de documentation et d'étude sur l'ancienne Égypte. Mémoires, Tome I [and] II; rev. *BiOr* 28 (1971), 50-51 (Sergio Donadoni); *Comptes rendus de l'Académie des Inscriptions et Belles-Lettres*. 1969, 257-258 (Jacques Vandier); *Pantheon* 28 (1970), 347-348 (Dietrich Wildung).

The Preface by Ahmad Badawi and Mme Desroches describes the work of the Centre de Documentation, the present volumes being its first complete study of a Nubian temple. The Introduction deals in general with travellers and modern scholars who have visited the temple, with its site and its history.

Part A (p. 7-107) carefully describes all parts of the architecture and all wall-scenes, with copies and translations of every text.

Part B (109-124) contains an attempt to interpret the temple and its meaning, stressing the notions of renewal of the kingship, the assimilation of Nofretari with Hathor, and the importance of the rites connected with the inundation. The date of the foundation may be early in Ramses' reign and may be connected with the beginning of a Sothis cycle. A particular section attemps to reconstruct the route of king and queen during their ritual visits to the speos.

In part C (125-230) one finds extensive notes to the preceding parts, two of them with the length of a short article: note 57 (136-145) about the homage to a person, either god, king or private person, and to a building, and note 566 (227-230) about the rise of the Nile.

Volume II contains photographs, line drawings and photogrammetic representations of all scenes as well as some reproductions from older books. Particularly useful are the architectural drawings facing the plates by which the exact place of each scene easily may be identified.

DESROCHES-NOBLECOURT, Christiane, see also our numbers 68006, 68059, 68060, 68359 and 68654.

DEWACHTER, M., see our numbers 68005, 68006, 68021, 68059, 68060 and 68167.

DIAKONOV, I., see our number 68056.

68170 DIENER, Lennart, Mumier i röntgenljus, *in*: *Medicinhistorisk Årsbok* 1967, Nyköping, 1968, 40-47, with 8 ill.

"Mummies X-rayed".
A lecture of 1966 being an account of observations in connection with the X-raying of mummies belonging to the Medelhavsmuseet in Stockholm. Included are a mention of the importance of the study of skeletal Harris-lines, the observation of a dislocation of the spinal column, and of residues of liquids inside the skull. A mummy modelled like a small child contained an ibis, another of similar shape the lower part of a human leg.
Cfr L. Diener, Beobachtungen bei der Röntgenuntersuchung einiger ägyptischer Mumien, *Orientalia Suecana*, Uppsala 17 (1968), 1969, 3-10. *B. J. Peterson*

68171 DIETRICH, Dieter, Die Ausbreitung der alexandrinischen Mysteriengötter Isis, Osiris, Serapis und Horus in griechisch-römischer Zeit, *Das Altertum*, Berlin 14 (1968), 201-211, with 3 fig.

The spread of the cults of the Alexandrinian mystery-gods, Serapis and especially Isis, in the Hellenistic and Roman World, is explained by the social and economic conditions of the period. These cults are considered to be a Hellenistic phenomenon, in which only remains of the Egyptian tradition can be perceived.
By the same author: "Der hellenistische Isiskult als kosmopolitische Religion und die sogenannte Isismission" (unpublished diss. Leipzig, 1966). *E. Ch. L. v. d. Vliet*

68172 DIOP, L.-M., Métallurgie traditionelle et âge du fer en Afrique, *Bulletin de l'Institut Fondamental d'Afrique Noire*, Dakar 30 (1968), 10-38, with 6 fig. and a map.

For Egypt and Nubia see especially p. 12-14, and p. 36.

68173 DIRINGER, David, The Alphabeth. A Key to the History of Mankind. Third Edition completely revised with the collaboration of Reinhold Regensburger, London, Hutchinson, [1968] (19.5 × 25.5 cm; volume 1: XXII + 473 p.; volume 2: [VI +] 452 p. with ill.).   Pr. set cased £ 12.60

Revised edition of our number 72.
Ancient Egyptian scripts are dealt with on p. 29-37, with an extensive bibliography on p. 37-39. The pertaining ill. in vol. II, p. 37-56. Meroitic scripts on p. 140-141 (ill. p. 141). The Coptic alphabet on p. 369-371 (ill. p. 331-339). The origin of the alphabeth is discussed on p. 145 ff. For the

Egyptian theory see p. 146-147, the Sinaitic theory p. 148-150.

68174 DOBROVITS, Aladár, I. Amenemhat Király Tanitása, *Philologiai Közlöny*, Budapest 14 (1968), 268-307.

"Die Lehre des Königs Amenemhat I".
Der Autor ist der Meinung, dass es sich eigentlich um eine Thronrede handelt, worin der Herrscher seinen Entschluss kundgibt, seinen Sohn, Sesostris I. als Mitregenten anzunehmen. Er tut dies mit dramatischer Offenheit, wobei seine bittere Enttäuschung von humanistischem Optimismus gemildert wird. Auch der König konnte schwach sein, und zieht die Folgerungen dieser Schwäche, aber schon 10 Jahre vor seinem Tode. Die Lehre ist im Stil eines *wḏ njswt*, "Königsbefehls", abgefasst. Seine Tragödie, die Verschwörung veranlasst ihn dazu, sich einen jungen, kräftigen Mitregenten beizugesellen, der nunmehr durch die feierliche Proklamation ebenfalls zum Herrscher geworden ist: "Als König stehe auf". *Vilmos Wessetzky*

68175 DOBROVITS, Aladár, Sur la structure stylistique de l'Enseignement de Ptaḥḥotep, *Acta antiqua academiae scientiarum hungaricae*, Budapest 16 (1968), 21-37.

Der Verfasser meint den Text P in die zweite Hälfte des A.R., vielleicht in die V. Dynastie, den Text L 2 in die zweite Zwischenzeit und L 1 vielleicht am Anfang der XVIII. Dynastie setzen zu können (Vgl. die Ausgabe von Z. Žába, *Les Maximes de Ptaḥḥotep*). Bei Ptahhotep muss die philosophische Seite seiner Lehre besonders betont werden. Das oft hervorgehobene schöne und gute Wort ist gleich das Gesetz der Welt in diesem Sinne. Seine Ethik ist nicht nur theoretisch, sondern auch praktisch. Der Autor untersucht einige Ausdrücke des Textes, und meint dass Ptahhotep nicht nur ein realer Humanist gewesen ist, sondern dass seine Lehre auch die spätere Idee des *logos spermatikos* enthält. *Vilmos Wessetzky*

68176 DOBROVOLSKAJA, I. A., Стела Сетау из собрания Государственного Эрмитажа, Тезисы докладов научной сессии, посвященной итогам работы Государственного Эрмитажа за 1966 год. 22-24 мая 1967 г., Ленинград, 1967, 21-22.

"Die Stele des Setau aus der Sammlung der Staatlichen Eremitage".
Stilistische Besonderheiten einer Stele des *St3w* (Eremitage N° 3937) aus der Zeit Tutankhamon's. *E. S. Bogoslovsky*

68177 DOLZANI, Claudia, Soda e incenso nei Testi delle Piramidi, *Aegyptus* 48 (1968), 5-18, with 1 pl.

La soude et l'encens, agents de purification, revêtent dans les *Textes des Pyramides* une importance identique. La première est jointe à l'eau, le second au feu. Leur fonction liturgique s'enracine dans la vie quotidienne. Quelques passages nous éclairent sur leurs origines et leur usage. Les deux termes présentent l'élément *nṯr*. La soude est le plus souvent appelée *bd*; ce mot répond au gisement de Nekheb. Comme pendant géographique figure la soude *ḥsmn* ou *smin* de Wadi el-Natrun. *Bsn*, un terme d'importance secondaire, pourrait désigner une substance différente. La première a été déifiée en *Bdw*. *Ḥsmn* reste absent des listes d'offrandes jusqu'à la VIe dynastie; ce terme s'emploiera pourtant comme verbe "(se) purifier". L'encens lui aussi devint dieu, avec jeu de mots sur *śn-nṯr* "frère divin". On le dit *mnwr* et peut-être *p3q/p3d*. L'épithète *wšr* "sec" caractérise une phase de conservation. L'analogie avec la soude porte à opposer l'encens du Nord à celui du Sud. Mais "l'odeur de Dedoun" fournit un repère chronologique: l'importation passait encore par la Nubie. La différence d'origine des deux produits ne les a pas empêchés de pénétrer en binôme dans les mécanismes rituels.
J. Custers

68178 DONADONI, F. S., A propos de l'histoire du texte de 'Merikarê', *Proceedings* 8-11.

The author compares several passages of the *Instruction for Merikare* in the three manuscripts P, C and M, suggesting that P, though containing many mistakes, presents the text as the writer found it, while M and C show signs of an ancient "edition".

68179 DONADONI, Sergio, Giuseppe Botti, *Rivista* 43 (1968), 379-382.

Obituary notice. Compare our number 68661.

68180 DONADONI, Sergio, Due lettere copte da Antinoe, *JEA* 54 (1968), 239-242.

The first letter is a small one with a few lines containing a greeting and mentioning a person called Enoch.
The second is on a larger piece of papyrus and in small writing but without naming anyone. *E. Uphill*

68181 DONADONI, Sergio, Traducendo la storia dell' "Oasita", *Annali dell' Istituto Universitario Orientale di Napoli*, Napoli 18 (1968), 441-443.

Short notes to words and passages in the *Story of the Eloquent Peasant*, particularly to B 1, 121; 149-150; 218-220; 221-224.

68182 DONADONI, Sergio — Silvio CURTO, Le pitture murali della chiesa di Sonki nel Sudan. La Nubia christiana, [Torino, 1968] (22 × 28 cm; 25 unnumbered p., 1 fig., 6 ill., 2 maps, 6 plans, colour ill. on cover) = Quaderno n. 2 del Museo Egizio di Torino.

In the Introduction Donadoni relates the find of a Christian church at Sonki (region Batn el-Haggar) during the first Italian campaign in 1967. Several mural paintings of the church have been removed and brought to Italy, where they are to be restored and studied, in order to be ultimately returned to Khartoum. During their stay in Italy they have been exhibited in Rome and Turin (February and March-April 1968). The booklet serves as guide to the Turin exhibition.

In ten unnumbered pages Curto sketches the history of Christian Nubia from 400 to 1323 A.D., its architecture and mural painting. The last part of the booklet contains photographs of the paintings. Two of them are given opposite related specimina of ancient Egyptian art. Two maps of Nubia and a bibliography are added.

DONADONI, Sergio, see also our numbers 68167 and 68612.

68183 DORESSE, Jean, "Le livre sacré du grand Esprit invisible" ou "l'Évangile des Égyptiens". Texte Copte édité, traduit et commenté, d'après le Codex I de Nagʻa-Hammadi/Khénoboskion, *Journal Asiatique*, Paris 256 (1968), 289-386.

Sequel to our number 66176. Part II: Commentary and notes and Part III: Additional Notices.

N.B. Codex I in the numeration of the author is Codex III in the numeration of Krause's inventory. *L. F. Kleiterp*

68184 DRENKHAHN, Rosemarie, Eine Bemerkung zur Nitokris-Stele, *MDAIK* 23 (1968), 115-116.

Der Text der *Nitokris-Stele* (unsere Nummer 64076) ist im 9. Jahr des Psametich I. geschrieben worden, und $Śm3 - t3.wj - t3j.f - nḫ.t$ ist der damals amtierende Schiffsmeister.
M. Heerma van Voss

68185 DROWER, Margaret S., Ugarit = *CAH* Volume II, Chapter XXI (b), §§ IV and V, 1968 (37 p.). Pr. 6 s.

In these chapters about Ugarit and its religion Egypt and Egyptian objects are mentioned on several pages, *e.g.* an alabaster jar with the pictures of king Niqmad and an Egyptian lady of rank, from the Amarna or post-Amarna period (p. 10), another alabaster jar with Horemheb's name (p. 10), and Egyptian stelae dedicated to Canaanite deities (p. 23).

68186 DROWER, Margaret S. and J. BOTTÉRO, Syria Before 2200 B.C. = *CAH* Volume I, Chapter XVII, 1968 (54 p.); rev. *Booklist* 1969, 13 (D. J. W[iseman]). Pr. 6 s.

The last two sections (by Miss Drower) are within the scope of the present bibliography.
In section V (p. 28-36), *Byblos and the Land of Negau*, the author deals with the commercial and religious relations between this city and Egypt.
Section VI (p. 36-47), *Egyptians in Sinai and Palestine*, discusses the Egyptian names for the nomads of the eastern desert, Egyptian remains in Sinai and Palestine, and the military campaigns of the Vth and VIth Dynasties. Attention is paid to the Deshasheh relief (43-44; cfr fig. 1) and the invasion of Uni.

68187 DUMMER, Jürgen, Angaben der Kirchenväter über das Koptische, *Probleme* 17-55.

The awareness of the existence of the Coptic language and the problem of intelligibility as testified by the writings of and about the fathers of the church.   *L. F. Kleiterp*

68188 DUNHAM, Dows, Department of Egyptian Art, *The Ninety-third Annual Report of the Museum of Fine Arts*, Boston, 1968, 35, with 3 ill.

Report of the activities and new acquisitions, particularly a headless statue of a squatting figure (*ca.* 650 B.C.).

68189 DUNHAM, Dows, William Stevenson Smith, February 7, 1907 — January 12, 1969, *Boston Museum Bulletin*, Boston 66, no. 346 (1968), 167-168, with portrait.

Obituary notice. Compare our next volume.

68190 DZIERŻYKRAY-ROGALSKI, Tadeusz, Une momie d'enfant de Basse Époque découverte à Deir el-Bahari en 1964, *Études et Travaux* II 107-113, with 11 ill. and 2 fig.

During the excavations carried out in 1964 on the area of the temple of Tuthmosis III at Deir el-Bahari, there was found in the ruins a small sarcophagus. The mummy in it was subject of exact anthropological examinations, which showed that this was a corpse of a 7-8 years old girl who died in the Late Period.   *A. Szczudłowska*

68191 DZIEWANOWSKI, K., Архангелы и шакалы. Репортаж накануне потопа, Москва, издательство "наука". Главная редакция восточнои литературы, 1968 (12.6 × 20 cm; 232 p., 11 ill). At head of title: Академия наук СССР.   Pr коп 66

"Archanges et chacals. — Reportage à la veille du déluge". Traduction abrégée du polonais (à comparer notre résumé 65342) par V.L. Kon. Ce compte-rendu des fouilles polonaises de Faras est dû à un journaliste. Préface de I. S. Katznelson.

68192 EDEL, Elmar, Bericht über die Arbeiten in den Gräbern der Qubbet El Hawa bei Assuan 1961 und 1962, *ASAE* 60 (1968), 77-89.

Inscribed pottery from the tombs no. 90, 92, 98, 102, 105 and 109 shows that they belonged to the families of *Sbk-ḥtp*, *'Iy-n-ḫnt*, *'Iy-šm3*, *Stt-k3*, *Ḥwyn-ḥnmw*, *Snnw*, and *3bby* respectively. The first of them was the son of *'Iy-n-ḫnt* and his wife *'Ipy*, and can only have been slightly younger than *Mṯnw* and his father *'Iy-šm3* who were buried in tomb no. 90 c. Thus all these tombs can now be safely dated to the second half of the VIth Dyn.   *Dieter Mueller*

68193 EDEL, Elmar, Bericht über die Arbeiten in den Gräbern der Qubbet El Hawa bei Assuan 1963, *ASAE* 60 (1968), 91-94.

Bones of three dogs were found in the pit of ʿnḫs-ny, wife of *Ny-sw-ḥwy* (no. 34 g). Tomb no. 107 led to a cult-chamber of the O.K., now completely filled with coffins from the Late Period. Also examined were the remains of a Coptic building in front of tomb no. 34 e.   *Dieter Mueller*

68194 EDEL, Elmar, Ein neuer Beleg für "Niniveh" in hieroglyphischer Schreibung, *Orientalia* 37 (1968), 417-420.

L'auteur avant reconnu le nom de Ninive dans un traité datant de Ramsès II (voir notre n° 63148). Une liste géographique de Louqsor, datant du même règne, en fait détacher le *n* du génitif. Les trois vases *nw* doivent s'y lire *nn*. Quant au classement des pays dans la liste, il suit en général la direction sud-est-ouest-nord, et *Nnw3* y côtoie le *Nhrn*.   *J. Custers*

EDEL, Elmar, see also our number 68219.

68195 EDWARDS, I. E. S., The Future of Annual Egyptian (sic) Bibliography, *Proceedings* 20-21.

Report of a meeting during which the present Bibliography was discussed.

68196 EDWARDS, I. E. S., Ḳenḥikhopshef's Prophylactic Charm, *JEA* 54 (1968), 155-160, with 2 pl.

This is written on a damaged sheet of papyrus, no. 10731, measuring approximately 33 cm × 19 cm that was presented to the British Museum by Mrs Newberry in 1950. It is inscribed on both sides with texts of different types and length which suggests that it may have come from Deir el-Medîneh. The shorter text is the opening of a letter written by the well-known scribe of the necropolis village, Kenhikhopshef who lived in the later part of the reign of Ramesses II. The spell is known from two hieratic ostraca of the same period and is a copy of an older work. It is an incantation against a demon called Sehak, while the magician who recites it takes the part of a foreign deity *Trws*. Directions on how to use the spell are appended but are partly missing. The papyrus was to be attached to a stem of flax serving as an arrow and shot away perhaps to get rid of the demon. Commentary and notes are given. *E. Uphill*

EDWARDS, Iorwerth Eiddon Stephen, see also our number 68159.

68197 The Egyptian Museum, Cairo. A Brief Description of the Principal Monuments, Cairo, General Organisation for Government Printing Offices, 1968 (13.6 × 17.7 cm; III + 210 + XXI p., 46 pl., 1 pl. in colour on cover, 2 plans). At head of title: United Arab Republic. Ministry of Culture. Antiquities Department.

A reprint (revised and enlarged) of our number 64133.
Compare our number 68429.

68198 EISSFELDT, Otto, Kleine Schriften. Vierter Band. Herausgegeben von Rudolf Selheim und Fritz Maass, Tübingen, J. C. B. Mohr (Paul Siebeck), 1968 (16 × 23.8 cm; VIII + 304 p., 1 ill., 2 maps, 4 pl.); rev. *Biblische Zeitschrift* 13 (1969), 284-285 (Joseph Scharbert); *BiOr* 26 (1969), 97-98 (A. A. Kampman); *Booklist* 1969, 4-5 (G. W. A[nderson]); *The Expository Times* 81 (1969-1970), 63 (H. H. Rowley); *Revue Biblique* 76 (1969), 437 (F. Langlamet); *Theologische Literaturzeitung* 94 (1969), 491-494 (Hans Bardtke); *ZAW* 81 (1969), 130 ([G. Fohrer]).   Pr. cloth DM 70

Sequel to our number 66188.
In this volume we find *e.g.* the studies *Baʿal Ṣaphon von Ugarit und Amon von Ägypten* (our number 62165) and *Gottesnamen in Personennamen als Symbole menschlicher Qualitäten* (our number 66187).

68199 EMERY, W. B., [Report by the Field Director of the Egypt Exploration Society] (= British Archaeology Abroad, 1967, 8), *Antiquity* 42 (1968), 99-102.

Report on the Society's excavations at North Sakkara (cfr our number 67187) and Tell al-Farâ'in (cfr our number 67508), and a visit to Qasr Ibrîm (cfr our number 67449).

68200 EMERY, W. B., Tomb 3070 at Saqqarâ, *JEA* 54 (1968), 11-13, with 2 fig. and 2 pl.

This large IIIrd Dynasty mastaba was partly cleared by Firth in 1931, and completely re-excavated by the writer in 1936. Although plundered it is of considerable architectural interest as it shows a return to the use of "palace facade" decoration. Deliberate archaising work is shown in the niches which use the techniques normal under the Ist Dynasty.
E. Uphill

68201 ENGELMAYER, Reinhold und Johann JUNGWIRTH, Eine Methode zur Härtung stark brüchiger Skelette aus Kulturschichten Unterägyptens, *Annalen des Naturhistorischen Museums in Wien*, Wien 72 (1968), 693-696.

The authors describe two different methods to preserve by hardening the skeletons found in Sayala and Tell ed Dab'a.

ENGELMAYER, Reinhold, see also our numbers 68311 and 68312.

68202 ERMAN, Adolf, Die Religion der Ägypter. Ihr Werden und Vergehen in vier Jahrtausenden. Nachdruck 1968. Mit einem Nachwort von Eberhard Otto, Berlin, Walter de Gruyter & Co, 1968 (XVI + 483 p., 186 fig., 10 pl.). Pr. cloth DM 48
Neudruck der 3. Ausgabe (1934).
Das Nachwort von Eberhard Otto gibt einen Überblick über das seit 1934 neu gefundene oder erschlossene Quellenmaterial und über neue Fragestellungen und Ergebnisse, die von der wissenschaftlichen Forschung seither erarbeitet wurden.
Nicht gesehen.

68203 Exhibition of Recent Discoveries in Egypt and the Sudan by the Egypt Exploration Society at The British Museum 16th October-30th November, 1968, London, The Egypt Exploration Society, [1968] (14 × 21.7 cm; 52 p., 7 ill., one map, ill. on cover).

The exhibition contained the Society's share of the discoveries from its excavations between 1952 and 1968, and an account of its activities in archaeological and epigraphical surveys and in securing material for Carbon 14 dating experiments.
There are the following sections: Saqqara 1952-56; Saqqara 1964-68; Buhen; Kor (Buhen South); the Nubian Survey,

1960-61; the Cemeteries of Qasr Ibrim, 1961-62; the Fortress of Qasr Ibrim; Tell el-Fara'in (Buto); Carbon 14; and the Archaeological Survey.

The first four sections deal with Emery's excavations; that on the Nubian Survey with the work of H. S. Smith; the first one on Qasr Ibrim again with Emery's work, the other with that of Plumley; and that on Tell el-Fara'in with the excavation of Mrs. Seton-Williams. The last sections describes Caminos' activities at Gebel es-Silsila, Buhen, Qasr Ibrim and Semna-Kumma.

68204 FAIRMAN, H. W., On the Origin of ϩⲓⲱⲙⲉ, *JEA* 54 (1968), 236-238.

The author discusses the origin of the Coptic word for 'palm, hollow (of the hand)' and whether a similar word *hnt* existed in Ptolemaic Egyptian. Examples are quoted which imply that there was and that it meant 'hand-breadth'.

E. Uphill

68205 FAULKNER, R. O., The Pregnancy of Isis, *JEA* 54 (1968), 40-44.

The author discusses the legend of the posthumous impregnation of Isis by Osiris and the subsequent birth of Horus, and cites an example found in Spell 148 of the *Coffin Texts*. He differs from the view of Gwyn Griffiths, expressed in *The Conflict of Horus and Seth*, and suggests Isis was not impregnated by physical means as in *P.T.* 632, 1636, or as shown on temple walls, but by a flash of lightning, this being a refinement comparable to that found in the creation of Shu. Parallels are to be found in classical authors. A translation and grammatical notes are included.

E. Uphill

68206 FAURE, Paul, Toponymes créto-mycéniens dans une liste d'Aménophis III (environ 1380 avant J.C.), *Kadmos*, Berlin 7 (1968), 138-149, with 2 folded maps.

The author discusses the topographical names of the fifth list from the statue bases in the temple of Amenophis III (compare our number 66181), suggesting new readings and interpretations. For no. 2 he reads *Bi-ša-ja* (= Pisaia ?), which cannot be Phaistos; no 4 (*Mu-ka-n*) may be Mycenai on Crete, in the neighbourhood of the preceding Kydonia; no 5, *D3-q3-j3-s*, may be either the Cretan Tegeas or Lynkeias; no 9, *Wi-ra-ja*, may be Feleia. The conclusions are that the five first names correspond with harbours on Crete's North coast, going from East to West; there follow three "lands" (Messenia, Argolis and Cythera); and then again five Cretan harbours or towns, this time from West to East. The author also discusses the name *Tj-n3-jj-w*, which occurs with *Kftiw* on the right side of the base, suggesting it to be Danaoi.

68207 FECHT, Gerhard, Zu den Inschriften des ersten Pfeilers im Grab des Anchtifi (Moʿalla), *Festschrift Schott* 50-60.

Translation with philological and historical comments of the inscriptions of the first pillar in the tomb of Ankhtifi, with an excursus about the writings for *rdi* and *šsp* in the tomb.

68208 FENNELLY, James M., Roman Involvement in the Affairs of the Egyptian Shrine, *Bulletin of the John Rylands Library*, Manchester 50 (1967-1968), 317-335.

General study of Roman Egypt, particularly of the temple of Soknopaiou Nesos in Karanis (Faiyûm), based on papyri as well as archaeological data. The author quotes *i.a.* from the *Instructions of Onchsheshonqy* and the *Story of Setne Khamuas*.

68209 FENSHAM, F. C., Die Nuutste Debat oor die Hyksos en die Bybel, *Ned. Geref. Teologiese Tyskrif*, Kaapstad 9 (1968), 1-8.

"The latest discussion about the Hyksos and the Bible." Proceeding from Josephus' story the author summarizes older and recent literature about the Hyksos, stressing the uncertainties with regard to the facts and indicating what influence modern theories may have on biblical chronology.

68210 FISCHER, Eberhard, Nackeanhänger bei den Dan in Liberia. Zur Verbreitung von Nackenschmuck in Afrika, *Baesller-Archiv*. Beiträge zur Völkerkunde, Berlin 16 (1968), 99-127, with 46 fig. and 4 ill.

For pendants in ancient Egypt see p. 117-119 and fig. 2 (= statue Brooklyn Mus. N° 53222).

68211 FISCHER, Henry G., Ancient Egyptian Representations of Turtles, New York, The Metropolitan Museum of Art, [1968] (23.6 × 30.7 cm; 35 p., 22 fig. [3 unnumbered], 20 pl., frontispiece in colour) = The Metropolitan Museum of Art Papers No. 13; rev. *AJA* 73 (1969), 379-380 (Hans Goedicke); *BiOr* 26 (1969), 196-198 (Dietrich Wildung); *CdE* XLIV, N° 87 (1969), 85-86 (Constant de Wit); *JARCE* 7 (1968), 133 (David O'Connor); *JEA* 56 (1970), 216-217 (Geoffrey T. Martin); *OLZ* 65 (1970), 246 (B. Brentjes). Pr. $ 6

In altägyptischen Sumpfdarstellungen begegnet man *Trionyx triunguis*, einer Wasserschildkröte, die sich heute fast ganz in südlichere Regionen des Niltals züruckgezogen hat.

Ihr Fleisch scheint in den prä- und protodynastischen Siedlungen Ägyptens sehr geschätzt gewesen zu sein. Umso auffallender ist ihr Fehlen in den Opferlisten und auf den reich beladenen Speisetischen. Die Erklärung liefert wohl ein Sargtext mit der Drohung: "Wenn du mir befiehlst, dies (Kot) zu essen, dann soll Rê Schildkröten essen!" Die Schildkröte war ein Abscheu für Rê und sein Feind während der Fahrt durch die Nachtstunden. Wir finden dies klar ausgedrückt in Texten des Neuen Reiches wie diesen: "Möge Rê leben und die Schildkröte sterben!" oder "So wahr Rê lebt und die Schildkröte stirbt, so wahr bleibt der, welcher in diesem Sarkophag ist." Seit der 19. Dynastie gibt es dann auch Darstellungen des Harponierens der Schildkröte als Götterfeind.

Dies hinderte den Ägypter nicht, ihr Bild bei Amuletten, Zaubermessen *etc.* zu verwenden; Verfasser liefert die umfangreiche Liste von 102 Beispielen (S. 21-35).

Ingrid Gamer-Wallert

68212 FISCHER, Henry George, Dendera in the Third Millennium B.C. down to the Theban Domination of Upper Egypt. Published under the auspices of the Metropolitan Museum of Art and the Institute of Fine Arts, New York University, Locust Valley, New York, J. J. Augustin Publisher, 1968 (21.9 × 29.7 cm; XXIV + 246 p., 43 fig. [2 on folding papers] including 2 plans, 30 pl., frontispiece, 1 folding plan); rev. *AJA* 74 (1970), 209-210 (John A. Wilson); *CdE* XLV, N° 90 (1970), 302-305 (Alexander Badawy); *JEA* 57 (1971), 209-210 (R. O. Faulkner).   Pr. cloth $ 16.50

The present book may be regarded as a second edition, revised and somewhat expanded, of the study summarized in our number 60239.

The principal new features are:

the transference of *Mni* and *I3wti/Rśi* from the VIth Dynasty to a point later than the Old Kingdom;

the inclusion of three appendices, A: on the Gozeriya Cemetery, B: on the nomarch *ꜥb-iḥ.w* (IXth Dyn.) and some others, C: on the composition of false doors and architraves.

More plates, line drawings, and references in the indices.

M. Heerma van Voss

68213 FISCHER, Henry G., Egyptian Art, *The Metropolitan Museum of Art Bulletin*, New York 26 (1967-1968), 62-64, with 1 ill.

Report of the activities of the Egyptian Department and its recent acquisitions, of which we mention two stelae from the

XIXth Dynasty, one of the Memphite scribe Ptahmose which had been brought to America by Lieutenant-Commander Gorringe, and the other of Wennenkhu.

68214 FISCHER, Henry G., Monuments of the Old Kingdom in the Cairo Museum, *CdE* XLIII, N° 86 (1968), 305-312, with 1 ill.

A propos du dernier volume paru des *Denkmäler des Alten Reiches* (notre numéro 64051) d'après le manuscrit de Ludwig Borchardt, terminé en 1899, l'auteur indique une série de compléments et de corrections concernant soit la provenance des objets, soit la bibliographie, qui peut facilement être complété naturellement des études parues pendant les soixante-dix ans qui séparent le manuscrit de son impression.

En particulier, il étudie la stèle 1652, dont les inscriptions copiées par Borchardt sont inintelligible dans la publication égyptienne par suite de la difficulté d'établir l'ordre de lecture des signes répartis autour de la figure, que la photographie reproduite ici permet de comprendre.

Ph. Derchain

68215 FOX, Michael V., Aspects of the Religion of the Book of Proverbs, *Hebrew Union College Annual*, Cincinnati 39 (1968), 55-69.

The author distinguishes three stages in the development of the religion in the Book of Proverbs, the first of which he calls the "Egyptian" stage. In this connection he discusses the Egyptian wisdom literature and its influence on Israelite wisdom (p. 58-63).

68216 FRIEDRICH, Ingolf, Ephod und Choschen im Lichte des alten Orients, Wien, Verlag Herder, [1968] (15 × 23 cm; 80 p.) = Wiener Beiträge zur Theologie 20; rev. *AfO* 23 (1970), 117-118 (Josef Scharbert); *BiOr* 27 (1970), 279 (anonymous); *ZAW* 81 (1969), 132-133 ([G. Fohrer]).

In this study about the ephod and the choshen (breastpiece) of the priests, later of the high priest of Israel, the author points for the origin of the word ephod as well as the object to ancient Egypt.

On p. 31-33 he discusses *ifd*, originally the word for a kind of cloth consisting of fourfold threads, later on meaning "linen" or "a square piece of linen". On p. 37-41 he discusses Egyptian garments as possible parallels for the ephod (compare for Egyptian dress our number 66565 and Elisabeth Riefstahl, *A Note on Ancient Fashion*, Boston Museum Bulletin, Boston 68, N° 354 [1970], 244-259).

For the choshen there appears to be no Egyptian equivalent (p. 35). In an appendix the Egyptian words are given in hieroglyphs and transcription (p. 73).

68217 GABALLA, G. A. and K. A. KITCHEN, Ramesside Varia I, *CdE* XLIII, N° 86 (1968), 259-270, with 3 ill. and 5 fig.

Les auteurs se proposent de publier des textes fragmentaires de l'époque ramesside provenant de Thèbes, qui présentent un intérêt historique. Le premier (*The Ancestry of Ramesses II*), provenant de Medinet Habou, fait connaître les parents de la mère de Ramsès II, un officier de la charrerie nommé Raia et sa femme ..... wia.

Le second est consacré à un chef de la police Amenemone, vivant sous le règne de Ramsès II, dont les auteurs ont réuni quelques monuments permettant de préciser sa carrière. Enfin est publié un fragment de stèle de Séthi II, trouvé en avant du 9e pylône, à propos duquel se pose la question de l'éventuelle communauté d'origine de ce bloc et des fragments publiés par Helck dans nos numéros 4594, 58278 et 63219.
Ph. Derchain

68218 GALLING, Kurt, Neue Mühlenostraka. Eine Nachbemerkung zum Aufsatz: "Datum und Sinn der graeco-koptischen Mühlenostraka im Lichte neuer Belege aus Jerusalem", ZDPV 82 (1966) S. 46-56, *Zeitschrift des Deutschen Palästina-Vereins*, Wiesbaden 84 (1968), 80-81.

In an addition to our number 66219 the author refers to an article by Herbert C. Youtie and William H. Worell in the *University of Michigan Studies. Humanistic Series*, vol. XLVI (1942), 255-294, where 77 more "etmoulon ostraca" had been published.

68219 GALLING, Kurt, in Verbindung mit Elmar EDEL und Riekele BORGER, Textbuch zur Geschichte Israels. 2., neubearbeitete Auflage, Tübingen, J. C. B. Mohr (Paul Siebeck), 1968 (16 × 23.5 cm; XII + 109 p., 1 loose map); rev. *Booklist* 1969, 14 (P. R. A[ckroyd]); *Journal of Biblical Literature* 88 (1969), 206-208 (George M. Landes); *Mundus* 5 (1969), 330-331 (Rainer Degen); *Nederlands Theologisch Tijdschrift* 23 (1968-1969), 377 (C. H. J. d[e] G[eus]); *ZAW* 80 (1968), 432 ([G. Fohrer]); *ZDMG* 120 (1970), 1971, 349-350 (Wolfgang Richter); *Zeitschrift des Deutschen Palästina-Vereins* 86 (1970), 103-104 (Siegfried Herrmann).
Pr. DM 17.50

New edition of our number 1313.
From Egypt are in this edition the numbers 1 (*Sinuhe*),

4, 5, 11-16 and 17 (*Wenamon*), all of which are newly translated by Edel.
Geographical indexes on p. 93-109.

68220 GARBINI, G., Alte Kulturen des Vorderen Orients. Architectur, Wandmalereien, Plastik, Keramik, Metallarbeiten, Siegel, Gütersloh, Bertelsmann Kunstverlag Reinhard Mohn, 1968 = Schätze der Weltkunst, 2; rev. *ZAW* 80 (1968), 432 ([G. Fohrer]). Pr. DM 19.50

German version of our number 66221 (not seen).

68221 GARTKIEWICZ, Przemysław Marek, On the Research and Preservation of Queen Hatshepsut Temple at Deir el-Bahari. Partial Reconstruction of the Eastern Wall of the Hypostyle Hall, *Études et Travaux* II 47-64, with 10 ill., 1 folding pl., and 2 fig. including a plan.

The author describes the early preservation works at the eastern wall and the doorway of the Hypostyle Hall, necessary for a correct reconstruction. Also new observations were made on the building craft, which had been applied at the temple's reconstruction. The measurement of the lean of the wall's face and other investigations show that the outer face of the eastern wall, on the portico side, had a slightly greater deviation than the inner wall face.
The plan attached to the article illustrates the survey and the project of a partial reconstruction of the Hypostyle Hall's northern part. *A. Szczudłowska*

GARTKIEWICZ, Przemysław Marek, see also our number 68148.

GAUTIER, A., see our number 68630.

68222 GEISSLER, Friedmar, Deutsche Asien-Afrika-Bibliographie. Herausgegeben unter Mitarbeit von..... Walter-Friedrich Reineke... 3. Folge, *MIO* 14 (1968), Heft 4 (XVI p. + 362 col.).

Cette bibliographie signalétique (voir aussi nos n°s 66223 et 67211) consacre cette année les colonnes 123-135 à l'égyptologie, les colonnes 135-137 au domaine copte. Comme la fois précédente, l'index par noms de personnes comprend outre les auteurs modernes, des personnages anciens, nommés dans les titres. *J. Custers*

GERSTER, Georg, see our number 68168.

68223 GHALIOUNGUI, Paul, La notion de la maladie dans les textes égyptiens et ses rapports avec la théorie humorale, *BIFAO* 66 (1968), 37-48.

Traçant la pensée rationnelle, l'auteur distingue cinq catégories de maladie interne.
Ce sont les malades dues au "vent", celles dues aux vers, celles dues au contenu intestinal, celles dues à des matières morbides, et les maladies du système vasculaire.

M. Heerma van Voss

68224 GHATTAS, Francis Abdel-Malek, Das Buch *Mk.t-ḥʿw* "Schutz des Leibes", Göttingen, no publisher, 1968 (14.9 × 20.9 cm; II + 107 + 7 unnumbered p., 1 folding pl., 1 plan).

Thesis for a doctor's degree in Göttingen.
The book "Protection of the body" is to be found on the inner face of the northern girdle wall of the Edfu temple. It consists of three parts: the ritual acts, their description, and the text for the "Protection of the body".
The last part begins with an invocation of the sun god, followed by a prayer for the king, the protective text itself, and a prayer for the temple god.
The text proper contains thirty phrases each identifying the protection of the living falcon with that of another deity.
The book is illustrated (see the pl.). It shows clearly that the divine image always stood in the centre of the temple cult. It was the god's living form and as such had to be protected by amulets against *e.g.* disease.
The author presents the texts in transcription and in translation with commentary.   *M. Heerma van Voss*

GHIRSHMAN, Roman, see our number 68307.

68225 GILULA, M., An Adjectival Predicative Expression of Possession in Middle Egyptian, *RdE* 20 (1968), 55-61.

La forme *nnk* exprimant la possession s'analyse d'ordinaire *nj ink* (adjectif nisbé du génitif + pronom indépendant). Cette interprétation est confirmée par une série d'exemples tirés des *Coffin Texts*, où la forme est également employée à la 2e et à la 3e personne, ne laissant aucun doute sur sa structure.   *Ph. Derchain*

68226 GISPEN, J. G. W., "Measuring" the Patient in Ancient Egyptian Medical Texts, *Janus*, Leiden 54 (1967), 1968, 224-227.

Text of a paper printed as well in *Acta Quinti Conventus Mosae Traiecti MCMLXVII*.
The diagnoses in medical texts contain the phrase "If you examine a man", using the verb *ḫ3i*, lit. "to measure". The author argues that is meant: Keeping an eye on the heart's

action by checking the canals to each member. He connects the notion of measuring (for controlling) with the main occupation of the Old Kingdom physicians, who were primarily builders and administrators.

68227 GIUSTOLISI, Vittorio, La "Pietra di Palermo" e la cronologia dell' Antico Regno, *Sicilia archeologica. Rassegna periodica di studi, notizie et documentazione a cura dell'Ente Provinciale per il Turismo di Trapani*, Anno primo 4 (Dicembre 1968), 5-14.

L'auteur publie une description détaillée de la pierre de Palerme, accompagnée d'une photographie du monument et de tous les fragments qui le complètent.

A suivre: *Sicilia Archeologica*, Anno secondo 5 (Marzo 1969), 38-55.   *Ph. Derchain*

68228 GIVEON, Raphael, The Egyptian funerary cones at the Israel Museum, *The Israel Museum News*, Jerusalem 3 (1968), 40-41, with 4 ill.

Note on two cones from the Walter Herz Collection, presented to the Israel Museum in Jerusalem.

The larger one belonged to '*In-ḥr.t-mś*, scribe of the works in the mortuary temple of Amenophis III.

The smaller one has been found at Deir el-Bahri. Its owner was *Dnrg*, a chief wab-priest (Dynasty XVIII).

M. Heerma van Voss

68229 GIVEON, R., Egyptian Tomb-Scenes on Phoenician Objects from the Near East and from Spain, *Archivo Español de Arqueologia*, Madrid 41 (1968), 5-15, with 10 ill.

Verfasser veröffentlicht eine mit hellblauer Glasur überzogene, in à jour-Technik gearbeitete Bronzetafel (3.5 × 3.5 cm), die angeblich bei Bauarbeiten im Flughafengelände von Churriana / Málaga gefunden wurde. Beide Seiten tragen Reliefdarstellungen. In den beiden Musikantinnen der einen Seite sieht der Verfasser die phönizische Kopie einer vergleichbaren Szene aus dem Grab des Rechmirê, in der Opferszene der anderen Seite die Kopie einer Darstellung im Tempel Sethos' I. von Abydos. Nach Meinung des Verfassers erbringt dieser Fund den Nachweis für die Echtheit einer Gruppe von vergoldeten Siegelzylindern (Slg. R. Jonas, Haifa und Walters Art Gallery, Baltimore 51.1489), die 1929 bzw. 1940 im Kunsthandel in Beirut auftauchten und deren Authentizität in Frage stand. *I. Gamer-Wallert*

68230 GIVEON, Raphael, New Acquisitions. A) Egyptian Seals, *Sefunim*. Bulletin (of) the Maritime Museum Haifa 2 (1967-8), 70-71, with 1 pl.

Publication of four seals recently acquired by the Maritime Museum, Haifa, all of them displaying a boat or a fish-design.

GIVEON, Raphael, see also our number 68375.

GLADFELTER, Bruce G., see our number 68109.

68231 GODRON, Gérard, A propos de la déesse Sédjémet-Nébet, *Rivista* 43 (1968), 319-326, with 1 pl.

Le bloc à relief publié ici et conservé au Caire, dans une collection privée, provient probablement d'un mur de temple. Il montre une déesse à coiffure hathorique. La courte légende permet de dater la pièce du règne de Ramsès II. L'auteur connaît jusqu'ici 15 exemples de la locution *Sḏmt-nbt*, le premier remontant peut-être au Moyen Empire, le dernier datant du règne d'Hadrien. Un complément phonétique éventuel (*m*) assure la transcription. Le sens proposé est "Celle-qui-entend-tout". Ce fut à l'origine une épithète de Iousaâs et le resta pendant un millénaire et demi au moins. Mais par l'effet du syncrétisme, *Sḏmt-nbt* est aussi devenue une vraie entité personnalisée. C'est le cas à Dendera et sur le fragment étudié ici. Sa popularité semble attestée en six endroits en dehors d'Héliopolis. La graphie tardive pour le nom de la ville (oreille, *t*, localité) se comprendrait comme mythologique: Cité de l'ouïe; la lecture a pu varier selon les époques. *J. Custers*

68232 GODRON, Gérard, A propos d'une inscription de l'Horus Khâsékhem, *CdE* XLIII, N° 85 (1968), 34-35, with 1 fig.

Godron corrige la lecture d'une inscription de Khâsékhem, lue en dernier lieu "sandale excellente contre le mal" par Grdseloff (*ASAE* 44 [1944], 300), en "sandale excellente contre les pays étrangers", après avoir reconnu que le dernier signe endommagé sur la pierre (publication Quibell, *Hierakonpolis* II, 58) ne peut-être *ḏw* mais *ḫ3st*. *Ph. Derchain*

68233 GOEDICKE, Hans, The Beginning of the Instruction of King Amenemhat, *JARCE* 7 (1968), 15-21.

The introduction (*Papyrus Millingen*, 1, 1-2) reads: "Beginning of the scroll containing the teaching which had made the majesty of King Amenemhat justified, as he speaks in revealing the truth, for his, the All-Lord's son; he speaks, having appeared as divinity . . .".
In an *Addendum* (p. 20-21), the author translates the first advice as follows: "Be wary now of the employees who had not been (before) and about whose scheming a thought had not been given" (*Millingen*, 1, 3-4). *M. Heerma van Voss*

68234 GOEDICKE, Hans, The Capture of Joppa, *CdE* XLIII, N° 86 (1968), 219-233.

Nouvelle traduction abondamment commentée de l'histoire de la prise de Joppé (Papyrus Harris 500, vs. 1-3).
A la suite du commentaire, l'auteur entreprend de fournir une nouvelle interprétation de l'histoire et analyse soigneusement les divers stratagèmes de Djehouti dans ses rapports avec le prince de la ville rebelle, puis examine le récit comme thème littéraire, d'où il ressort que Djehouti représente très exactement le parallèle d'Ulysse et d'Ali Baba, que l'on peut encore rapprocher des récits bibliques de la prise de Jéricho (Josué 6, 3, 16 et 20) et de la cité d'Ai (*id.* 8, 3-8). *Ph. Derchain*

68235 GOEDICKE, Hans, *Dbt* "work-bench", *JARCE* 7 (1968), 128.

The author concludes from the context that *db.t* (*Papyrus Lansing*, 5, 5-6) is the instrument used in the cutting of boards. It is to be identified with the sawing-post, well known from pictures. *M. Heerma van Voss*

68236 GOEDICKE, Hans, Four Hieratic Ostraca of the Old Kingdom, *JEA* 54 (1968), 23-30, with 1 pl.

These rare Old Kingdom ostraca of unknown provenance are in the Anastasi Collection in the Rijksmuseum in Leiden. They are of grey limestone and their form suggests that they were intended for use before the burial of the persons concerned, after the fashion of later mummy-labels. The inscriptions are in black ink with red additional sections, paleographical considerations suggesting a date of later Fourth or early Fifth Dynasty. J 426 mentions the director of the crew from *Ḥwwt* in the Snake-district, J 427 another from ʿ*rk-int* in the Harpoon-district. J 428 only mentions the deceased's name and J 429 has a date, the year of the 10th count, *etc.* *E. Uphill*

68237 GOEDICKE, Hans, Papyrus Lansing 3,9-3,10, *JARCE* 7 (1968), 128-130.

Šsȝ in the underlying passage and elsewhere refers to the Bedouin. Either it is an incorrect spelling of the late word *Šȝsw*, or the bubalis represents the ethnic group (a case of heraldry). *M. Heerma van Voss*

68238 GOEDICKE, Hans, Remarks on the Hymns to Sesostris III, *JARCE* 7 (1968), 23-26.
Compare our number 2844.

Preceded by a number of discussions, the author offers a translation of the four poems. *M. Heerma van Voss*

GOEPFERT, Eva-Maria, see our number 68271.

68239 GOFF, Beatrice L., The "Significance" of Symbols. A Hypothesis Tested with Relation to Egyptian Symbols, *in*: *Religions in Antiquity*. Essays in Memory of Erwin Ramsdell Goodenough, Leiden, E. J. Brill, 1968 (= Studies in the History of Religions. Supplements to *Numen*, 14), 476-505, with 6 fig.

The author distinguishes three levels in the use of symbols: 1) symbols without verbal explanation; 2) with a few words of very general nature; 3) with more words, sometimes elaborated in a myth. This hypothesis is tested with relation to Egyptian symbols of the XXIst Dynasty, mainly appearing in the funerary papyri, particularly the *Mythological Papyri* translated by Piankoff (our number 57380).

The author studies *i.a.* the use of the numbers two, four, three and seven, in which either the number itself appears to be potent, or there is an explanation with the scene suitable for a variety of designs, or the number has a specific meaning (*e.g.* the four corners of heaven). As another example she discusses scarabs, potent in themselves, more potent when inscribed with the name of a famous person, and even more when inscribed with a spell. Thus also the designs in the papyri can stand alone without text, or be accompanied by quite simple texts such as a name, or they are standardized designs adapted to a particular spell.

GOODENOUGH, Erwin Ramsdell, see our preceding number.

68240 GORDON, Ayala, Youth Wing Exhibition, *The Israel Museum News*, Jerusalem 3 (1968), 8-9, with 1 ill.

Contains *i.a.* a note to a didactic "Pharaoh's Egypt" exhibition combining models made by children, diagrams and photographs with original objects from various collections in Israel.

There is also mentioned an exhibition of Egyptian art of the Amarna Period in another hall of the Museum.

We mention here some new acquisitions by the Samuel Bronfman Biblical and Archaeological Museum, among which Egyptian predynastic vessels, the statue of a seated man (XXVth Dynasty) and an Amarna relief showing blindfolded musicians (see p. 37).

68241 GORDON, Cyrus H., Forgotten Scripts. How they were

deciphered and their impact on contemporary culture, New York, Basic Books, inc., Publishers, [1968] (14.8 × 22 cm; XVIII + 175 p., 10 pl., map on endpapers); rev. *The Antiquaries Journal* 49 (1969), 407-408 (W. C. Brice); *Antiquity* 43 (1969), 150-151 (John Chadwick).

In chapter 2 (p. 19-40) the author describes the system of hieroglyphic writing and the history of its decipherment, until its final confirmation by the discovery of the decree of Canopus in 1866.

There is also an English edition, London, Thames and Hudson, 1968 (Pr. 52 s. 6 d.).

68242 GOYON, J. C., Le cérémonial pour faire sortir Sokaris. Papyrus Louvre I. 3079, col. 112-114, *RdE* 20 (1968), 63-96 (including 11 p. with hieroglyphic texts), with 1 pl.

En dehors du présent texte, le papyrus I 3079 du Louvre contient encore un Livre des Morts (Rougé, *Rituel Funéraire* [1861-76] pl. 5-20) et le cérémonial de glorification d'Osiris dans l'Empire des Morts (voir notre numéro 67228).

Le présent texte est un doublet du Pap. Bremner-Rhind 18,1-21,6, dont il existe encore trois autres copies inédites, dont l'auteur a eu connaissance. Outre la photographie et la transcription avec apparat critique, l'édition comprend une traduction et un commentaire à la fois grammatical et fondamental où l'on trouvera de nombreuses références bibliographiques concernant les mots rares et les toponymes apparaissant dans le texte. *Ph. Derchain*

68243 GOYON, Jean-Claude, Les cultes d'Abydos à la Basse Époque d'après une stèle du musée de Lyon, *Kêmi* 18 (1968), 29-44, with 2 pl. and 3 fig.

La petite stèle cintrée I.E. 328 de Lyon paraît être une copie d'époque romaine, sinon un faux récent. Elle fournit malgré tout une contribution à l'onomastique abydénienne ou thinite ainsi qu'aux titres sacerdotaux. Le défunt Hor est représenté avec son fils sous un tableau où Isis et Horus figurent devant Min et le saule. L'épigraphie du verso laisse à désirer, et des éléments semblent omis. *B3st.t nb.t hn*, qui n'est pas attestée avant Nectanébo serait, en tant que Bastet-Isis ou Mehit, protectrice du *hn* osirien, sanctuaire censé renfermer le corps du dieu et surmonté d'une colline plantée d'arbres. *J. Custers*

GRÄF, Erwin, see our number 68279.

68244 GRAY, P. H. K., Bone Infarction in Antiquity, *Clinical Radiology*, Edinburgh & London 19 (1968), 436-437, with 3 fig.

X-rays of Greco-Roman mummies in the Horniman Museum in London showed one case of symmetrical bone infarction, and one possible case of solitary bone infarction. Both are almost certainly not the result of an occupational hazard such as tunneling or deepsea diving, and may have been caused by some vascular disturbance, emboli from the heart, or pancreatitis. *Dieter Mueller*

68245 GRAY, P. H. K. and Dorothy SLOW, Egyptian Mummies in the City of Liverpool Museums, [Liverpool], Liverpool Corporation, 1968 (18.6 × 24.9 cm; II + 77 p. containing 101 pl. [2 in colour] and 1 table) = *Liverpool Bulletin*, Liverpool 15 (1968); rev. *BiOr* 27 (1970), 347-348 (Lennart Diener); *CdE* XLV, N° 89 (1970), 91-94 (Suzanne Ratié).

Sixteen of the eighteen mummies in the City of Liverpool Museums (XXIst Dynasty—Roman Period) are published here in the order in which they were radiographed in 1966 and are numbered accordingly.

A description with pictures of the coffins, cartonnages and amulets is given likewise, as well as of a stela, a canopic chest and a Ptah-Sokar-Osiris figure (see p. 42-43), and a head and a hand with rings, both from mummies.

A review of Egyptian embalming will be found on p. 1-6, medical data on 69, bibliography on p. 70-71.

Appendix 1 contains the exposure factors. Appendix 2 (by K. B. Priestman) deals with the examinations and conservation of mummies (p. 72-74). *M. Heerma van Voss*

GRAY, Peter H. K., see also our number 68159.

GREENWOOD, P. H., see our number 68630.

68246 GRIFFITHS, J. Gwyn, The Relative *NTY* with Generic Reference, *JEA* 54 (1968), 60-66.

Egyptian grammarians following Gardiner and Erman and unlike Latin and Greek scholars have devoted much discussion to the question of whether the antecedents of relative clauses are defined or undefined. Greek has a definite article and the point is thus superfluous in that language, while Latin lacks both articles thereby occasionally causing ambiguity. Possibly Hebrew and Arabic grammar have given prominence to the subject in Egyptian, thus Gardiner laid down in his Grammar that virtual relative clauses are said to have undefined antecedents, this view in general being followed by Erman in the 4th edition of his Egyptian Grammar. But the latter used the procedure found in Late Egyptian and Coptic, projecting it backwards into Old and Middle Egyptian, which may not necessarily have been the

case. The article taking Edel's lead sets out to show that a generic reference of *nty* is often attested and cites many examples from Old Kingdom and later texts in support of this view.
E. Uphill

68247 GRIMM, Günter, Eine verschollene Apisstatuette aus Mainz, *ZÄS* 95, 1 (1968), 17-26, with 4 ill., 1 fig., and 1 pl.

Verfasser veröffentlicht zwei Beispiele des "bewegten Apis", einer römischen "Erfindung". Die beiden Bronzen sind:
Bonn, Rheinisches Landesmuseum, Inv.-Nr. 1254, aus Alt-Trier bei Luxemburg;
Frankfurt am Main, Liebieghaus, Inv.-Nr. 444, aus dem Kabirion beim griechischen Theben.
Die Ikonographie wird eingehend erörtert.
M. Heerma van Voss

68248 GRIÑÓ, Raimundo, Sobre un cono funerario egipcio con inscripción del Museo Arqueológico de Barcelona, *Ampurias*, Barcelona 30 (1968), 253-261, with 1 ill. and 1 fig.

Verfasser publiziert einen Grabkegel des Museo Arqueológico von Barcelona (ehem. Slg. Miret i Sans), der zu dem Grab des Nacht (Theben Nr. 52) gehörte (Macadam, *Corpus Funerary Cones*, Nr. 157). Einleitend wird kurz die Entwicklung und Bedeutung der Grabkegel referiert.
I. Gamer-Wallert

GROLLENBERG, Luc. H. see our number 68436.

68249 GUÉPIN, Jean-Pierre, The Tragic Paradox. Myth and Ritual in Greek Tragedy, Amsterdam, Adolf M. Hakkert, [1968] (17.4 × 25.7 cm; XVI + 364 p.).

The purpose of this thesis for a doctor's degree at the University of Amsterdam is to inquire into the relation between the cult of Dionysus and the tragedies which were performed as part of this cult.
Part III deals with the influence of Orphism on myth and ritual of the Dionysus cult, chapter V (p. 252-260) discussing the Egyptian origins. The author quotes Herodotus and the *Ramesseum Papyrus* and demonstrates the connections between the cult of Osiris and that of Dionysus, which appear *e.g.* from the physical interpretation of the *sparagmos* as vintage and the search for the *membra disiecta*.

68250 GUERRINI, Lucia, Rilievi copti nella Università di Roma, *Rivista* 43 (1968), 131-134, with 2 pl.

Publication of five relief-blocks recently acquired by the Egyptian collection of the University of Rome, all dated to the mid fifth century A.D.

GUICHARD, Jean and Geneviève, see our number 68630.

68251 GUNDEL, Hans Georg, Papyri bibliothecae Universitatis Gissensis. Eine Einführung, = *Kurzberichte aus den Giessener Papyrus-Sammlungen*, Giessen Nr. 27 (1968), 1-43, with 2 pl.

Enlarged and corrected edition of our number 4570.
For the numbers of Hieratic, Demotic and Coptic papyri see p. 16-19. A list of publications of some of the texts on p. 20-25. We mention our numbers 58226 and 63463.

J. F. Borghouts

68252 GUNDEL, Hans Georg, Weltbild und Astrologie in den griechischen Zauberpapyri, München, C. H. Beck'sche Verlagsbuchhandlung, 1968 (16.5 × 23.9 cm; X + 100 p., 1 pl.) = Münchener Beiträge zur Papyrusforschung und antiken Rechtsgeschichte 53; rev. *BiOr* 27 (1970), 217-220 (Dierk Wortmann); *CdE* XLIV, N° 87 (1969), 162 (Philippe Derchain); *The Classical Review*, N.S. 21 (1969), 358-360 (J. Gwyn Griffiths); *Latomus* 27 (1968), 978-980 (Robert Turcan); *ZDMG* 120 (1970), 165-167 (Manfred Errens).

Pr. DM 14.50

Although this analysis of the cosmic, astral and astrological lore of the Greek magical papyri is outside the scope of the present bibliography we mention it because of its many allusions and references to ancient Egypt.
Moreover, in an appendix the author deals with a papyrus fragment (Pap. Giss. Inv. 1080) previously published by him together with Jozef M. A. Janssen (our number 62242).

68253 GUNDLACH, Rolf, Maschinelle Philologie als historische Hilfswissenschaft, *Folia Linguistica. Acta Societatis Linguisticae Europaeae*, The Hague 2 (1968), 230-256.

Discussion of the methods according which the computer may be used for historical studies, particularly for the philology as auxiliary historical science.
The author refers to some projects of the department Nichtnumerik of the Deutsches Rechenzentrum, Darmstadt, *i.a.* that of *Coffin Texts*, Spell 335a, demonstrating the kind of results which may be achieved. Compare Rolf Gundlach und Wolfgang Schenkel, *Lexikalisch-grammatische Liste zu Spruch 335a der altägyptischen Sargtexte. LL/CT. 335A*, Darmstadt, Deutsches Rechenzentrum, 1970 (2 vols).

68254 GUNDLACH, Rolf, Zur maschinellen Erschließung historischer Museumsbestände, *Museumskunde*, Berlin (1968), 135-146, with 2 fig. and 1 table (= p. 138).

The author discusses the possibilities of processing data on museum holdings for computers, and describes a project to document the Egyptian antiquities in German museums.

Dieter Mueller

68255 von GYNZ-REKOWSKI, Georg, Hasenhieroglyphe und Hasengöttin in Ägypten, *Klio*, Berlin 50 (1968), 5-28, with 6 ill. and 1 fig.

Study of the function of the hare in the Egyptian religion. After mentioning the representations of hares, particularly the female, in the African rock-drawings the author indicates the role of the hare-goddess in the 15th Upper-Egyptian nome, her connections with re-birth, with Thoth and the moon, with the lion-goddess and Onuris. He even suggests that there is a fundamental reason why both verbs *wn*, "to open" and "to exist", are written with the hare-sign, and that the same may hold for the writing of the name Osiris as *Wn-nfr*, the hare being the symbol of fertility and vital strength.

At the end the author suggests that in the legend of St. Onuphrius these conceptions may have been preserved.

HAAG, Herbert, see our number 68105.

68256 HABACHI, Labib, Nakht, propriétaire de la tombe N° 397 de la nécropole thébaine et sa famille, *Kêmi* 18 (1968), 51-56, with 5 fig.

Cette tombe de Qournah est extrêmement dégradée. Les inscriptions livrent les noms du *wʿb* Nakht et de son épouse Senhotep. D'autres monuments permettent de regrouper les membres de trois générations de cette famille. On peut ajouter, à une stèle de Nakht, au Musée du Caire, et à une stèle d'Amenhotep, à New York, une statue d'Ahmosé dit Rourou, à Brooklyn (voir notre n° 68529) et une inscription rupestre à Assouan. Cette dernière représente Nakht, sa femme et leur fils Qenamon, qui est *wʿb* d'Amon, comme son frère Mery. Le titre de "premier fils royal d'Amon", qui semble lié à la fonction de porteur de la barque d'Amon, a été porté sous Hatshepsout et Thoutmès III par Rourou, ensuite problablement par Kamosé, père de Nakht, et enfin par ce dernier.

J. Custers

68257 HABACHI, Labib, The Owner of Tomb No. 282 in the Theban Necropolis, *JEA* 54 (1968), 107-113, with 4 fig.

This rock tomb was originally partly cleared by Clarence Fisher for the University of Philadelphia over 45 years ago. The decorations have suffered and the inscriptions are really illegible. Fisher and Greenlees believed the owner was

Ḥeḳanakhte, viceroy of Kush under Ramesses II. The writer differs, however, and suggests the titles agree with one Anḥernakhte who left three rock-inscriptions on Seheil Island. An examination of the tomb itself supported this reading of the owner's name. He also probably dedicated a now broken stela in the Temple of Horus at Aniba.

E. Uphill

68258 HABACHI, Labib, Tomb No. 226 of the Theban Necropolis and its Unknown Owner, *Festschrift Schott* 61-70, with 6 fig. (including a plan) and 1 pl.

The author tries to identify the owner of the badly destroyed Theban tomb no 226. He publishes a graffito from Aswân representing a man standing in front of Amenophis III and his mother. A similar scene is found in tomb 226. Since in Aswân the man is called Hekareshu, and a person of this name according to Theban tomb no 64 was the "nurse of the king's sons", which is also one of the titles in tomb 226, the author suggests that the latter belonged to the same Hekareshu, nurse of the sons of Tuthmosis IV, and possibly also owner of tomb 64 which is usually ascribed to his son Hekerneheh.

68259 HAGEDORN, D.—M. WEBER, Die griechisch-koptische Rezension der Menandersentenzen, *Zeitschrift für Papyrologie und Epigraphik*, Bonn 3 (1968), 15-50.

Der Beitrag beschäftigt sich mit drei Zeugen der *Monosticha Menandri*, wovon zwei zum ersten Mal völlig veröffentlicht, übersetzt und kommentiert werden. Das sind ein Papyruskodex im Vatikan und im Tiroler Landesmuseum Ferdinandeum (Nr. 7) in Innsbruck, und ein Papyrusblatt des British Museum, *Pap. Lond.* VIII fol. 1a + fol. 3b. Sie gehören dem 6-7. Jahrhundert. M. *Heerma van Voss*

68260 HAMBURGER, Anit, Gems from Caesarea Maritima, *'Atiqot.* English Series, Jerusalem 8 (1968), 1-38, with 8 pl.

Description of 165 gems in the possession of the author, some of which show Egyptian motifs, such as Chnoubis (110-112 and 125), Harpocrates (116-117) and Pantheos (121).

68261 HAMMERSCHMIDT, Ernst, Einige Beispiele zu den Wiederbelebungsversuchen des Koptischen im heutigen Ägypten, *Probleme* 225-231.

Attempts are made to regenerate the Coptic language. The author quotes and translates a contemporary Coptic poem and gives examples of neologism, e.g. ⲡⲓⲉⲧϩⲁⲗⲓ, aeroplane and ⲙⲁⲛⲟϩⲓ, station. *L. F. Kleiterp*

68262 HAMMERSHAIMB, E., Some remarks on the Aramaic letters from Hermopolis, *Vetus Testamentum*, Leiden 18 (1968), 265-267.

Some remarks on our number 66084.

HANSEN, Carl L., see our number 68109.

68263 HARRIS, J. R., How Long was the Reign of Ḥoremḥeb ?, *JEA* 54 (1968), 95-99.

The author uses an ostracon in the form of a letter now in Toronto as evidence for rejecting the generally held view that Ḥoremḥeb reigned for nearly 30 years. Only three regnal years have survived intact from contemporary inscriptions, the highest being year 8 in a graffito in the tomb of Tuthmosis IV. Manetho appears unreliable on this and a graffito from the king's mortuary temple may indicate a year 27, thus being in agreement with the Mes inscription, but has been disputed as contemporary evidence. The burial of two Apis bulls in this reign and the apparent quantity of large architectural remains are both discounted.

The letter is in the form of a scribal exercise from a chief of police Mininiwy stating that he has been in the Vizier's service since year 7 of Ḥoremḥeb. The Vizier Khay who is mentioned cannot be in office earlier than year 16 of Ram. II, so assuming that Mininiwy was serving as a necropolis worker in his youth under Ḥoremḥeb, the period cited suggests a shorter reign than 27 years, although this is not impossible if the "aged" petitioner was 75 to 80 years old.

E. Uphill

HARRIS, John R., see also our number 68655.

68264 HARTMAN, Thomas Charles, The Ḳadesh Inscriptions of Ramesses II: An Analysis of the Verbal Patterns of a Ramesside Royal Inscription, *A Dissertation Abstracts*, Ann Arbor, Michigan 28, Number 10 (1968), 4150.

Abstract of a thesis (Brandeis University, 1967), obtainable in microfilm and xerography (119 pages).

In order to analyse and characterize the verbal patterns of the texts concerning the Kadesh battle as a fair representation of Ramesside royal inscriptions the author deals with: I. morphology and auxiliary verbs; II. the affirmative verb; III. the infinitive, participle, and relative; IV. the negatives; V. style; VI. subordinate *iw* clauses and independent present I; VII. particles.

The author concludes that the verbal pattern of the Kadesh texts stands between the normative Middle and Late Egyptian stages of the language. The grammar of the texts should be considered an integral part of that stage of the language which is the direct ancestor of Demotic and Coptic.

68265 HAYCOCK, B. G., Towards a Better Understanding of the Kingdom of Cush (Napata-Meroe), *Sudan Notes and Records*, Khartoum 49 (1968), 1-16.

The aim of this study is to present reasons for supposing that during the Napatan stage the Cushite culture was much more complex than usually supposed.

The author demonstrates that several scholars have described Cushite culture as second-rate and derived from the Egyptian civilisation, interesting only because of its influence on more southern Africa. He strongly defends, however, the continuity between Napatan and Meroitic culture and the achievements of the former. In this context he discusses the royal Napatan stelae, *e.g.* those of Aspelta and Nastaseñ, which contain in general reliable historical material. He also discusses the theocratic position of the Napatan rulers and their relationships with the priests.

68266 HEERMA VAN VOSS, M., De dragers zijn tevreden, *Phœnix*, Leiden 14 (1968), 128-132, with 2 fig.

This article deals with the Old Kingdom representations of the tomb-owner being carried in a sedan-chair and with the texts accompanying them.

Special attention is paid to the song of the bearers. To Ipi's copy (fig. 48; Cairo C.G. 1536) the author adds two variants both as well from Dynasty VI. One is given in our number 3204, Pl. XXXI and LIX; the other version belonged to Nekhebu's mastaba (G 2381) and is now in the store rooms of the Museum of Fine Arts, Boston (see fig. 49). A fresh translation with commentary is offered of what turns out to be an invocation of Sokaris. The nature of this god is investigated on p. 130-131.

The author argues that the scenes in question are to be situated in the hereafter. With their act of lifting up and carrying around the lord the servants imitate Sokaris' procession. In doing so they realise new life for their master and for themselves. *M. Heerma van Voss*

68267 HEERMA VAN VOSS, M., On the Meaning of the Shipping of Sand by the Shawabtis, *Proceedings* 21.

Summary of our number 63215.

68268 HEERMA VAN VOSS, M., Een scherf uit het Dodenboek, *Phœnix*, Leiden 14 (1968), 165-171, with 3 fig.

Publication, discussion and translation of an ostracon

(12 × 9.5 cm) from the Collection Beekmans, Melissant (Holland). It was found at Baliana and dated by the editor to the end of the XIXth, eventually to the XXth Dynasty. The piece bears eight names with epithets of judges from the *Negative Confession* in *Book of the Dead* 125. The author proves that the text was copied from the *Papyrus of Ani* (British Museum 10470), sheet 31. He comments upon the character of the judges, and surveys the ostraca with passages from the *Book of the Dead*.   M. Heerma van Voss

68269 HEERMA VAN VOSS, M., Viglius en Canopus. Penningen en politiek, *Spiegel Historiael*, Bussum 3 (1968), 443, with a fig.   Pr. of separate copy fl. 3.75/b. fr. 60

A note on the god "Canopus" and on the way of representing him.

de HEINZELIN, Jean, see our number 68630.

68270 HELCK, W., Die Bedrohung Palästinas durch einwandernde Gruppen am Ende der 18. und am Anfang der 19. Dynastie, *Vetus Testamentum*, Leiden 18 (1968), 472-480.

The author demonstrates from various Egyptian texts, *e.g.* the inscriptions in the Memphite tomb of Horemheb at Leiden, that since the mid XVIIIth Dynasty the outcasts who troubled the cities of Palestine were called *ḫabiru*, while in the south the roads were attacked by similar gangs of nomads, called *š3sw*. When afterwards organized tribes invaded the country it took some time before the new element was recognized by the Egyptians, and even longer until the terminology has been adapted. Thus the names of Edom, Moab and Israel appear for the first time in the reign of Ramses II.

68271 HELCK, W., Geschichte des Alten Ägypten, Leiden/Köln, E. J. Brill, 1968 (16.6 × 25.1 cm; XII + 291 p., 26 ill. [on 8 pl.], 1 table on folding page) = Handbuch der Orientalistik. Erster Abteilung. Der nahe und der mittlere Osten. Herausgegeben von B. Spuler. Erster Band. Ägyptologie. Dritter Abschnitt; rev. *Aegyptus* 48 (1968), 250-251 (Edda Bresciani); *BiOr* 27 (1970), 18-19 (Hans Goedicke); *CdE* XLIV, N° 88 (1969), 274-278 (Luc Limme); *Mundus* 6 (1970), 313-314 (Hellmut Brunner).   Pr. fl. 110

In the introduction the author states that, within the framework of the *Handbuch*, the main facts are presented without final interpretation, the subject being the political history since all other aspects are reserved to other volumes of the *Handbuch*. The manuscript, completed in 1962, was revised in 1967.

Chapter 1 about the prehistory is followed by the protohistory (Thinitenzeit) in chapter 2 and the IIIrd and IVth Dynasty (Pyramidenzeit) in chapter 4, with an excursus on the history of the royal family of the IVth Dynasty. The remainder of the Old Kingdom is dealt with in chapter 4 and 5, while chapter 6 is devoted to the administration and social development of the Old Kingdom.

Chapter 7 on the Heracleopolitan Period contains also the history of the XIth Dynasty. In chapters 8-10 the Middle Kingdom is dealt with, together with its chronology, and its administration and economy. After a chapter (11) on the Hyksos there follows a lengthy discussion of the XVIIIth Dynasty (chapter 12) and a shorter on the Ramesside Period (chapter 13), again accompanied by a chapter (14) on administration and economy, this time of the New Kingdom.

Chapter 15 deals with the decline of the state (XXIst-XXIInd Dynasties); chapter 16 with Egypt as the stage of foreign conflicts; chapter 17 with the Saite Restoration; chapter 18 with the clashes between Egyptian nationalism and Persian domination. In the last chapter (19) the place of Egypt in the world history is sketched.

Indexes composed by Eva-Maria Goepfert on p. 276-291.

68272 HELCK, Wolfgang, Die Ritualszenen auf der Umfassungsmauer Ramses' II. in Karnak, Wiesbaden, Otto Harrassowitz, 1968 (Text: 17.5 × 25 cm; [IV +] 131 p., 2 plans, 1 ill.; Abbildungen: 21 × 29.7 cm; 88 p. containing 151 ill.) = Ägyptologische Abhandlungen herausgegeben von Wolfgang Helck und Eberhard Otto 18; rev. *BiOr* 26 (1969), 67 (Constant de Wit); *JNES* 30 (1971), 315-318 (Edward F. Wente); *Mundus* 6 (1970), 314-315 (Schafik Allam); *OLZ* 66 (1971), 5-14 (W. Barta); *Orientalia* 39 (1970), 159-169 (Jürgen Osing).   Pr. DM 54

Publication of the two registers of ritual scenes on the exterior of the girdle wall around the eastern half of the Amon temple of Karnak.

After a short introduction (p. 1-2) the 62 scenes of the south wall are described, with text and translation of the inscriptions (4-68, with a folding table on p. 69). Scenes 1-9 appear to constitute a separate group, at present separated from the following scenes by a big gap. The author attemps to indicate the contents of the lost reliefs by comparison with similar scenes on other temples (13-14). The ritual represented in scenes 11-63 is summarized and studied on p. 70-80.

The second part contains the scenes 63-88 on the east wall (81-105), again with a folding table (106) and summary (107-109), after which the north wall is dealt with (scenes

90-100, p. 110-116). For the last series, which is full of lacunae, the author publishes photographs and descriptions of several fragments.

Added are texts and translations of the inscriptions in the bottom register of the walls (124-131).

68273 HELCK, Wolfgang, Ritualszenen in Karnak, *MDAIK* 23 (1968), 117-137, with 3 ill. (including a map) and 6 pl.

Verfasser legt die auf der Westwand im Cachette-Hof in Karnak erhaltenen 13 Szenen auf Tafeln vor. Die schönen Reliefs stammen wohl aus der Zeit Ramses II.

Die außerdem autographierten Texte sind übersetzt. Bei der Hymne des "siegreichen Theben" hat Helck zwei spätere Kopien hin zugefügt und Bemerkungen zu dieser Göttin und zum Text. *M. Heerma van Voss*

68274 [HELCK, Wolfgang], Siegfried Schott zum 70. Geburtstag, *Festschrift Schott* [V].

68275 HELCK, Wolfgang, Zur Chronologie Amenophis' I, *Festschrift Schott* 71-72.

Some ostraca and papyri mention the dates of anniversaries of king Amenophis I. The author attempts to establish what events have been commemorated.

68276 HEMMERDINGER, Bertrand, Noms Communs Grecs d'Origine Égyptienne, *Glotta*, Göttingen 46 (1968), 238-247.

The author draws up a list of words occurring in Greek, from the Mycenean language until Xenokrates, which to his opinion are derived from Egyptian. Most of them are well known, such as κόμμι = *Kmyt*, or βορεύς = *br*, while others may be less certain.

Cfr our number 68390.

68277 HENRICHS, Albert, Vespasian's Visit to Alexandria, *Zeitschrift für Papyrologie und Epigraphik*, Bonn 3 (1968), 51-80.

Shortly after having been proclaimed emperor at Alexandria (1 July 69) Vespasianus visited Egypt. According to the sources his stay was accompanied by conspicuous events such as an oracle received by him in the temple of Sarapis, his healing of a blind man and one having a crippled hand, and an unusual rise of the Nile. Although some of them may have been mere inventions they reflected Egyptian conceptions of kingship. The author refers to Ptolemaic, but also to some older parallels.

68278 HENTZE, Carl, Die zerstückelte Schlange, *Antaios*, Stuttgart 9 (1968), 253-261, with 3 fig. and 5 ill. on 3 pl.

Study of the motives: tree of life and the snake which is cut to pieces, in Mexico, Egypt (Apophis), China, *etc.*

68279 HERMANN †, A., 'Stummer Handel' im alten Ägypten, *in*: *Festschrift Werner Caskel* zum siebzigsten Geburtstag, 5. März 1966 gewidmet von Freunden und Schulern. Herausgegeben von Erwin Gräf, Leiden, E. J. Brill, 1968, 184-195.

Bei dem "Stummen Handel" ("silent trade", "commerce de dépôt" oder "à distance") handelt es sich um einen Umschlag, der ohne persönliche Berührung der Partner vor sich geht.

Verfasser beschäftigt sich mit der Inschrift des *Ḥnw* (Hammamat Nr. 114), der dritten Reise des *Ḥrw-ḥwj.f*, dem *t3-3ḥtj.w*, und dem Verbum *3ʿj* c.s.   M. *Heerma van Voss*

HERMANN †, Alfred, see also our number 68162.

68280 HERMISSON, H.-J., Studien zur israelitischen Spruchweisheit, Neukirchen-Vluyn, Neukirchener Verlag des Erziehungsvereins, 1968 (16 × 24 cm; 208 p.) = Wissenschaftliche Monographien zum Alten und Neuen Testament, 28; rev. *Biblica* 51 (1970), 266-267 (Luis Alonso Schökel); *Booklist* 1969, 34 (R. N. W[hybray]); *Theologische Literaturzeitung* 94 (1969), 744-746 (Rosario Pius Merendino).

Pr. cloth DM 24.80

On p. 103-107 the author deals with the school in Egypt, summarizing the study of Brunner about education (our number 57071). There are also several references to Egyptian wisdom literature throughout the book.

68281 HERRMANN, Siegfried, Mose, *Evangelische Theologie*, München 28 (1968), 301-328.

The first part of this study about Moses deals with the historical background. The author discusses *i.a.* the name Moses (p. 303-304), the Semites in Egypt (305-309), influence of the Amarna theology on Moses, which he denies (313-315), and the possible relations between the *Š3sw* and the Israelites.

68282 HERZOG, Rolf, Punt, Glückstadt, Verlag J. J. Augustin, 1968 (21.2 × 22.9 cm; 101 p., 6 pl.) = Abhandlungen des Deutschen Archäologischen Instituts Kairo. Ägyptologische Reihe. Band 6; rev. *BiOr* 28 (1971), 53-56 (Gerald E. Kadish); *Mundus* 6 (1970), 315-316 (Hellmut Brunner); *OLZ* 66 (1971), 459-466 (W. Helck); *Orientalia* 40 (1971), 184-207 (K. A. Kitchen); *ZDMG* 121 (1971), 1972, 115-117 (Winfried Barta).

Pr. DM 38

Verfasser ist nicht Ägyptologe, sondern Ethnologe. Er

versucht die völkerkundlich wägbaren Aussagen über Punt, besonders die bildlichen von Deir el-Bahri, für die Bestimmung der geographischen Lage und der ethnischen Zugehörigkeit zu nutzen.
Seine wohl wichtigste Folgerungen sind:
Punt hat in der jetzigen Republik Sudan bzw. in den angrenzenden Landschaften Äthiopiens am Weißen oder Blauen Nil oder am Flusse Atbara gelegen;
bereits 1481 v. Chr. war dort eine negroide Population durch Hellfarbige (wohl Kuschiten) überschichtet.
Vier aus sechs Tafeln zeigen Pfahlbauten im Sudan des zwanzigsten Jahrhundert. *M. Heerma van Voss*

HESS-von WYSS, Jean-Jacques, see our number 68559.

68283 HEWARD, Grant S.—Jerald TANNER, The Source of the Book of Abraham identified, *The Joseph Smith Egyptian Papyri* 92-98.

The authors demonstrate that Joseph Smith used one of the recently rediscovered fragments from the "Breathing Permit" of Hor as the source for the Mormon Book of Abraham. *Dieter Mueller*

HEYLER, André, see our numbers 68373 and 68595.

68284 HINTZE, Fritz, Musawwarat es Sufra. Vorbericht über die Ausgrabungen des Instituts für Ägyptologie der Humboldt-Universität zu Berlin, 1963 bis 1966 (vierte bis sechste Kampagne), *Wissenschaftliche Zeitschrift der Humboldt-Universität zu Berlin.* Gesellschaftliche-Sprachwissenschaftliche Reihe, Berlin 17 (1968), 667-684, with 28 ill., 1 loose map, 5 loose plans, 1 loose fig. and 1 loose diagram; summaries in German, Russian, English and French on p. 684.

Sequel to our numbers 62273 and 63226.
Preliminary report of the fourth to sixth campaign at Musawwarat es Sufra. The building history of the Great Enclosure has been largely clarified. Five periods could be distinguished, comprising the entire Meroitic age from the 5th century B.C. until the 4th century A.D.
Some other buildings have also been investigated: a small house of the 1st century B.C., the remains of an old sanctuary, and a sacral construction of an unknown type.
The excavation of the north cemetery proved the graves to be post-meroitic ("Noba").
The author concludes from the absence of larger remains of inhabitation and the low number of burials that Musawwarat has been predominantly a sacral place, and the Great Enclosure with its spacious court a centre for pilgrims.

Over 120 graffiti, mainly Meroitic, may also point in that direction.

68285 HINTZE. F. and U. HINTZE, Civilizations of the Old Sudan. Kerma, Kush, Christian Nubia. Translated from the German by P. Prochnik, Leipzig, Edition Leipzig, 1968 (146 p., including 112 ill. [24 in colour], 2 maps); rev. *Phœnix* 14 (1968), 194 (K. R. Veenhof). Pr. bound DM 38.50

English edition of our number 66283. Not seen.

HIRMER, Max, see our number 68359.

68286 Histoires et légendes de l'Egypte mystérieux. Textes recueillis et présentés par Pierre du Bourguet, [Paris], Tchou, éditeur, [1968] (14.3 × 21.6 cm; 320 p. containing numerous ill.); series: Histoires et légendes noires. Collection dirigée par Denis Roche; rev. *BiOr* 27 (1970), 26 (Tito Orlandi); *Revue Biblique* 77 (1970), 301-302 (B. Couroyer).

Ce livre contient, annotés, illustrés et préfacés, des contes pharaoniques, des récits chrétiens et des contes musulmans. Les traductions dans le premier groupe sont données d'après notre numéro 953, d'après *Les Contes populaires* de G. Maspero (*Rhampsinite* et *Khaemouast*) et d'après E. Talbot (*Eucrate* de Lucien de Samosate).
L'histoire de *Saint Pisentius et la momie* a été traduite par Jean-Luc Benoziglio d'après B. Gunn dans notre numéro 561.
M. Heerma van Voss

68287 HODZHASH, S. I. and N. A. POMERANTSEVA, Всеволод Владимирович Павлов. К 70-летию со дня рождения, Вестник Московского государственного университета 4 (1968), 86-88.

"Vsevolod Vladimirovich Pavlov. The Seventieth Birtday". Compare *ВДИ* 3 (105), 1968, 216.

68288 HOFMANN, Inge, Die historische Bedeutung der Niltal kulturen zwischen Aswân und Sennar, *Saeculum*, Freiburg/ München 19 (1968), 109-142, with 3 maps and 10 pl.

The author summarizes the historical implications of her archaeological thesis (our number 67269), particularly stressing the relations of the various Nubian cultures with other countries. The cultures are dealt with in a chronological order, from the so-called "mesolithic" civilisation of Khartoum (in fact early neolithic) to the Christian period. An extensive bibliography on p.138-142.

68289 HORNUNG, Erik, Altägyptische Höllenvorstellungen, Berlin, Akademie-Verlag, 1968 (21.2 × 29.9 cm; 42 p.,

6 fig., 7 pl.) = Abhandlungen der Sächsischen Akademie der Wissenschaften zu Leipzig. Philologisch-historische Klasse. Band 59. Heft 3. Pr. DM 10.30

Wer auf Erden der Maat nicht folgte, ihr vielmehr widerstrebte, fiel nach dem Tode der Verdammnis anheim. Die Teilung des Jenseits in ein Reich der Verklärung und ein Reich der Vernichtung findet sich zum ersten Mal in den Jenseitsbüchern des Neuen Reiches. In diesem wird der Verbannte seiner Bestrafung übergeben. Die Strafen richten sich zum Teil gegen den Körper: Sie bestehen u.a. in Aufhebung der Bestattung, Verlust der Sinnesorgane, Gottesferne, Fesselung oder Einkerkerung, Bestrafung durch Feuer und Schwert. Feuerstrafen werden besonders vielfältig geschildert und ausgeführt durch flammenspeiende Schlangen, feuersprühende Schwerter, das Sonnenauge, den Feuersee, große Feueröfen, in denen blutrote Flammen züngeln, siedende Kessel! Die "Seele" $b\vec{3}$ und der "Schatten" šwt können, vom Körper getrennt, die gleichen Strafen erhalten wie jener. Zudem findet die gewünschte Vereinigung der Teile nicht statt: die Seele wird geraubt, der Schatten findet nicht zu dem Leichnam zurück. Schließlich wird der Verdammte ausgelöscht in seiner Existenz, indem er an der Vernichtungsstätte der Fresserin anheimgegeben wird.

Die ägyptische Hölle kennt also keine Tantalus- oder Sisyphusqualen, keine unendliche Folterung; die Qualen sind vielmehr nur der Auftakt zu völliger Austilgung.

Ingrid Gamer-Wallert

68290 HORNUNG, Erik, Das Tal der Könige, *Bild der Wissenschaft*, Stuttgart 5 (1968), 774-783, with 9 ill. (2 in colours).

A richly illustrated description of certain wall decorations of tombs in the Valley of the Kings (especially from the tomb of Haremhab). Scenes described here are of cultic character or illustrate the netherworld (*Amduat*; *Book of Gates*; *Book of Caverns*).

Unchanged reprint in *Neue Funde aus alter Zeit*, Stuttgart, Deutsche Verlags-Anstalt, 20-29 (biographical notice on p. 8).

J. F. Borghouts

68291 HUARD, Paul, Nouvelles figurations sahariennes et nilosoudanaises de bœufs porteurs, montés et attelés, *Bulletin de la Société Préhistorique Française. Comptes rendus*, Paris 65 (1968), 114-120, with 3 fig.

For ancient Egypt see p. 119-120.

68292 HUGHES, George R., A Demotic Plea to Thoth in the Library of G. Michaelidis, *JEA* 54 (1968), 176-182, with 1 pl.; rev. *Enchoria* 1 (1971), 60 (Heinz-Josef Thissen).

This is one of eight appeals to Thoth in this collection and is written on linen. It probably came from Hermopolis where it may have been 'posted' in the underground ibis galleries at Tûna el-Gebel. Palaeographically it can be dated to the reign of Darius I or at the earliest to that of Amasis. The translation suggests that the man who petitions is asking for protection against an Evil Genius who has brought him ill luck. Grammatical notes are included. *E. Uphill*

HUS, Alain, see our number 68081.

68293 **IBRAHIM**, Mohiy E. A. E., Miscellaneous Passages about King and Kingship According to the Inscriptions of the Temple of Edfu, *ASAE* 60 (1968), 297-300.

Though the divine nature of kingship is emphasized throughout Egyptian history, a clear distinction is made between the king acting in a priestly function "like" (*mi*) a god, and the king acting "as" (*m*) the head of state. *Dieter Mueller*

68294 ISCHLONDSKY, N. Dorin, The Saga of a Bronze and the Story of a Friendship, *JNES* 27 (1968), 51-60, with 4 fig.

The writer describes his friendship with the late Günther Roeder which arose out of his research of a bronze figure of Anubis given to him by Mrs Chester Beatty. This object known as Anubis X had an unusual tail (see our number 66301). Specimens of letters and correspondence are reproduced. *E. Uphill*

68295 IVERSEN, Erik, Diodorus' Account of the Egyptian Canon, *JEA* 54 (1968), 215-218, with 1 pl.

Diodorus stated that the Egyptians unlike the Greeks divided "the structure of the body into twenty-one parts and one-fourth in addition", and then separated these afterwards using them in the sizes they wanted, but in such a way that they corresponded. Lepsius first showed the relation of these figures to the grid employed in the Late Egyptian art canon, but was unable to explain the meaning of the additional fourth. The author uses the measures shown on a standard cubit-rod to answer this difficulty and demonstrates the correctness of Diodorus's statement. *E. Uphill*

68296 IVERSEN, Erik, Obelisks in Exile. Volume I. The Obelisks of Rome, Copenhagen, G. E. C. Gad Publishers, 1968 (22.8 × 35.5 cm; 207 p., 175 ill. and fig. on 62 pl., 1 map on pl. 63, 1 unnumbered ill. on p. 7); rev. *BiOr* 26 (1969), 194-196 (B. van de Walle); *Rivista* 44 (1969), 54-56 (Sergio Donadoni).

Study on the thirteen obelisks at present erected in Rome. In contrast to the book on the same subject by D'Onofrio

(our number 67428) Iversen also deals with the Egyptian origin of the monuments. In an introductory chapter their architectural and cultic significance is sketched. There follows a discussion of each of the monuments, which mentions its Egyptian provenance, though mainly devoted to their Roman history and their significance for the development of the conceptions about ancient Egypt from the Middle Ages until today. In a last chapter the lost obelisks are dealt with.
Extensive indexes on p. 189-203.
We mention particularly the splendid illustration of the book which seldom overlaps and usually amplifies that of D'Onofrio's study.

68297 JACQUET-GORDON, Helen, Two Stelae of Horus-on-the-Crocodiles, *The Brooklyn Museum Annual* 7 (1965-1966), 53-64, with 4 ill., 1 fig., and 2 p. with hieroglyphic texts (= p. 60-61).

One of the two stelae (Brooklyn acc. no. 60.73), of unknown provenance and dated to the 3rd century B.C., is well preserved, while of the other (Brooklyn acc. no. 57.21.2), also of unknown provenance, the upper part is missing. The author describes the stelae and gives the text of the later one in hieroglyphs and in translation. The older one contains as the most important element of the text, which is an abbreviated version of text B of the other, the name of a pharaoh Osorkon. For the rest the texts do not greatly differ from those of other versions of the same inscriptions which appear on numerous prophylactic stelae.

68298 JAIN, Ramchandra, Śramaṇic Foundations of Ancient Egypt, *Proceedings* 21.

The author suggests that the earliest Egyptian immigrants came from Punt under the leadership of Menes, a Paṇi leader, who took his Śramaṇalogical culture to Egypt. *Śrama* is the name given to "the right driving force of the soul".

68299 JAMES, T. G. H., An Early Middle-Kingdom Account, *JEA* 54 (1968), 51-56, with 2 pl.

This small papyrus in private ownership in England shows an interesting relationship with the XIth Dynasty Heḳanakhte documents discovered at Deir el-Baḥri. It was probably acquired in Luxor about 1923. Attached to it is a small mud sealing with the impression of a scarab whose design although commonplace is identical with a sealing on one of the Heḳanakhte letters. The text deals with barley measures and had names similar to some in the Hekanakhte texts. Translation and commentary are appended.

E. *Uphill*

68300 [JAMES, T. G. H.], Editorial Foreword, *JEA* 54 (1968), 1-2.

68301 JANSEN, H. Ludin, Der Begriff ⲡⲧⲏⲣϥ, "das All", im Evangelium Veritatis, *Acta Orientalia*, Havniae [Copenhagen] 31 (1968), 115-118.

With the word ⲡⲧⲏⲣϥ is indicated that part of man which is of transcendental origin; its antithesis is Matter (ϯϩⲩⲗⲏ).

L. F. *Kleiterp*

68302 JANSSEN, Jac. J. The Smaller Dâkhla Stela (Ashmolean Museum no. 1894. 107 b), *JEA* 54 (1968), 165-172, with 2 pl.

This monument inscribed with abnormal hieratic was found by Captain Lyons. It is of sandstone and measures 81.5 cm high by 39.5 cm wide, the upper left side being missing. It shows a figure called the great chief of the Sha(m)in, Esdhute offering to the falcon-headed god Setekh. It is dated to year 24 of a Pharaoh called Py, possibly to be equated with Piankhi, in whose period epithets such as are found on this stela can be adduced.

E. *Uphill*

68303 JANSSEN, Jac. J. and P. W. PESTMAN, Burial and Inheritance in the Community of the Necropolis Workmen at Thebes (Pap. Bulaq X and O. Petrie 16), *Journal of the Economic and Social History of the Orient*, Leiden 11 (1968), 137-170, with 2 pl.

The article consists of three parts, the first part containing a short introduction on Deir el-Medina and the texts of Pap. Bulaq X and O. Petrie 16 (= *Hieratic Ostraca* 21,1). The papyrus is given in photograph and transcription, but the translation with notes and the commentary on the recto and the verso are separate since both texts are complete in themselves, although related to each other. The recto is to be dated to the end of the XIXth or the early XXth Dynasty, and records the dispute over an inheritance between members of a family, while the verso, dated in a year 8 (of Ramses III), contains the will of one of them, consisting of a list of the divided property and of the beneficiaries concerned. The ostracon is translated and commented upon, and contains two disputes concerning inheritances, the second of which is referred to in the Pap. Bulaq as a precedent.

The second part discusses the Egyptian words for the properties, *i.e.*, several buildings, while in the last part the law of inheritance is studied.

L. M. J. *Zonhoven*

68304 JANSSEN, Jozef M. A., Ägypten, *in*: *Geschichte und Religion des Alten Testament* herausgegeben von P. J. Cools, Olten und Freiburg im Breisgau, Walter Verlag, [1968] (= Das moderne Sachbuch 77), 149-162.

German translation of our number 57272.

68305 JANSSENS, Yvonne, L'Évangile selon Philippe, *Muséon* 81 (1968), 79-133.

In this article a translation is given of the Gospel of Philip (the third tractate in Codex II of the Nag-Hammadi papyri). Compare our numbers 67391 and 68331. *L. F. Kleiterp*

68306 JARRY, Jacques, Inscriptions grecques et coptes de Nubie (1964-1965), *BIFAO* 66 (1968), 143-146, with 7 pl.

Publication of some fragmentary texts (inscriptions, graffiti, ostraca and a stela) from es-Sebua' containing only very little information.

68307 JÉQUIER, [Gustave], En Perse 1887-1902. Journal et Lettres de Gustave Jéquier publiées et annotés par Michel Jéquier. Avec une préface du professeur Roman Ghirshman et une note biographique du professeur Eddy Bauer, [Neuchâtel], A la Baconnière, [1968] (15.4 × 21.6 cm; 206 p., 3 fig., 3 maps, 56 ill., 5 colour pl., 2 colour ill. on cover); rev. *BiOr* 26 (1969), 449 (anonymous).

Though only concerned with Jéquier's Persian years (1897-1902) during which he was attached to de Morgan's Mission at Susa the Egyptologist may find something of value to him in the biography (p. 185-186) and bibliography (187-192) as well as in the annotated index to the persons quoted, *e.g.* Gautier and de Morgan (193-198).

68308 JESI, Furio, Letteratura e mito, [Torino], Giulio Einaudi editore, [1968] (10.7 × 18 cm; 247 p.) = La ricerca letteraria. Serie critica 4. Pr. L. 1200

In this anthology two essays are related to ancient Egypt. The former is a reprint of our number 64252 to be found on p. 85-94. The latter (215-241) is entitled *L'esperienza religiosa di Apuleio nelle Metamorfosi*, "Apuleius' religious experience in the *Metamorphoses*".

P. 247 presents a concise biography and bibliography of the author. *M. Heerma van Voss*

68309 JESI, Furio, Note sul pessimismo egizio, *Aegyptus* 48 (1968), 1970, 19-30.

The *Dialogue of a Man With His Ba* reflects the deep pessi-

mism caused by the disastrous upheavals that marked the end of the Old Kingdom. Although the virtuous man must reject the *carpe diem* attitude proposed by his ba, the latter is willing to guarantee his immortality after the suicide, albeit with profound scepticism toward the promise of a blissful life in the hereafter. Compared to this genuine outburst of tragic despair, the *Songs of the Harper* reflect the fashionable scepticism of the sophisticated upper class expressed in conventionalized modes.
See now also Gertrud Thausing, Aegyptiaca, *WZKM* 62 (1969), 11-29. *Dieter Mueller*

68310 JIDEJIAN, Nina, Byblos through the ages, Beirut, Dar el-Machreq Publishers, [1968] (22 × 28 cm; XXII + 223 p. [including 10 unnumbered pl.], 130 ill. and fig. [= p. 150-208; 1 unnumbered ill.; 2 plans included], pl. on endpapers, folding pl., map on p. XXII); rev. *Antiquity* 44 (1970), 65-66 (Diana Kirkbride); *BiOr* 27 (1970), 122 (anonymous); *JEA* 55 (1969), 230-231 (G. T. Martin); *Mélanges de l'Université Saint Joseph* 44 (1968), 243-244 (M. Tallon); *Orientalia* 38 (1969), 584-585 (Robert North); *Phoenix* 15 (1969), 236-237 (anonymous); *ZAW* 81 (1969), 136 ([G. Fohrer]).

The account of the Phoenician city contains by its very nature several chapters which are of interest to the Egyptologist.
Chapter 3 (The Early Bronze Age) deals with the relations between Byblos and Egypt during the Old Kingdom, and discusses the temple of Baalat-Gebal, the goddess represented in a manner similar to Hathor-Isis, in whose sanctuary many objects from Egypt have been found.
Chapter 4 (The Middle Bronze Age) is devoted to the royal necropolis and the Temple of the Obelisks. In the necropolis again many Egyptian objects have been discovered, but also *i.a.* the famous sarcophagus of Ahiram, which is amply discussed. There is also a survey of the history of the period quoting the *Story of Sinuhe* and the *Execration Texts*.
Chapter 5 (The Late Bronze Age) is completely devoted to the relations with the XVIIIth Dynasty (*Annals of Tuthmosis III* and *Amarna Tablets*). The curious lack of archaeological material from the city between the Middle Kingdom and the Roman levels is discussed in chapter 6, where we also find a paragraph about the *Story of Wenamon*.
The rest of the book is mainly outside the scope of the present bibliography.

68311 JUNGWIRTH, Johann und Reinhold ENGELMAYER, Die anthropologischen Ergebnisse der Grabungskampagne 1967 in Tell ed Dab'a, Unterägypten, *Annalen des Naturhistorischen Museums in Wien*, Wien 72 (1968), 697-702, with 2 pl.

Preliminary report on 22 skeletons found by the Austrian expedition in Tell ed Dab'a, 12 of which pertain to children. It was impossible to define the race in the field, but there may be rather uncommon types among them.

68312 JUNGWIRTH, Johann [und] Reinold ENGELMAYER, Der Beitrag Österreichs zur Erforschung der Rassengeschichte Ägyptens, *Bustan*, Wien 9, Heft 3-4 (1968), 33-38.

Survey of the archaeological and anthropological results of the Austrian excavations in the district of Sayala, Nubia. Altogether 650 skeletons have been found, preserved and studied, of which 38 from the C-Group, 13 from the Pan-Graves culture, 443 from the Roman period and the others from the 8th-10th century A.D. The authors mention *i.a.* the contrast between the fairly pure Europoid type of the C-Group and the negroid characteristics in the Pan-Grave people.

At the end the authors mention recent Austrian excavations at Tell ed-Dab'a near Khata'na (eastern Delta), which may or may not be the city of Avaris (see our number 68075).

JUNGWIRTH, Johann, see also our number 68201.

68313 KAISER, Martin, Herodots Begegnung mit Ägypten, *in*: Siegfried Morenz, *Die Begegnung Europas mit Ägypten*, Berlin, Akademie-Verlag, 1968, 200-247.

Herodotus was impressed by the magnitude of everything in Egypt: the Nile, the population, the monuments, and particularly the length of its history. For its tradition he felt a profound respect. The connection between god and man dates back to the primeval times, which stood in contrast to the Greek conceptions. The relation between natural and human history found in Egypt agreed with his rational mind. He therefore used Egyptian history in order to insert the Greek past into the universal history, replacing the Greco-centred picture by an Egypt-centred conception, particularly in the field of religion, where his rationalism also leads to concentration on the cult, the myths being for him reflections of historical events.

68314 KAISER, Martin, Literarische Traditionen in den Apophthegmata Patrum, *Probleme* 125-144.

The history of the form of the *Apophthegmata Patrum* is essentially part of the Greek literary history. The form was further influenced by the Bible and the Logia-collections;

little or no Egyptian influence can be indicated. Many of the motives however can be traced back to Egyptian stories and the Wisdom-literature. *L. F. Kleiterp*

68315 KÁKOSY, László, A Cheops piramis feltörésének kérdése, *Archaeologiai Értesítő*, Budapest 95 (1968), 82-89, with a summary in English on p. 89.

"The Problem of The Breaking Open of Cheops' Pyramid." Though a great number of pyramids and tombs were plundered during the First Intermediate Period, it cannot be convincingly proved that the Cheops pyramid was forced in times previous to the XXVIth Dynasty. Even subsequently to this era certain information is available only for the underground chamber and the descending corridor. The most probable inference seems to be that the burial chamber was rifled in the second half of the 5th century, in any case after Herodotus' time, or subsequently to the time of the second Persian rule. *Vilmos Wessetzky*

68316 KÁKOSY, László, Az idő az állat-szimbolikában, *Művészet*, Budapest 9, N° 3 (1968), 3-5, with 4 fig.

"Die Zeit in der Tier-Symbolik".
Der Ewigkeits- und Zeitbegriff der Ägypter wird oft durch das Symbol verschiedener Tiere ausgedrückt. Die ihren Schwanz beissende Schlange (Uroboros) ist das Zeichen der Ewigkeit. Die Hieroglyphe des Jahres, der knospende Zweig wurde später als Ziegenhorn gedeutet, und dadurch auch zum Ewigkeitssymbol. Die mit Sothis identische Isis kann in der Spätzeit in Kuhgestalt auch die Zeit bedeuten. Ewigkeitssymbole können weiterhin sein der Aasgeier, der auf der Wasseruhr sitzende Affe, der Ibis, der Phönix, der Skarabäus. Die Hieroglyphe des Krokodils bedeutet auch die Zeit.
Zahlreiche Elemente dieser Symbolik gehen über die römische Kultur in die europäische Kunst ein.

Vilmos Wessetzky

68317 KÁKOSY, L., Imhotep and Amenhotep son of Hapu as patrons of the dead, *Acta orientalia academiae scientiarum hungaricae*, Budapest 21 (1968), 109-117.

Proceeding from a mention of the sages Amenhotep and Imhotep in Pap. Boulaq III (see our number 2554) the author discusses their cult in Thebes, particularly their connection with the belief in the netherworld. He explains their role in the embalming rites by pointing out that in the Late Period a mysterious, ancient science was thought to be necessary in order to avoid destruction, and the sages were supposed to be keepers of this secret knowledge. Since these were also familiar to the Greeks, they contributed to the rapprochement between both religions.

68318 KÁKOSY, László, Nemetközi Kollokvium a késő-egyiptomi vallásról (Strassburg, 1967, május 16-18), *Antik Tanulmányok. Studia Antiqua*, Budapest 15 (1968), 174-175.

"Internationales Kolloquium über die spätägyiptische Religion".
Kurze Zusammenfassung der Vorträge der religionsgeschichtlichen Konferenz in Strasbourg, 16-18 Mai 1967.
Vilmos Wessetzky

68319 KÁKOSY, László, Pythagoreus hatás Apuleius Metamorphoses XI-ben?, *Antik Tanulmányok. Studia Antiqua*, Budapest 15 (1968), 243-245.

"Pythagoreische Einwirkung in die Metamorphoses XI von Apuleius?"
Nach Apuleius wurde am Isisfest in Kenchreai von einem Priester der Göttin eine Hand als Zeichen der Gerechtigkeit getragen. Neben der apotropäischen Bedeutung soll auch der mit der Hand zusammenhängende symbolhafte Sinn der Zahl 5 beachtet werden. Seit dem 1. Jahrhundert v. Chr. berufen sich mehrere Werke auf pythagoreische Überlieferung, die sich mit der Zahlenmystik beschäftigen; in der Spätzeit wurden diese Spekulationen in Ägypten ebenso populär.
Vilmos Wessetzky

68320 KÁKOSY, László, Varázslás az ókori Egyiptomban, Budapest, Akadémiai Kiadó, 1968 (19 × 12.5 cm; 202 p., 33 ill.) = Kőrösi Csoma Kiskönyvtár, Vol. 7.

"Zauberei im alten Ägypten".
Der Autor gibt eine Übersicht der Stellung der Magie in der ägyptischen Religion, im Leben des Alltags und des Staates. Nach einer Zusammenfassung der ägyptischen Religion behandelt das II. Kapitel die Charakteristik der ägyptischen Magie, III. die Geschichte der Zauberei, IV. die Metternich-Stele, den Budapester Zauberpapyrus und den Berliner koptischen Zaubertext, V. die in der ägyptischen Literatur auftretenden "Zauberer", VI. die Amulette und Zaubermittel. Das reiche Anmerkungenmaterial (1-421) verweist auf die literarischen Angaben.
Vilmos Wessetzky

68321 KÁKOSY, László, Zu einer Etymologie von Philae: die «Insel der Zeit», *Acta antiqua academiae scientiarum hungaricae*, Budapest 16 (1968), 39-48, with a fig. and 3 ill.

Eine Inschrift des Trajanus-Kioskes in Philae deutet den Namen *P jw rk* als "Insel der Zeit". Diese Volksetymologische Namenserklärung passt gut zu den Lehren des späteren, dem Aion gleichgesetzten Osiris und dem Osiriskultes. Osiris hat im Götterdekret über das Abaton auch den Beinamen "göttlicher Phönix" als Ausdruck des Symbols für Auferstehung und Ewigkeit. Der neben dem grossen Tempel von Philae stehende Torbau des Hadrian enthält ebenfalls eine Relief-Darstellung, wo die Hieroglyphe im Osirisgestalt als $ḏt$ "Ewigkeit" zu deuten ist.

Vilmos Wessetzky

68322 KAMEL, Ibrahim, A Bronze Hoard at Athribis, *ASAE* 60 (1968), 65-71, with 15 pl. (including 1 plan) and 1 fig.

In April 1963, a hoard of 55 Ptolemaic bronzes, most of them representing Harpokrates or Isis, was discovered at Tell el-Athrib. The find was made in an area north of the Great Temple of Horus Khenti-kheti, the patron-god of Athribis.

Dieter Mueller

68323 KAPLONY, Peter, Eine neue Weisheitslehre aus dem Alten Reich (Die Lehre des $Mṯṯj$ in der altägyptischen Weisheitsliteratur), *Orientalia* 37 (1968), 1-62, with 3 pl.; (Zusätze und Nachträge), 339-345, with 1 pl.

I. La collection Kofler-Truniger, à Lucerne, contient une plaque de calcaire haute d'un mètre, provenant de la tombe de Methethi, à Saqqara. Methethi est représenté avec son fils Ihy. L'inscription comprend dix lignes verticales, plus une ligne horizontale: le nom et les titres du personnage. Kaplony donne la transcription, une traduction allemande et un commentaire.

Methethi laisse peu de données biographiques. Voici en gros son enseignement. Honorer le roi assure le bonheur dans les deux vies. Je fus un serviteur loyal, et deviens ainsi un médiateur, un "ancêtre" exemplaire.

II. L'auteur rapproche la distribution d'or figurée sur un relief du Virginia Museum et le rôle médiateur de Shou. Methethi a reçu du roi une litière, et donne en son nom le collier d'or. Notes sur la nécessité d'apprendre au visiteur de la tombe le nom de son propriétaire; le culte du roi de son vivant; l'idée du corps de l'Etat. La crise se montre peut-être dans des conventions entre particuliers et prêtres-lecteurs. L'influence des esprits de la nécropole, même sur les vivants, indique peut-être déjà l'autorité affaiblie. Et l'importance du tribunal de Neith à Saïs pourrait remonter à une institution de haute époque. *J. Custers*

68324 KAPLONY, Peter, Neues Material zu einer Prosopographie des Alten Reichs, *MIO* 14 (1968), 192-205, with 3 fig., 10 pl. and an English summary on p. 205.

L'auteur publie le texte de huit monuments. Un relief porte l'inscription "Maison de ka de $Ḥḥ(j)$-$k3$: 5 aroures de terre arable". La livraison de produits à des privilégiés aurait peut-être remplacé l'impôt, le roi attribuant de nombreux petits biens dispersés, et morcelant des localités entre plusieurs bénéficiaires. Mais le nom Hehy pourrait désigner le propriétaire du tombeau.

Un chevet de calcaire et un plat à offrandes, en marbre rouge, appartiennent respectivement au fonctionnaire '$Ippy$ et à $Snny$. Un bassin fut offert pour Mrt-$it.s$ par sa petite-fille $Ḥnty$-$k3w.s$, "nourrice du Palais". Le $K3.s$ à qui appartient un bassin pourrait porter un nom abrégé. Les autres bassins (Louvre et Caire) sont aux noms de Ny-$m3ʿt$-$Rʿ$ de $Snḏm$-ib et de (*$Ḥp$-m-)$hnn.f$.   *J. Custers*

68325 KAPLONY, Peter, Steingefässe mit Inschriften der Frühzeit und des Alten Reichs, Bruxelles, Fondation Égyptologique Reine Élisabeth, 1968 (22.8 × 28.5 cm; 78 p., 34 pl.) = Monumenta Aegyptiaca 1; rev. *BiOr* 26 (1969), 333-335 (Wolfgang Helck).   Pr. bound b. fr. 750

Catalogue of a private Swiss collection of 42 stone vases with inscriptions, to which are added some pieces with similar inscriptions from other collections. Of each item the author gives a photograph, an outline drawing, a drawing of the inscription, an extensive description and discussion.

The inscriptions are divided into five groups: documents from the time of the uniting of the country (nos 1-4); royal names from the archaic period (5-21); personal names from this period (23-29); royal names from the Old Kingdom (30-37) and personal names of this time (38-42). No 22 only contains the indication of an office without a personal name. In Excursus I the author deals with the sequence of the pharaohs of the late IInd Dynasty and the development of the royal titulary. Excursus II discusses the problem of the genuineness of stone vases.

68326 KAPLONY-HECKEL, Ursula, Die Demotische Tempeleide der Berliner Papyrussammlung, *Forschungen und Berichte* 10 (1968), 133-184, with 2 pl.

Publication of 40 Demotic ostraca containing a temple-oath from the Papyrussammlung of the Museum in East Berlin. Each text is published in facsimile (4 also in photograph) with translation and commentary. Only the first one (Berlin P. 770) has previously been published (Revillout, *Mélanges sur la métrologie*...., Paris, 1895, 189 ff.).

The author gives a survey of the temple-oath in general on p. 136-137 and short introductions to three different categories on p. 150, 170 and 177. Index of names on p. 183, list of museum numbers on p. 184.

68327 KARIG, Joachim Selim, Die Kultkammer des Amenhotep aus Deir Durunka, *ZÄS* 95, 1 (1968), 27-34, with 1 pl. and 3 fig.

Veröffentlichung einer Kammer, nur einige Jahre zuvor noch im Museum in Assiût aufgestellt. Die Blöcke sind jetzt in Berlin-Charlottenburg, Cleveland, Toledo und Zürich; cfr unsere Zusammenfassung 66250.
Man vergleiche jetzt H. Wild, *Note concernant des antiquités trouvées, non à Deir Dronka, mais dans la nécropole d'Assiout*, *BIFAO* 69 (1971), 307-309. *M. Heerma van Voss*

68328 KARIG, Joachim Selim, Das neue Ägyptische Museum in Charlottenburg, in: *Jahrbuch Preussischer Kulturbesitz* 1967, Band V [1968], 227-236, with 2 pl.

The author relates the history of the Egyptian collection in Berlin, which was divided after the war between East and West Berlin, and describes the exhibition of the western part in the Charlottenburger Schloß.

68329 KASSER, Rodolphe, Bibliothèque gnostique V. Apocalypse d'Adam, *Revue de théologie et de philosophie*, Lausanne, 3ᵐᵉ série, 17 (1967), 316-333.

Sequel to our number 67308.
After a short introduction the author presents a translation of the Apocalypse of Adam (codex V of the Nag Hammadi Manuscripts).

68330 KASSER, Rodolphe, Bibliothèque gnostique VI. Les deux apocalypses de Jacques, *Revue de théologie et de philosophie*, Lausanne, 3ᵐᵉ série, 18 (1968), 163-186.

Sequel to the preceding number, in which the author translates the two apocalypses of James (Codex V of the Nag Hammadi Manuscripts).

68331 KASSER, Rodolphe, L'Évangile selon Philippe. Propositions pour quelques reconstitutions nouvelles, *Muséon* 81 (1968), 407-414.

The author, while observing that the work on the reconstruction of the text of the Gospel of Philip (Nag-Hammadi Codex II, third tractate) is by no means completed, hereby submits a series of emendations. *L. F. Kleiterp*

68332 KASSER, Rodolphe, Morphologie Copte. Les substantifs ⲃⲁⲉⲓⲉ, ⲃⲁⲕⲉ (ou ⲃⲁⲕⲏ, ⲃⲉⲕⲉ), ⲉϧⲱ, ⲕ̄ⲣⲕⲏⲟⲩ, le verbe ⲥⲟⲉⲓⲩ, et les verbes causatifs ⲑⲉⲙⲟⲟ et ⲧⲥⲁⲙⲓⲟ, *BIFAO* 66 (1968), 105-111.

The author connects ⲃⲁⲉⲓⲉ "brooklet" with ϥⲟ (Crum 623 a), ⲃⲁⲕⲉ with ⲃⲟⲕⲓ "pregnant" (Crum 31 a), ⲉⲟⲱ "residence" with ⲁⲟ (Crum 24 b), k̄ⲣⲕⲏⲟⲩ "foundation" with ⲥⲱp̄ⲥ (Crum 831 b), and ⲥⲟⲉⲓⲩ "to copulate" (?) with the noun ⲥⲟⲉⲓⲩ (Crum 374 b). He debates whether ⲑⲉⲙⲟⲟ "to commit suicide" is related to ⲙⲟⲩⲟⲩⲧ "to kill", and discusses the origin of ⲧⲥⲁⲙⲓⲟ "to create".

Dieter Mueller

KASSER, Rodolphe, see also our number 68397.

68333 KATZNELSON, Isidor, Аркамон (Эргамен) и ритуальное убийство царя в Куше, *Klio*, Berlin 50 (1968), 29-38.

"Arkamon (Ergamenes) and the ritual killing of the king in Kush".
Ritual killing of the king after a certain period of reign is a well-known custom with some African peoples (Shilluk, Funga, Nuba, Ewe) and from antiquity it is reported for the Darfur oasis, as well as for the Meroitic kingdom. According to Strabo (XVII, 2,3) the power of the priests to take the decision of killing the king was finally broken, and Diodorus (III, 6) attributes this to the reign of Ergamenes, a contemporary of Ptolemy II. In the so-called (Ethiopic) Stela of Banishment (*Urkunden III*, 108-113, here translated on p. 36) which may be ascribed to king Aspelta (c. 590) a verdict is given by the king over a certain group of priests (*mhw.t twy msd ntr*, "that ungodly clique", = *Urkunden III*, 111, 8-9 = line 5) which had planned to kill somebody without the god's consent. The author argues, that this might be an early testimony of the custom; the premeditated ritual murder of the king was, however, prevented and punished by the latter, thus anticipating the conflict between Ergamenes and the priests with some centuries.

J. F. Borghouts

68334 KATZNELSON, I. S., Царица Хатшепсут и храм в Фивах, Азия и Африка Сегодня, 6 (1968), 50-51.

"Königin Hatschepsut und ein Tempel in Theben".
Populär-wissenschaftlicher Artikel.

KATZNELSON, I. S., see also our number 68191.

68335 KAYSER, Hans, Die Opfertafel des Minpriesters Dedhor in Heidelberg, *Festschrift Schott* 73-79.

Publication of the offering-table of Djedhor (Heidelberg,

Inv. Nr. 11), which may originate from Akhmim. The object is carefully described; the texts are transcribed and translated, followed by a commentary.

68336 KEMP, Barry J., Canopic Jars in the Lady Lever Art Gallery, *Orientalia* 37 (1968), 63-74, with 3 pl.

Ces quatre vases d'un beau fini ont connu une longue histoire depuis leur découverte. L'ensemble ne constitue pas une série homogène, mais les couvercles "chacal" et "babouin" semblent appartenir aux vases correspondants. Les formules, du type XIX de Sethe, nomment un Iahmès, ainsi qu'un Djehouty. La tête de "chacal" très peu caractérisée et la gorge du faucon atteignant le rebord sont de type peu connus. Au groupe de Iahmès appartenait le canope Hapy, Bibl. Nat. 79, devenu Louvre E 13137, qui est également présenté. Mrs Moss publie dans notre n° 68418 le quatrième canope du groupe. *J. Custers*

68337 KEMP, Barry J., Merimda and the Theory of House Burial in Prehistoric Egypt, *CdE* XLIII, N° 85 (1968), 22-33, with 1 map.

L'auteur s'élève contre la théorie selon laquelle les habitants de Merimde Beni Salame auraient enterré leurs morts dans les maisons ou à proximité de celles-ci, et constitué ainsi une exception significative pour l'histoire religieuse, parmi les autres occupants préhistoriques de l'Égypte.
En réalité, la sépulture auprès des habitations n'est certaine que pour des nourrissons, selon un usage encore attesté chez les Coptes. Tous autres cas paraissent contestables, faute d'une stratigraphie suffisante. Il est beaucoup vraisemblable d'admettre qu'à Merimde, comme dans de nombreux autres sites répartis à travers la Basse et Haute Égypte, la proximité des tombes et des maisons est le résultat de la rotation des villages sur des aires limitées d'une certaine étendue, rotation par ailleurs bien attestée, qui aurait amené parfois les habitations au-dessus d'anciennes nécropoles oubliées. Il n'existerait ainsi aucune relation entre les tombes trouvées sous les maisons et ces dernières. *Ph. Derchain*

68338 KEMP, Barry J., The Osiris Temple at Abydos, *MDAIK* 23 (1968), 138-155, with 4 fig. (comprising 2 plans) and 3 pl.

A reconsideration of decisions made by Petrie on the spot and before publishing *Abydos* I and II.
The author had access to a field notebook (1903, unpublished) and to the negatives of Petrie's photographs. He spent a day in the area concerned (1968).
According to him, New Kingdom wealth was spent for the

royal mortuary temples, not for the "popular" temple or tomb of Osiris himself.

The archaic temple of the "Foremost among the Westerners" has been lost beneath the late Old Kingdom sanctuary.

Kemp concludes with remarks on the "First Dynasty" deposits. Compare our number 365, p. 543-546.

M. Heerma van Voss

68339 KENNA, V. E. G., Studies of Birds on Seals of the Aegean and Eastern Mediterranean in the Bronze Age, *Opuscula Atheniensia*, Lund 8 (1968), 23-38, with 7 ill.

The author discusses representations of birds in Egyptian tomb painting since here, rather than on Egyptian seals, he suggests to search for the prototypes of the naturalistic bird forms on Aegean seals.

68340 KERRN LILLESØ, Ebba, Wolja Christian Erichsen 21. november 1890 - 25. april 1966, *Acta Orientalia*, Havniae [Copenhagen] 31 (1968), 1-7, with a portrait.

Obituary notice, with a bibliography. See our number 66648.

KHAWAM, Roger, see our number 68119.

68341 el-KHOULI, Ali, A Preliminary Report on the Excavations at Tura, 1963-64, *ASAE* 60 (1968), 73-76, with 14 pl., including 1 plan.

Continuation of the work at the Tura Cement Factory yielded several more tombs, ranging from the Archaic Period to Roman times. Also discovered were the remains of a brick-paved Roman road. *Dieter Mueller*

68342 KINK, H. A., Об особенностях связей Египта и стран Ханаана с окружающими странами в IV и начале III тысячелетий до Н.Э., IV Сессия по Древнему Востоку, 38-39.

"Über die Besonderkeiten der Beziehungen Ägyptens und der Kanaanitischen Länder zu den umgrenzenden Ländern im IV. und in dem Anfang des III. Jahrtausends".

Der Import einiger Materialien (Obsidian, Kupfer), Keramik und dekorierter Material hat weniger ökonomische Bedeutung für Ägypten als für Kanaan. Die lokale Bodenschätze waren erschöpfend für die Bedürfnisse Ägyptens.

E. S. Bogoslovsky

68343 KITCHEN, Kenneth A., Further Notes on New Kingdom Chronology and History, *CdE* XLIII, N° 86 (1968), 313-324.

Article suscité par la lecture du dernier livre de Redford

(notre numéro 67465). En particulier, il étudie et critique très en détail la démonstration de l'inexistence d'une corégence d'Aménophis III et d'Aménophis IV, dont il montre certaines faiblesses, qui interdisent malheureusement de considérer cette étude comme la solution définitive du problème.

De même, en ce qui concerne la tentative de solution de la question de la date d'accession au trône de Ramsès II (1304 ou 1290), l'auteur montre également que Redford n'a pas réussi à lever tous les doutes.

Il conclut en reconnaissant que les sources dont on dispose actuellement ne permettent pas de réponse définitive aux deux questions posées. *Ph. Derchain*

68344 KITCHEN, K. A., Ramesside Inscriptions. Historical and Biographical. IV. Fascicle 1, Oxford, B. H. Blackwell Ltd, [1968] (19.8 × 28.2 cm; 32 p.); rev. *BiOr* 27 (1970), 349-351 (W. Helck); *JARCE* 8 (1969-1970), 99 (Hans Goedicke); *JEA* 56 (1970), 220 (C. H. S. Spaull); *RdE* 21 (1969), 170-171 (F. Le Corsu). Pr. 15 s.

This is the first fascicle that has been published of a series in which the author intends to present all Ramesside historical and biographical inscriptions.

The present fascicle contains the Amada stela of Merenptah, his Karnak inscription about the Libyan war, his triumph-hymn from the Cairo-stela (Cairo Cat. 34025 vs. = the *Israel Stela*) and that from the Karnak cachette, the Kom el-Ahmar stela, and the stela from Hermopolis with the festival-song of Thoth, together with some smaller texts. At head of each text there are the relevant references to Porter-Moss and earlier publications.

Prior to the present fascicle the author had privately published 24 pages of the same edition, with a prefatory note in which he proposes to cite the series as *KRI*.

Volume I will cover the period of Ramses I and Sethy I; vol. II the royal inscriptions of Ramses II; vol. III the biographical inscriptions of his contemporaries; vol. IV the time of Merenptah and the late XIXth Dynasty; vol. V the reigns of Sethnakht and Ramses III; vol. VI those of Ramses IV to IX; while vol. VII is planned to follow with indexes and addenda.

At present there have been further published: I, 1 (1969); II, 1 (1969); II, 2 (1970); II, 3 (1970); II, 5 (1971); II, 6 (1971); V, 1 (1970) and VI, 1 (1969).

KITCHEN, Kenneth A., see also our number 68217.

68345 KLÄMBT, Hans, Eine Fahrt nach... Ismailia, *Armant*, Köln 1, 1968, 36-43, with 2 plans.

Quelques indications sur Ismailia et description rapide de son musée, ainsi que du jardin des stèles. *Ph. Derchain*

68346 KLASENS, Adolf, A Social Revolution in Ancient Egypt, *Études et Travaux* II 5-13; rev. *BiOr* 27 (1970), 186-187 (Egon Komorzynski).

The situation described in the *Admonitions of an Egyptian Sage* seems to point at a social revolution which broke out in the region of Memphis shortly after the collapse of the Old Kingdom, caused by an increasing desintegration since the Vth Dynasty, culminating under the extremely long and weak reign of Pepi II. There may have been three parties: 1) a revolutionary group, possibly headed by a revolutionary committee of 5 man, 2) the old reigning class, to which Ipuwer belongs, and 3) the indifferent ones.

Ipuwer, putting the question who is guilty of having disturbed the established social order, blames both God and mankind (cfr *Coffin Texts*, Spell 1130).

Basing on information from the Leiden Papyrus, Manetho on the VIIth Dynasty and the *Teaching for Merikare*, the author considers it probable that the revolution has taken place in the First Intermediate Period.

L. M. J. Zonhoven

KLASENS, Adolf, see also our number 68040.

KOCH, Leo, see our number 68648.

68347 KOENEN, L., Die Prophezeiungen des "Töpfers", *Zeitschrift für Papyrologie und Epigraphik*, Bonn 2 (1968), 178-209, with 4 pl.

New edition of a Greek text containing the prophecies of the "potter", known from two manuscripts of the 2nd and 3rd centuries A.D. In the introduction Koenen points at the genuine Egyptian character of the text which originally may have been written in Egyptian.

Cfr the additions, *Zeitschrift für Papyrologie und Epigraphik* Bonn 3 (1968), 137-138.

KOENEN, L., see also our number 68404.

68348 KOLTA, Kamal Sabri, Die Gleichsetzung ägyptischer und griechischer Götter bei Herodot, [Tübingen], 1968 (15 × 20.7 cm; XVI + 203 p.).

In this thesis for a doctor's degree in Tübingen the author

studies Herodotus' identification of Egyptian and Greek divinities.

The introduction is devoted to the sources of Herodotus and the problem of his reliability. For the present subject the author accepts the data of the historian.

In Part I the author deals with seven pairs of divinities whose names are explicitly connected by Herodotus, *e.g.* Zeus-Amon, Bubastis (Bastet)-Artemis, Isis-Demeter, Osiris-Dionysus. Each section is followed by a summary in which the corresponding features of the pair are enumerated. An addendum is devoted to *Her.* II, 170,1, where Osiris may be meant.

Part II deals with twelve more divinities for which Herodotus mentions the Greek name only, though conclusions as to their Egyptian counterparts are possible; *e.g.* Aphrodite-Hathor, Athena-Neith, Hermes-Thoth. Again each section is followed by a summary containing the conclusions. The author had to be more careful than in part I, some identifications being rather uncertain.

In a short third part the author discusses the problem of the identification in general. For its main cause he points to the derivation of gods and cults by the Greeks from the Egyptians, the role of Herodotus in this respect being rather small (cfr our number 68313).

68349 KOROSTOVTSEV, M. A., Категория переходности и непереходности глаголов в египетском языке, *ВДИ* 4 (106), 1968, 109-118.

"The categories transitive and intransitive in Egyptian". To determine whether a verb in Egyptian is of transitive (with direct object) or intransitive (with prepositional object) meaning can as little be used as an absolute criterium as in other languages. Transformation into the passive voice yields no help, for it is clear enough that intransitives can also be used passively. The author thinks it possible to discern with much cautiousness (basing himself on verbs and uses thereof recorded in the *Wörterbuch*!): I. exclusively "direct" verbs (DV, *i.e.*, with only direct object), exclusively "indirect" verbs (IV, similarly with indirect object) and exclusively "absolute" verbs (AV, *i.e.*, unable to be constructed with any object at all). The latter two species are of intransitive order, the first of transitive. But next to these classes with their exclusive character, there are II. "diffuse" verbs, admitting several of the aforesaid constructions, of course with semantic shift. Thus out of the *Wörterbuch* entries 193 diffuse verbs are listed. Among these, there are threevalent verbs (DV/IV/AV) and bivalent verbs (DV/AV and DV/IV; no IV/AV examples were found). A lot of verbs of movement may *i.a.* function DV, their object being conceived "spatially". *J. F. Borghouts*

68350 KOROSTOVTSEV, M.A., Некоторые факты новоегипетского языка в освещении трансформационной грамматики, Вопросы Языкознания, Moscow 17, 2 (1968), 101-105.

"Some facts of Late Egyptian in the light of transformational grammar".
About the subordinate clauses introduced by the auxiliary verb *iw* as elementary nuclear clauses.

68351 KOROSTOVTSEV, M. A. "Поучения" древнеегипетские, Советская историческая энциклопедия, X1, Москва, 1968, 486.

"Ancient Egyptian Instructions".

68352 KOSACK, Wolfgang, Hieroglyphen — die Entzauberung ihres Geheimnisses, *Armant*, Köln 2, 1968, 69-100, with 1 ill. and 3 fig. (one in colour).

Présentation, pour le lecteur profane, du système hiéroglyphique égyptien. *Ph. Derchain*

68353 KOSACK, Wolfgang, Eine neue Droge in der altägyptischen Medizin, *Armant*, Köln 1, 1968, 2-10.

L'auteur examine quelques passages des papyrus médicaux où apparaît le mot *wꜥḥ*, et propose de le traduire par "pavot", car le remède semble employé essentiellement comme analgésique. Il ne fait pas état dans son article des autres identifications proposées autrefois par Loret (Caroube) et Dawson (Coloquinthe) et des discussions auxquelles elles ont donné lieu, alors que le problème a été réexaminé sans qu'une solution définitive soit posée du reste, par Grapow-von Deines, *Wörterbuch der ägyptischen Drogennamen*, 134, que l'auteur ne cite du reste pas. *Ph. Derchain*

68354 KOSACK, Wolfgang, Ein satirischer Briefwechsel zwischen Hori und Amenemope, *Armant*, Köln 2, 1968, 104-112.

Paraphrase et résumé du Pap. Anastasi I.

KREIßIG, Heinz, see our number 68096.

68355 KRIVCHENKO, V. I., Аменхотеп и Раннаи, Москва, Советский художник, 1968 (10 × 15 cm; 19 p. with ill.). Series: Щедевры Государственного музея изобразительных искусств имени А.С. Пушкина. Pr. 8 коп.

KROPP, Angelicus, see our number 68162.

68356 KRUPNOV, E. I., К 60-летию Бориса Борисовича Пиотровского, Советская Археология 1, 1968, 115-118, with portrait.

"In commemoration of the 60th anniversary of Boris Borisovich Piotrovski".
See also Anonymous, *ВДИ* 3 (105), 1968, 216.

KUENTZ, Charles, see our number 68169.

68357 LACARRIÈRE, J., Hérodote et la découverte de la terre, [Paris], Arthaud, [1968] (15.7 × 21.1 cm; 272 p., 20 pl., 4 maps [one folded]) = Collection signes des temps 20.

The author gives translations of several pages from Herodotus' *Historiae*, particularly those related to geography and ethnography, connecting them by his comments.
The chapter on. p. 85-151 is devoted to the Second Book dealing with Egypt.
See also the Indexes on p. 247-261, where more information is given about persons and geographical names.

LAFONTAINE-DOSOGNE, Jacqueline, see our numbers 68378 and 68621.

68358 LAMPL, Paul, Cities and Planning in the Ancient Near East, New York, George Braziller, [1968] (16.2 × 34.2 cm; 128 p., 165 ill. [including maps and plans], 3 maps). Series: Planning and Cities.

A particular chapter of this study is devoted to ancient Egypt (p. 23-32).
After a few remarks about the history and role of cities in the Egyptian civilisation the main cities are briefly described. In the section "Planning in Ancient Egypt" the author argues that funerary complexes, temples, palaces, fortresses and workmen's quarters bear the imprint of directed and controlled planning according to established rules, with predelection for axial balance and symmetry, whereas in other districts of the cities a "laisser faire" attitude prevailed. The author illustrates his argument with many examples from various buildings, while ill. 66-88 present their plans and some pictures.

68359 LANGE, Kurt and Max HIRMER, Egypt. Architecture. Sculpture. Painting in Three Thousand Years. With Contributions by Eberhard Otto and Christiane Desroches—Noblecourt, London. New York, Phaidon, [1968] (24 × 31.3 cm; VII + 219 p., 86 fig. [including many plans], 2 maps, 330 pl. [60 in colour]); rev. *Connaissance des Arts* N° 203 (Janvier 1969), 23 (anonymous); *Phoenix* 15 (1969), 239 (anonymous); *Times Literary Supplement* 67 (1968), 1356 (anonymous).

English edition of our number 67357.
We did not see the French edition, Paris, Flammarion, 1968.

68360 LAUER, J.-Ph., L'harmonie dans l'architecture égyptienne, *CdE* XLIII, N° 85 (1968), 94-103.

Article de critique des théories numériques appliquées à l'architecture égyptienne par Alexander Badawy dans divers livres et articles parus depuis 1961 (nos 61038, 62039, 62041 et 65040).
Là où ce dernier découvre l'application rigoureuse de proportions régies par le nombre d'or et la série de Fibonacci, Lauer montre qu'il faut aussi faire une place très importante aux séries décimales et aux fractions simples. Contrairement à Badawy, il pense que ce dernier système est le seul en usage sous l'Ancien Empire, à l'exception peut-être du règne de Mykérinos, qui choisit le triangle 8:5 pour la section méridienne de sa pyramide. Ce triangle donne en effet à peu de chose près le rapport Φ mais rien ne prouve qu'il ait été choisi en fonction de ce dernier. A partir de l'époque amarnienne, en revanche, Lauer admet que certaines séries de Fibonacci aient été tentées. Pour en obtenir la certitude, toutefois, de nouvelles mesures précises des monuments s'imposeraient souvent.
En revanche, les tracés modulaires pour Lauer auraient pu être utilisés dès la XIe dynastie, mais non plus tôt (contra Badawy), tandis que les tracés harmoniques ne deviennent plausibles que dans les grandes constructions du Nouvel Empire après Amarna. *Ph. Derchain*

68361 LAUER, Jean-Philippe, Recherche et découverte du tombeau sud de l'Horus Sekhem-khet dans son complexe funéraire à Saqqara, *RdE* 20 (1968), 97-107, with 1 plan, 1 fig., 2 ill. and 2 pl.

Texte d'une communication présentée au 27e congrès des Orientalistes à Ann Arbor, 1967.
La fouille systématique du complexe funéraire de l'Horus Sekhemkhet à l'ouest de celui de Djeser à Saqqarah a révélé l'existence d'un souterrain inachevé surmonté de superstructures très ruinées dans la cour située au sud de la pyramide, dans lequel l'auteur reconnaît un tombeau analogue par sa disposition au "tombeau sud" de Djeser. On y a retrouvé les restes d'une caisse à canopes. Il paraît donc vraisemblable de considérer cet édifice comme le second tombeau du roi, substitut de celui que les pharaons

des deux premières dynasties se faisaient ériger à Abydos et ramené à Memphis en signe de la centralisation poussée du royaume sous la 3e dynastie. On y verra l'origine de la petite pyramide, qui, dès la fin de la troisième dynastie à Meidoum, puis sous la 4e dynastie, accompagne au sud le monument funéraire principal des rois. *Ph. Derchain*

68362 LAUER, J.-Ph., Travaux et recherches à Saqqara. Campagnes 1966-67 et 1967-68, *BSFE* N° 52 (Juillet 1968), 15-26, with 2 pl., 2 fig. and 1 ill.

Suite de notre n° 66380. Ces deux campagnes ont porté sur trois chantiers: les complexes funéraires de Zoser et de Sekhemkhet, la pyramide de Pépi Ier.

I. *Zoser*. Dans la cour du Heb Sed, le pavillon à toiture plate a pu être restauré jusqu'à la corniche. A l'arc de cercle de la terrasse, les blocs malades ont été remplacés; l'angle N.-O. de la cour est également protégé.

II. *Sekhemkhet*. Le mastaba du "tombeau sud" a été mis au jour, avec puits et descenderie. L'appartement funéraire, à l'état d'ébauche, contenait les ossements d'un jeune enfant. Le mobilier est typique de la IIIe dynastie. Il y aurait alors inhumation et remploi, pour un jeune prince, du tombeau abandonné.

III. *Pépi Ier*. On a pu dégager l'entrée par le bas, enlever les éboulis contenant des fragments inscrits, déblayer et consolider l'antichambre. Le nombre total des fragments inscrits dépasse 500. Les pavages de la cour et de la salle des offrandes ont été retrouvés, ainsi que des fragments de bas-reliefs. *J. Custers*

68363 LAUFFRAY, Jean, Nouvelles découvertes par le centre franco-égyptien d'étude des temples de Karnak, *Comptes rendus de l'Académie des Inscriptions et Belles-Lettres*. 1968, Paris, 337-351, with 3 ill. and 2 plans.

Report on the activities of the recently created Franco-Egyptian centre for the study of the temples of Karnak by its director.

The following subjects are mentioned: investigation of the sub-soil; preparations for a definite plan; discovery of a monumental gate near the temple of Opet; excavations in the passage of the 3rd pylon; works at the 9th pylon, and in the Festival Temple of Tuthmosis III.

For more detailed studies of these subjects cfr the following numbers and *Kêmi* 19 (1969).

68364 LAUFFRAY, Jean et Serge SAUNERON, La création d'un centre franco-égyptien pour l'étude des temples de Karnak, *Kêmi* 18 (1968), 103-104.

La montée des eaux souterraines, conséquence du nouveau barrage d'Assouan, posait pour Karnak des problèmes nouveaux de sauvegarde. Le centre, créé en juillet 1967, poursuivra l'étude archéologique, étudiera les travaux de consolidation et de restauration nécessaires, et en dirigera l'exécution.
Voir notre n° suivant. *J. Custers*

68365 LAUFFRAY, Jean et Serge SAUNERON, Mission à Karnak (mars-juillet 1967), *Kêmi* 18 (1968), 93-97.

Les travaux préparatoires, pour l'étude et la conservation des temples, par le nouveau centre franco-égyptien, ont porté sur trois points.
I. Deux techniciens ont établi les bases du quadrillage métrique et de la photogrammétrie.
II. On a fixé un programme de recherches au sujet des matériaux.
III. Des sondages et relevés ont eu lieu sur une section effondrée de l'enceinte, au sud du premier pylône, et à l'extérieur du mur, où une maison copte ou islamique a été dégagée. On a étudié les stades de construction du troisième pylône et entrepris l'étude de la grande enceinte. *J. Custers*

LAUR-BELART, Rudolf, see our number 68597.

68366 LECLANT, Jean, Du Nil au Rhin. De l'antique Égypte au cœur de l'Europe, *in*: *Mélanges offerts à Polys Modinos*. Problèmes des droits de l'homme et de l'unification européenne, Paris, Éditions A. Pedone, 1968, 71-84.

In this article the author attempts to demonstrate that the Egyptian influence reached the Rhine. Leclant refers to a study called *Alsatia Illustrata*, by J. D. Schoepflin, which appeared in 1751 and in which Egyptian and Egyptianized objects are depicted, though most of them incorrectly ascribed to ancient Egypt. He further mentions several objects found along the Rhine, from Swiss to the Netherlands, which allow the conclusion that the spread of the Isis cult followed the river.

68367 LECLANT, Jean, Éléments pour une étude de la divination dans l'Égypte pharaonique, *in*: *La Divination*. Études recueillis par André Caquot et Marcel Leibovici. Tome Premier, Paris, Presses Universitaires de France, 1968 (series "Rites et pratiques religieuses"), 1-23.

The first part of the study (p. 1-10) mainly consists of an annotated bibliography of books and articles concerning oracles. There follows a description of the various methods: movements of the sacred bark, oracles given by the god in the form of a decree, the conduct of animals, *etc.* The author also discusses the subjects on which oracles are given: political questions (particularly during the Late Period), questions about a theft, *etc.* At the end there are short sections about oniromancy, incubation, prophecy, astrology, *etc.*, each with references to the pertinent literature.

68368 LECLANT, Jean, Fouilles et travaux en Égypte et au Soudan, 1966-1967, *Orientalia* 37 (1968), 94-140, with 27 pl.; rev. *ВДИ* 1 (111), 1970, 177-180 (N. E. Semper); *Comptes rendus de l'Académie des Inscriptions et Belles-Lettres*. 1968, 334-335 (Jacques Vandier).

Pour cette année, les notices sur l'Égypte sont au nombre de 36, les plus étendues portant sur Mendès, Tell el-Dab'a (avec 8 ill.), Abydos, la rive gauche de Thèbes et principalement sur Saqqarah (plus de 5 pages, 14 ill.). Au Soudan, des travaux ont eu lieu sur 18 sites. On signalera en particulier Mirgissa, Semna sud, Soleb et Musawwarat es-Sufra. Hors de la vallée du Nil, parmi 15 rubriques, les plus développées se réfèrent à Chypre, à la Grèce, à la France et à l'Algérie. Le triple index habituel couronne cette précieuse chronique. *J. Custers*

68369 LECLANT, Jean, Histoire de la diffusion des cultes égyptiens, *École Pratique des Hautes Études*. V^e *section—Sciences religieuses. Annuaire*, Paris 76 (1968-1969), 1968, 122-131.

Suite de notre n° 67364.

68370 LECLANT, Jean, Histoire de la diffusion des cultes égyptiens, *in*: *Problèmes et méthodes d'histoire des religions*. Mélanges publiés par la Section des Sciences religieuses à l'occasion du centenaire de l'École Pratique des Hautes Études, Paris, Presses Universitaires de France, 1968, 87-96.

The department of the É.P.H.É. concerned with the diffusion of the Egyptian cults embraces the southern spread (Meroe) as well as the northern (the Roman Empire). The author presents a survey of the present state of the Meroitic studies and those of the Egyptian cults in the Roman Empire, stressing the activities of his department in these matters.

68371 LECLANT, Jean, Les relations entre l'Égypte et la Phénicie du voyage d'Ounamon à l'expédition d'Alexandre, *The Role of the Phoenicians* 9-31, with 5 pl.

The author stresses the provisional character of his study owing to the lack of monographs concerning the subject.
Proceeding from a discussion of the *Story of Wenamon* and its implications for the relations between Egypt and

Phoenicia Leclant first deals with the Third Intermediate Period (fragments of royal statues from Byblos, alabaster vases found in Spain and Assur). Whether Egypt dominated the Phoenician cities is still uncertain. In two more sections the author summarizes the history of the Near East during the Assyrian Empire, the Saite Dynasty and the Persian domination of Egypt, with particular attention to the scanty data for the relations between Phoenicia and Egypt.
Notes with bibliographical references on p. 22-31. Cfr also for the preceding period our number 68121.

68372 LECLANT, Jean, Les rites de purification dans le cérémonial pharaonique du couronnement, in: *Proceedings of the XIth International Congress of the International Association for the History of Religions*. Volume II. Guilt or Pollution and Rites of Purification, Leiden, E. J. Brill, 1968, 48-51.

Summary of a lecture.
The author deals with resemblance and difference between purification in the ritual of the coronation and baptism.

68373 LECLANT, Jean et André HEYLER, Préliminaires à un Répertoire d'Épigraphie Méroitique (REM), *Meroitic Newsletter. Bulletin d'Informations Méroitiques*, Paris 1 (Oct. 1968), 9-18.

REM gibt ein systematisches Inventar aller bis 1966 publizierten meroitischen Inschriften. Auf eine chronologische Abfolge wird jedoch manchmal verzichtet, da in einigen Werken bereits große Gruppen meroitischer Texte zusammengestellt sind. REM 0001 *sq.* bis REM 0551 *sq.* umfassen die von Griffith publizierten Inschriften (1911-1925); REM 0601 *sq.* = Macadam, *Kawa* I, 1949; REM 0801 *sq.* = Dunham, *The Royal Cemeteries of Kush*, 1950 *sq.* Einige problematische Stücke werden jedoch noch in den nachfolgenden Listen wieder aufgenommen. REM 1001 bis REM 1015 umfaßt die zwischen 1912 und 1922 veröffentlichten Inschriften, u.a. aus Faras und Gemai, sowie ihre Beschreibung und eine kurze Bibliographie. *Inge Hofmann*

LECLANT, Jean, see also our numbers 68378 and 68595.

68374 LEE, G. M., Demotica et Coptica, *Aegyptus* 48 (1968). 139-140.

I. Le mot *ꜣntwge* pourrait ne pas désigner une taxe spécifique mais refléter *endikè*, "taxe légale". Pour la syllabe inexpliquée *sal-* de *salbanaka*, l'auteur propose la valeur *snb*: le *salus* des monnaies romaines. Il étudie le passage sémantique

de l'expression *e.mn hypś* du sens premier "sans épaule" au sens dérivé "sans détour".
II. Dans un papyrus magique copte d'Aberdeen, les noms Marie et Marthe représenteraient les auteurs de la *defixio*. Un long mot mystérieux pourrait y signifier "Donne-moi la bonne Fortune", le š notant l'aspiration du grec.

J. Custers

68375 LEIBOVITCH, Joseph, Modèles de barques funéraires au Musée Maritime de Haifa, *Sefunim*. Bulletin (of) the Maritime Museum Haifa 2 (1967-8), 9-16, with 5 fig. and 3 pl.

Description of three recently acquired model boats in the Maritime Museum in Haifa.
1. A boat with a double mast and a very long prow, 6 men aboard, and a canopy with a chair. The author quotes some parallels, *e.g.* Copenhague, National Museum N° 5488 (= pl. Ib).
2. A similar boat without mast and with 8 sailors.
3. A very simple model, with 20 sailors listening to a speech of the captain.
On p. 16 a short biography (by R. Giveon) of the author, who died on the 3rd of April, 1968. See our number 68662.
A Hebrew version of this article entitled חצריות סירות־קבורה is to be found on p. 9-15 of the Hebrew section of the same volume.

LEIBOVICI, Marcel, see our number 68367.

68376 LEIBOWITCH, J., Quelques griffons demeurés inédits, *Israel Exploration Journal*, Jerusalem 18 (1968), 126-129, with 3 fig. and 3 pl.

Publication of some more representations of the griffin (cfr our numbers 58405 and 65063). One of them is called *srṭ* (Newberry and Griffith, *El Bersheh* II, pl. XVI). An example in the Brooklyn Museum (cfr our number 4816) appears to differ from the usual type in having human breasts instead of animal teats on the belly.

LEIGH, Egbert G., see our number 68109.

68377 LENGER, Marie-Thérèse, La XXIIe Session de la Société internationale Fernand de Visscher pour l'histoire des droits de l'Antiquité. Pérouse, 11-14 septembre 1967, *Revue Internationale des Droits de l'Antiquité*, Bruxelles serie 3, tome 15 (1968), 505-522.

Voir la communication de M. Aristide Théodoridès, *La magistrature ouvrière en Égypte au Nouvel Empire*, p. 508-509.

68378 LEROY, Jules und Jean LECLANT, Nubien, *in*: Wolfgang Fritz Volbach und Jacqueline Lafontaine-Dosogne, *Byzanz und der christliche Osten* (= Propyläen Kunstgeschichte, Band 3), Berlin, Propyläen Verlag, 1968, 361-366, with 2 plans, 14 ill. (= nos 408-417) and 1 colour pl.(= no. LI).

After a short note about the Christian art in Nubia, architecture and wall paintings, the second author describes several examples of both which are represented by photographs.

68379 LINDSAY, Jack, Men and Gods on the Roman Nile, [London], Frederick Muller, [1968] (14.2 × 21 cm; X + 458 p., 100 fig., including a map); rev. *American Historical Review* 74 (1968-1969), 1256-1257 (Alan R. Schulman); *BiOr* 28 (1971), 200 (H. Leclercq); *Latomus* 28 (1969), 797-798 (Michel Malaise).   Pr. 65 s.

The theme of this book is the Nile, the activities on its waters and banks, and the ideas and emotions it aroused. Though the main point of focus is the world of Roman Egypt, and thus the book would be outside the scope of the present bibliography, the author is convinced that "there was a development of continuity of Egyptian life and thought", and therefore quotes throughout pharaonic sources of various nature.

In chapter 11, for instance, called "The Insatiable Sea", the author translates and discusses the *Story of Astarte*, illustrating his argument with quotations from the *Tale of the Two Brothers*, the *Medical Papyrus Hearst*, various religious papyri, *etc.* He deals with subjects such as the introduction of foreign gods (Astarte) and words (*ym*), the character of the god Seth (quoting *i.a.* te Velde, *Seth, God of Confusion*, our number 67575), so that in fact it is more a popular, though extremely well founded description of pharaonic life and thought than a study of Roman Egypt. The same holds true for other chapters, though not for all of them.

References to the sources in the notes (p. 377-438). Bibliography on p. 439-448, indexes p. 449-457.

68380 LING, Trevor, A History of Religion East and West. An Introduction and Interpretation, London-Melbourne-Toronto, Macmillan [and] New York, St Martin's Press, 1968 (14.4 × 22.4 cm; XXX + 464 p., 4 maps); rev. *Booklist* 1969, 55-56 (J. B[lythin]).   Pr. cloth 80 s.

Ancient Egypt and its religion are very briefly dealt with on p. 4-6, while some remarks to it are made in the subsequent sections.

68381 LIPIŃSKA, Jadwiga, The Granite Doorway in the Temple of Tuthmosis III at Deir el-Bahari. Studies on reconstruction, *Études et Travaux* II 79-97, with 13 ill., 1 fig. and 2 plans.

During the excavation season of 1964-1965 the lower part of a huge doorway which led from the great colonnade hall to the antechamber of the main sanctuary of the temple of Tuthmosis III was discovered. The preserved part of the doorway consists of a threshold and two partly preserved jambs (about 2.11 m high), mounted directly upon it.
Basing on the preserved fragments of the doorway the author reconstructs the inscriptions that had been cut on the jambs of the doorway. *A. Szczudłowska*

68382 LIPINSKA, Jadwiga, A List of Objects Found at Deir el-Bahari in the Area of the Temple of Tuthmosis III. IVth Season of Excavations 1964/65, *ASAE* 60 (1968), 153-204, with 69 pl.

A brief description of 129 from the 2500 objects discovered in 1964/65. *Dieter Mueller*

68383 LIPINSKA, Jadwiga, List of Objects Found at Deir el-Bahari in the Temple of Tuthmosis III. Vth Season of Excavations 1966, *ASAE* 60 (1968), 205-212, with 19 pl.

A brief description of 31 from the 372 objects discovered in 1966. *Dieter Mueller*

68384 LIPINSKA, Jadwiga, Preliminary Report on the Reconstruction Works of the Temple of Hatshepsut at Deir el Bahari During the Season 1964-1965, *ASAE* 60 (1968), 139-152, with 11 pl.

Besides restoring the Osiride pillars of the upper terrace, further excavations were carried out at the temple of Thutmosis III which had been destroyed by a rockslide at the end of the XXth Dynasty, and was subsequently used as a quarry. By now, the whole preserved *in-situ* part of the temple has been cleared. During these excavations, innumerable fragments of inscribed and decorated blocks and about 2000 other larger objects including several statues came to light. Among the more important discoveries are hundreds of hieratic graffiti from the XIXth and XXth Dynasty. *Dieter Mueller*

68385 LITTAUER, Mary Aiken, A 19th and 20th Dynasty Heroic Motif on Attic Black-figured Vases?, *AJA* 72 (1968), 150-152, with 1 pl.

The author studies a peculiar pose of the chariot warrior,

called "the-foot-on-the-chariot-pole", which occurs on XIXth and XXth Dynasty reliefs and on Attic black-figured ware. Since it seems unlikely that a chariot warrior was ever standing in this way the motif may have been borrowed from the Egyptians by Greek artists.

68386 LORTON, David, The Expression Šms-ib, JARCE 7 (1968), 41-54.

There is no sceptical and hedonistic attitude in the passages where the present compound occurs. The author surveys them, and concludes that šms ib has more than one application. He distinguishes: "follow the conscience", "serve (someone else's) will (or: desires)", "exercise (one's own) will", and undecided meaning(s). Compare now the Velde, De Goede Dag der Oude Egyptenaren, Leiden, E. J. Brill, 1971.
M. Heerma van Voss

68387 LÜDDECKENS, Erich, Wolja Erichsen. 21. November 1890-25. April 1966, ZÄS 95, 1 (1968), I-V.
Obituary notice. Compare our number 66648.

68388 LÜDDECKENS, Erich, Gottesdienstliche Gemeinschaften im pharaonischen, hellenistischen und christlichen Ägypten, Zeitschrift für Religion und Geistesgeschichte, Köln 20 (1968), 193-211; rev. ZAW 81 (1969), 122-123 (G. Wanke).

Inaugural lecture (with notes) delivered at the University of Würzburg in December 1965.
The author deals with the religious community in different periods of the Egyptian history: from the national community building the pyramid of Cheops and the community of necropolis workmen in the New Kingdom to the cult society in Tebtynis dedicated to the service of Suchos, which is discussed in detail and compared with the Christian monasteries of Pakhom and Shenute. The author stresses the traditional Egyptian character of the latter.

68389 LÜDDEKENS (sic), Erich, Urkunde eines Soldaten über den Verkauf seines Ernteertrages, Festschrift Schott 80-86, with 1 fig. and 1 ill. (on pl. IV); rev. Enchoria 1 (1971), 61 (Heinz-Josef Thissen).

Publication of a Demotic text (Pap. dem. Lüddeckens 1), with transcription, translation and commentary. The text is from 246 B.C. and contains the receipt for the sale of a field.

LÜDDECKENS, Erich, see also our number 68162.

MAASS, Fritz, see our number 68198.

68390 McGREADY, A. G., Egyptian Words in the Greek Vocabulary, *Glotta*, Göttingen 46 (1968), 247-254.

After pointing out the difficulties for the Greek in translitterating Egyptian words the author draws up a list of more or less certain loan-words. They are given in three groups: those used by Herodotus and his contemporaries, those used by later writers, and those occurring in papyri. The majority appears to belong to the following categories: fauna and flora peculiar to Egypt; Egyptian products; weights and measures; terms relating to Egyptian culture and religion.
The author stresses the Greek preference for translating if possible, pointing at words such as ὀβελίσκος (= *thn*) and νομός (= *spt*). Even Egyptian terms for digging and irrigation works have been translated by the Ptolemaic administration. McGready also stresses the uncertainty of the derivations.
Cfr our number 68276.

68391 MACLAURIN, E. C. B., Date of the Foundation of the Jewish Colony at Elephantine, *JNES* 27 (1968), 89-96.

In *JNES* 14 Cyrus Gordon rejected the general view that the Jewish colony at Yeb was a military garrison established by Cambyses on the grounds that documents from the site appear to date only from this period or slightly later. There is, however, clear evidence from the O.T. that there were Hebrews living in Egypt at an earlier date, *i.e.* before the fall of Jerusalem in 581 B.C. Deities worshipped by the Hebrews at Yeb belong to an ancient group and exclude Baal and other gods known in Egypt in the 12th century B.C. Yahu, Bethel and Anath were worshipped at Yeb suggesting its early separation from the rest of the Hebrews and Canaan. Yahu represents an earlier form of YHWH and the general picture thus seems to indicate a date of before 1500 B.C. for their entry into Egypt and a pantheon belonging to the Patriarchal Age. By analogy the language spoken at Yeb was the vernacular Aramaic and that was used to correspond with the priests at Jerusalem Aramaic, as they knew little Hebrew. This colony may therefore have been composed of the descendants of a body of Hebrews left behind at the time of the Exodus. *E. Uphill*

68392 MALAISE, Michel, Pline l'Ancien a-t-il séjourné en Égypte?, *Latomus*, Bruxelles 27 (1968), 852-863.

As the evidence afforded by the inscription from Arados is contradictory, only the work of Pliny can show whether he ever actually visited Egypt. The numerous errors in his *Historia Naturalis* concerning the geography and archaeology of Egypt indicate that he has never seen this country with his own eyes, and his use of *videmus* elsewhere shows that the verb "to see" does not necessarily introduce an eye-witness account. *Dieter Mueller*

68393 MALAMAT, A., The Last Kings of Judah and the Fall of Jerusalem. An Historical-Chronological Study, *Israel Exploration Journal*, Jerusalem 18 (1968), 137-156, with a table (= p. 156).

The reconstruction of the chronological sequence of events that led to the fall of Jerusalem involves a discussion of the role played by Egypt in this historical drama. When Josiah had died after the battle against Necho II at Megiddo, Jehoahaz was appointed King of Judah in 609 B.C., to be replaced by his pro-Egyptian brother Jehoiakim only three months later. The Egyptian defeat at Carchemish in 605 B.C. opened Judah to the Babylonian forces which captured Jerusalem in 603 B.C. Presumably prompted by Hophra, who had succeeded to the Egyptian throne in Febr. 589, Jehoiakim's successor Zedekiah rebelled against Nebuchadnezzar and brought about the siege of Jerusalem that was only temporarily relieved by Egyptian intervention in the spring of 587 B.C., and ended with the destruction of the temple in Aug. 586 B.C. *Dieter Mueller*

68394 MALININE, Michel, Un contrat démotique de société (Pap. Loeb n° n° 47 et 46), *Festschrift Schott* 87-93; rev. *Enchoria* 1 (1971), 62-63 (Heinz-Josef Thissen).

Publication with transcription, translation and comments of Pap. dem. Loeb 47 (488 B.C.) and Pap. dem. Loeb 46 (487 B.C.). The former contains a contract by which two goose herds constitute a partnership for the usufruct of a property consisting of ten geese of the Divine Offering of Amon. The other is a receipt for the sale of these geese by a son of one of the partners.

The author adds some remarks concerning the rights of property in Egypt.

68395 MALININE, Michel, Une livraison d'oies au domaine d'Amon (Pap. dém. Strasbourg N° 2), *JEA* 54 (1968), 188-192, with 1 pl.; rev. *Enchoria* 1 (1971), 62 (Heinz-Josef Thissen).

This document is a contract in which the goose keeper Petemestur of the Domain of Amon at Gebelên associated with his colleagues in exploiting twenty-one geese in his possession. It is dated to year 2 of Psammetichus III. A commentary is appended. *E. Uphill*

68396 MALININE, M. - G. POSENER - J. VERCOUTTER, Catalogue des stèles du Sérapéum de Memphis. Tome Premier (Texte) [and] (Planches), Paris, Imprimerie Nationale, 1968 (24.8 × 31.9 cm; Texte: XVI + 192 p., 2 pl. [one folding] containing plans; Planches: [IV p.], 67 pl. containing 252 + 5 ill.); at head of title: Ministère d'État. Affaires culturelles. Musées Nationaux. Département des Antiquités Égyptiennes du Musée du Louvre; rev. *Comptes rendus de l'Académie des Inscriptions et Belles-Lettres.* 1969, 76-78 (Jacques Vandier).

The preface deals with the history of the Serapeum stelae since they have been found by Mariette between 1851 and 1853. It also discusses the attempt to arrange them in a chronological order, complicated by the loss of Mariette's diary so that their exact provenance is uncertain.

The authors have arranged them into groups, either based on similarities in the style of the representations or on the pertinence of the owners to one family. A particular section deals with the different systems of numbering the stelae. The authors have given them entirely new numbers.

The present volume contains 252 stelae, found in the isolated tombs and in the Lesser Vaults, with exclusion of a few posterior to year 21 of Psammetichus I which in fact will not have belonged here. For each stela the following data are given; material and measurements, provenance according to Mariette, date, technique and colour, present state, description with a line drawing indicating the place of representations and texts and the texts themselves in printed hieroglyphs; at the end of each entry the bibliography and the old numbers, if any.

Each of the stelae is reproduced in photograph in the plate volume, unless nothing anymore is discernable.

68397 MALININE, Michel, Henri-Charles PUECH, Gilles QUISPEL, Walter TILL †, Rodolphe KASSER, adiuuantibus R. McL. WILSON [et] Jan ZANDEE, Epistula Iacobi Apocrypha. Codex Jung F. Ir- F. VIIIv (p. 1-16). Ediderunt, Zürich und Stuttgart, Rascher Verlag, 1968 (21.8 × 32.7 cm; XXXI + 139 p., 16 pl.); rev. *Revue Biblique* 77 (1970), 304-306 (B. C[ouroyer]).

Publication of the Epistula Jacobi Apocrypha from the Codex Jung, in 16 full-sized photographic plates, followed by the printed (Subakhmimic) text and a French translation

(p. 2-33). Critical notes on p. 35-94, a German and an English translation on p. 97-112 and 115-130.
The introduction is given on p. VII-XXXI, indices of Greek words, proper names and Coptic words on p. 131-139.
Compare our numbers 3499, 4524 and 63341.
L. F. Kleiterp

MANCINI, M., see our number 68142.

68398 MARAGIOGLIO, Vito [and] Celeste RINALDI, Note sulla piramide di Ameny 'Aamu, *Orientalia* 37 (1968), 325-338, with 10 pl.

Le nom du roi, '*3mw*, le désigne comme Asiatique, et la disposition de sa tombe le situe sûrement à la IIe Période Intermédiaire. L'état incomplet de la pyramide à Dahchour indiquerait un règne assez bref. Fouillé en 1957, le monument n'avait pas été édité.
Les deux premières planches montrent le plan, dans l'état actuel puis reconstitué. Les blocs ne sont pas restés à leur place. Il semble qu'à la mort du roi la pyramide commencée reçut en hâte l'aspect d'un mastaba. Les appartements funéraires, de dimensions réduites, étaient terminés sauf à l'entrée, où l'on procéda à des modifications hâtives et au comblement du puits. La description des auteurs prend la crypte comme point de départ. On trouve employés du calcaire, des briques, du quartzite. Une herse fut brisée au sommet, une autre semble n'avoir jamais été fermée, un éventuel projet de troisième n'a pas été réalisé. La couleur rouge d'un mortier serait due à l'altération chimique.
L'existence d'un temple haut est quasi certaine, mais apparemment aucune rampe n'a été commencée. Les voleurs ont pénétré par le haut, dès l'antiquité. La démolition des appartements funéraires pour réutiliser les matériaux pourrait remonter au Nouvel Empire. *J. Custers*

68399 MARCINIAK, Marek, Quelques remarques sur la formule *IR NFR, IR NFR, Études et Travaux* II 25-31.

During the Polish excavations at Deir el-Bahri the mortuary temple of Tuthmosis III was discovered, the columns of which were covered with hieratic graffiti left by visitors from the Ramesside Period.
The author studies the formula *ir nfr, ir nfr* occurring in the graffiti. He traces back its origin, defines its function as an acclamation and gives a translation. *L. M. J. Zonhoven*

MARKS, Anthony E., see our number 68630.

MARTIN, Francine, see our number 68630.

68400 MARTIN, Geoffrey T., A New Prince of Byblos, *JNES* 27 (1968), 141-142, with 1 pl.

The author publishes a scarab-seal of unknown provenance bearing the number 5945 in the Egyptian collection of the State Hermitage Museum, Leningrad. It has the name of a prince of Byblos Ka-in of the second millenium B.C., and has parallels in Hall's types A 1 and C2-C3, *E. Uphill*

68401 MAUNY, R., Le Périple de la Mer Érythrée et le problème du commerce romain en Afrique au sud du limes, *Journal de la Société des Africanistes*, Paris 38,1 (1968), 19-34, with 2 maps.

Der berühmte "Periplus des Erythräischen Meeres", der in zwei Handschriften vorliegt und ein Handbuch für Handelsschiffahrten auf dem Roten Meer und dem Indischen Ozean ist, wirft auch ein Licht auf das meroitische Reich. Zumindest die Stadt Meroe war zur Zeit des "Periplus", dessen Datierung immer noch umstritten ist, bekannt und berühmt. Nach einer zusammenfassenden Darstellung der Küstenbeschreibung bis Azania werden die Handelsgüter untersucht, die auf die afrikanischen Märkte kamen. Demgegenüber ist wenig bekannt über die römisch-westafrikanischen Handelsbeziehungen. Es ist aber wahrscheinlich, daß der transsaharanische Handel, der von den Garamanten getragen wurde, beträchtlich war. *Inge Hofmann*

68402 MAZAR, B., The Middle Bronze Age in Palestine, *Israel Exploration Journal*, Jerusalem 18 (1968), 65-97.

Study of some problems connected with the history and culture of Palestine in the Middle Bronze Age, in which evidence from Egypt is quoted.

68403 MEEUSSEN, A. E. – J. VOORHOEVE, Im memoriam H. P. Blok (28 maart 1894-25 augustus 1968), *Jaarboek der Leidse Universiteit 1968/1969*, [Leiden, 1968], 268-269, with portrait.

Obituary notice. Cfr our number 68660.

68404 MERKELBACH, R., Ein ägyptischer Priestereid, *Zeitschrift für Papyrologie und Epigraphik*, Bonn 2 (1968), 7-30.

Study of a Greek papyrus from Oxyrhynchos (2nd century A.D.), the recto of which contains the oath which priests had to swear at their entrance into the office. The oath shows resemblances to some passages of chapter 125 of the *Book of the Dead*. In a separate section the author discusses the ethical value of the judgment of the dead.
See also the additions in *Zeitschrift für Papyrologie und Epigraphik*, Bonn 3 (1968), 136.

Cfr also L. Koenen, Die Unschuldbeteuerungen des Priestereides und die Römische Elegie, *Zeitschrift für Papyrologie und Epigraphik*, Bonn 2 (1968), 31-38, which discusses three passages of Lydamus (Tibullus III, 5; I, 3; III, 2) with similar meaning.

68405 MERRILLEES, R. S., The Cypriote Bronze Age Pottery Found in Egypt, Lund, Studies in Mediterranean Archaeology, 1968 (23 × 31.5 cm; XVIII + 217 p., 37 pl., 4 maps) = Studies in Mediterranean Archaeology, vol. 18; rev. *CdE* XLV, N° 90 (1970), 315-317 (Claude Vandersleyen); *Orientalia* 38 (1969), 592-593 (R. North); *Revue Biblique* 77 (1970), 150-151 (R. de Vaux); *Syria* 46 (1969), 153-156 (Liliane Courtois et Jacques Lagarce). Pr. sw. kr. 150

Thesis for the degree of Doctor of Philosophy at the London University (April, 1965).

The book contains a purely archaeological study of Cypriote hand- and wheel-made pottery found in Egypt without any reference to Alasia and the problem whether this is Cyprus or not.

Chapter I (p. 1-144) contains a description catalogue of the pottery arranged according to its finding places in Egypt, from the North to Buhen, with descriptions of the relevant evidence concerning its provenance.

In chapter II (145-190) an analysis is given of the pottery types, their shapes, decoration and sizes, including the Egyptian copies, whether in metal, stone, pottery or any other material. There is also reference to the representations of Cypriote pottery in Egyptian tombs. The chapter concludes with a section on ships and navigation, the pottery being witness to a specialized trade conducted by foreign merchants, either Syrians or Cypriotes.

Chapter III (190-202) discusses the historical background of Cypriote and Syrian trade to Egypt, constituting an important study of the history of the Egyptian Empire in Asia. The first Cypriote pottery appears on the Egyptian scene in the second half of the Second Intermediate Period, demonstrating that there were peaceful relations between the North and Southern Egypt, in spite of the Hyksos rule. The author then describes the vicissitudes of the trade during the XVIIIth Dynasty, arguing that its decline under Tuthmosis III and his successor was due to the domination of Ras Shamra by the Mitanni, and its recovery under Tuthmosis IV by the improvement of relationships between Egypt and this country. The import of Cypriote ware appears to have abruptly ceased by the conquest of Ras Shamra by the Hittites under Suppiluliuma.

Bibliography on p. 204-209, indexes p. 210-217.

68406 de MEULENAERE, H., La famille du roi Amasis, *JEA* 54 (1968), 183-187, with 1 pl.

Al the standard historical documents available suggest that the Saite king Amasis was a usurper. Herodotus only tells us that he originated from Siuph in the Saite nome. Egyptian documents now allow a dossier to be made on his family. The British Museum statue no. 775 gives the king's mother as Tacherenêse. Amasis had several wives in addition to Ladike princess of Cyrene. Tentkheta was the mother of Psammetichus III, another was called Nekht-bastet-eru, another, Tadiuser, became the mother of a daughter Tacherenêse. A famous daughter was the last Divine Adoratrix at Thebes, Ankhnesneferibrēʿ. *E. Uphill*

68407 de MEULENAERE, H., Pyramidions d'Abydos, *JEOL* VII, 20 (1967-1968), 1968, 1-20, with 25 ill. on 7 pl.

Les pyramidions de Basse Epoque, beaucoup moins nombreux que ceux du Nouvel Empire, paraissent tous être d'origine abydénienne. L'auteur en décrit 14, dont plusieurs restaient inédits, et dégage l'essentiel de leur décoration. Celle-ci demeure semblable, dans le choix des thèmes, à celle du Nouvel Empire. Le dédicant, qui à Thèbes était représenté en ronde bosse, est à la Basse Epoque gravé généralement en bas-relief. La face Est, la principale, continue à être consacrée à Rê-Horakhti; les autres témoignent d'une variété plus grande. a) Des motifs du culte solaire peuvent accompagner les trois formes du soleil. b) Tout un groupe est décoré "symétriquement", c'est-à-dire de manière analogue sur les faces opposées. c) Les documents 4 et 9 semblent avoir eu un caractère exclusivement funéraire. Mais l'un d'eux n'est plus connu que par une description incomplète, l'autre pourrait être resté inachevé. Le classement qui précède n'a aucune prétention de chronologie. *J. Custers*

68408 MEYER, Ernst, Einführung in die antike Staatskunde, Darmstadt, Wissenschaftliche Buchgesellschaft, 1968 (13.5 × 21.5 cm; 313 p.); series: Die Altertumswissenschaft. Einführungen in Gegenstand, Methoden und Ergebnisse ihres Teildisziplinen und Hilfswissenschaften; rev. *Deutsche Literaturzeitung* 91 (1970), 47-48 (Victor Ehrenberg); *Latomus* 28 (1969), 747-748 (Paul Petit).

In the first chapter of the Introduction (p. 9-22) the author deals with ancient Egypt. He discusses the divine kingship as an institution, to be distinguished from the royal person; the state officials, the vizier, the court, the administration, *etc.* He also pays attention to the historical developments.

68409 MICHAÏLIDIS, G., Bès aux divers aspects, *BIE* 45 (session 1963-1964), 1968, 53-93, with 32 fig. and 20 pl.

Les documents sur Bès n'apportent plus guère de traits nouveaux. Le nain au visage bestial peut répondre aussi aux noms de *H3ty*, *ꜥh3wy*, *'Iḫty*. Bes préside, comme Thouéris, aux divers aspects de la maternité. On le trouve parfois accompagné de sa fidèle réplique, ou avec une parèdre à visage humain; la Béset tardive illustrerait sa nature androgyne. Quelques figurines représentent un quadrupède à tête de Bès. Sur la couronne du Bès traditionnel figurent maintes fois des animaux; ailleurs la couronne peut être formée de palmes plutôt que de plumes. Le nain apparaît en outre tenant deux rameaux ou une guirlande. Nous le verrions donc transformé en dieu de la nature, présidant aussi à la naissance des animaux et des plantes.

Bès est la seule divinité à manier des instruments autres que le sistre: il joue là un rôle cultuel. Il peut encore être assimilé à *Šsmw*, ancien dieu du pressoir, et gesticuler ou danser. Il écarte les mauvais esprits, surtout lors du sommeil, et peut rendre le dormeur plus clairvoyant, d'où sa figuration sur des chevets et pieds de lits, son association avec l'*oudjat* et les ivoires magiques. Avec Hathor Bès est la seule divinité à constituer un motif décoratif. Dans tout cela et sous les divers noms, on serait tenté de voir un pluriel: des génies associés à la vie courante. Cet être modeste mais familier et non spéculatif se hausse parfois au niveau d'Amon, ou s'identifie à Reshef. Si le corps se modifie, le facies reste caractéristique; il apparaît seul sur les stèles d'Horus. Même le grotesque et le comique font partie de l'énergie universelle, mais bien plus le rythme, auquel ne saurait échapper rien de matériel. *J. Custers*

68410 MICHAÏLIDIS, Georges, Éléments de synthèse religieuse gréco-égyptienne, *BIFAO* 66 (1968), 49-88, with 12 pl. and 9 fig.; rev. *CdE* XLIV, N° 87 (1969), 163 (Jean Bingen).

L'auteur publie quatre statuettes de divinités égyptiennes à inscriptions grecques:
bronze d'Osiris provenant d'Abydos;
Isis avec enfant en granit noir (région de Memphis);
Horus en calcaire blanc, vu à Alexandrie;
base d'un bronze: Horus (?) perçant (?) un animal.
Les pièces témoignent d'une dévotion particulière des Hellènes consacrée aux divinités les plus populaires en Égypte (VIe au Ve siècle avant notre ère).
A l'occasion de cette publication, l'auteur offre les résultats de son examen comparatif de la notion du divin chez les Égyptiens et chez les Grecs. *M. Heerma van Voss*

68411 MICHAŁOWSKI, Kazimierz, L'Art de l'ancienne Égypte, Paris, Éditions d'Art Lucien Mazenod, Éditio, 1968; series: L'Art et les grandes civilisations, collection créée et dirigée par Lucien Mazenod; rev. *Archeologia* 26 (janvier-février 1969), 89 (R[égine] P[ernoud]).

We did not see this original edition. For the German and English versions see our next volume.

68412 MICHAŁOWSKI, Kazimierz, The Labyrinth Enigma: Archaeological Suggestions, *JEA* 54 (1968), 219-222.

The writer discounts the accepted identification of the site of the Labyrinth with the pyramid temple of Hawâra and also the idea of its being a funerary temple built in the time of Ammenemes III or a royal palace or governmental centre of the same period. He postulates a Saite foundation of vast size possibly built in the Hawâra area and makes a plea for methodical excavation in the vicinity. *E. Uphill*

MODINOS, Polys, see our number 68366.

68413 MODRZEJEWSKI, Joseph, Histoire des institutions de l'Antiquité (à propos d'un ouvrage récent), *Revue internationale des droits de l'antiquité*, Bruxelles 15 (1968), 489-504.

Review article of Jean Gaudemet, *Institutions de l'Antiquité* (our number 67210).

68414 MONTET, Pierre, Egipt i Biblia, Warszawa, Inst. Wyd Pax, 1968 (116 p.); rev. *Przegląd Orientalistyczny* 3 (71), 1969, 288-290 (Albertyna Szczudłowska).

Polish version of our number 59433 (not seen).
There is also an English translation, Philadelphia, Fortress Press, 1968 (not seen).

68415 MONTET, Pierre, Lives of the Pharaohs, London, Weidenfeld and Nicolson, [1968] (19.5 × 25.7 cm; 288 p., 3 maps, frontispiece, 3 fig., numerous ill., 32 colour pl.). Pr. 63 s.

Description of the lives of several pharaohs from Snefru to Amasis (not seen).

68416 MORENZ, Siegfried, Die Begegnung Europas mit Ägypten. Mit einem Beitrag von Martin Kaiser, Herodots Begegnung mit Ägypten, Berlin, Akademie-Verlag, 1968 (14.8 × 21.6 cm; 247 p., 20 pl.) = Sitzungsberichte der Sächsischen Akademie der Wissenschaften zu Leipzig. Philologisch-historische Klasse. Band 113. Heft 5; rev. *Deutsche Literaturzeitung* 92 (1971), 331-334 (Ingrid Gamer-Wallert); *OLZ* 65 (1970), 244-246 (W. Wolf).

In the Introduction the author explains that in the encounter of Europe with ancient Egypt two stages have to be distinguished: the Antiquity, during which Egypt was a living partner, and the European civilisation since the Middle Ages, during which it was a "living dead". He also discusses here the main contributions of Egypt to the world: writing and calendar.

Part I deals with Egypt's influence in the European Antiquity. After stating that the conception "Europe" has been unknown to Egypt itself, so that the present study makes only sense from a modern European point of view, the author deals with Crete and the Aegean, which show signs of the Egyptian influence though the styles of art remain basically different. In the chapter on Ancient Greece Herodotus and Plato, various kinds of literature, religion and arts pass in review, each of them demonstrating the consequences of the encounter, though in various degrees. The main products of the Egyptian influence are to be found in Hellenism and the Roman Empire, up to very successful examples of mutual penetration. The author deals successively with science, religion, philosophy, literature and arts, mentioning several instances of Egyptian influence in the various fields.

Part II describing the encounter with the European culture since the Middle Ages, is divided into three chapters. During the Middle Ages Egyptian legacy appears to be found in the under-current: Hermetism, Physiologus, descriptions of the hell and love-poetry. From the Renaissance onwards there was again a conscious contact, though for the literature only through the classical authors, while in the plastic arts we find mainly imitations, adapted to the European taste (*e.g.* obelisks). While the Baroque was still in search for the mysteries of Egypt (Kircher), it was with Herder, and to a less extent with Winckelmann, that an adequate understanding of the Egyptian civilisation has begun, of which the science of Egyptology itself has been a product. But, though in the 19th century European art derived in a correct way elements of the architecture, it were still only motifs that were borrowed (the author demonstrates the differences with the 18th century by comparing the "Zauberflöte" with "Aïda"). In more recent times the encounter has been source of inspiration for painters (Gauguin) and authors (*e.g.* Rilke, Feuchtwanger and Thomas Mann), by whom not so much external forms as well the spirit of the Egyptian civilisation has been represented.

The study is accompanied with 20 plates illustrating various points of the author's argument. See also for the study of Herodotus' encounter with Egypt our number 68313.

A revised and enlarged edition of this study appeared in 1969 (Zürich and Stuttgart, Artemis Verlag) in the series Die Bibliothek der alten Welt.

68417 MORENZ, S., La religione egizia, a cura di Chr. M. Schröder. Trad. di G. Glässer e W. Perretta, Milano, 1968.
Italian version of our number 60503. Not seen.

68418 MOSS, Rosalind, By-products of Bibliography, *JEA* 54 (1968), 173-175, with 2 pl.
Robert Hay examined what was later known as the 'Lepsius mummy' and recorded some details. This was actually an elaborate set of late coffins with the mummy, belonging to Pedeamūn called Ipu Some while after Sir Gardner Wilkinson noted other features on them before they were presented to Gloucester City Museum. Two of the coffins subsequently went to Liverpool Museum in 1953, one having again been published by Dr. Margaret Murray in *Historical Studies* II (1904), 39-40. In 1719 Dom Bernard Montfaucon drew and published three alabaster canopic jars belonging to Ahmosi, son of Pediptah, and the writer traces their history to their present locations in the Lady Lever Art Gallery, Port Sunlight, Musée Calvert at Avignon and Bibl. Nationale, Paris. *E. Uphill*

MOUKHTAR, Gamal, see our number 68167.

68419 MRSICH, Tycho, Untersuchungen zur Hausurkunde des Alten Reiches. Ein Beitrag zum altägyptischen Stiftungsrecht, Berlin, Verlag Bruno Hessling, 1968 (20 × 29 cm; XIV + 222 p.) = Münchner Ägyptologische Studien herausgegeben von Hans Wolfgang Müller und Wolfhart Westendorf 13; rev. *BiOr* 28 (1971), 40-41 (S. Allam); *Mundus* 7 (1971), 36-37 (Schafik Allam); *Revue historique de droit français et étranger* 47 (1969), 699-700 (Ibrahim Harari). Pr. DM 44.50
Ziel der Arbeit ist es, "anhand von einigen Beispielen dem frühen Vermögensrecht nachzugehen, nämlich der Begründung, Art und Organisation des durch Hausurkunde übertragbaren Vermögens sowie den diesbezüglichen Geschäftsformen". Zu diesem Zweck wird der Terminus *jmyt-pr* "das was das Haus darstellt", der seit der 3. Dynastie belegt ist, im Kontext einiger Steininschriften des Alten Reiches untersucht. Die Organisation der Familie des Alten Reiches — beruhend auf der religiös begründeten Familienhoheit — wird "mit der Denkfigur eines funktionell teilbaren und abstufbaren Eigentumes im Verband umschrieben". Der Verband kann sich um einen Stifter-Ahnen eines Totenkultes oder einen lokalen Götterkult organisieren und erscheint wie

eine Verewigung der Grundherrschaft des Stifters vermittels der ihm angehörigen Personen, denen dieses System der Versorgung größere Stabilität in ihrer jeweiligen Position bieten sollte. Rechtlich ist zwischen dem begründenden Akt, der den Stiftungsverband konstituiert, und den später nötigen Rechtsgeschäften, die seiner Erhaltung dienen, zu unterscheiden. Eine solche Stiftungsgründung kann durch das *wḏt-mdw*-Formular verordnet werden: In subjektiver Stilisierung wird hier ein einseitiger, befehlsartiger, förmlicher Zuwendungsakt innerhalb des familiären Hausbereiches verfügt, also kein gegenseitiger Vertrag. Die Zuwendung kann schon bei Lebzeiten erfolgen und in ihre Wirkung eintreten; mangels Widerruflichkeit wird eine Deutung des *wḏt-mdw* als Testament ausgeschlossen. Ausdrücklich können im Nachfolgefall gewisse Inhaber von Herrschaftspositionen des Eigentumsverbandes zum Abschluß bestimmter Geschäfte, z.B. vermittels Hausurkunde, ermächtigt werden, obwohl solche Geschäfte grundsätzlich untersagt sind. Gegenstand der frühen Hausurkundenverfügung sind Vermögenskomplexe, das heißt Grundbesitz und Naturalienrenten-Anteile umfassendes Amtsvermögen; genaue Details über den Bestand sind nicht angegeben. Die Beteiligten des Rechtsgeschäftes *m jmyt-pr* des Alten Reiches sind Verwandte oder eine Totenpriesterschaft. Auch beim *jmyt-pr* ist ein Widerruf so gut wie ausgeschlossen und daher die Deutung "Testament" abzulehnen. Auch hier ist die Einseitigkeit und Befehlsartigkeit der Verfügung vorauszusetzen. Ergänzend zur Hausurkunde wird die einfachere Form NN *ḏd.f* gebraucht.   *E. M Wolf-Brinkmann*

68420 MÜLLER, C. Detlef G., Die Homilie über die Hochzeit zu Kana und weitere Schriften des Patriarchen Benjamin I. von Alexandrien. Herausgegeben, übersetzt und beschrieben, Heidelberg, Carl Winter Universitätsverlag, 1968 (17.5 × 25.2 cm; 393 p., 8 pl.) = Abhandlungen der Heidelberger Akademie der Wissenschaften. Philosophisch-historische Klasse, Jahrgang 1968,1.   Pr. DM 78

Publication of the homily of patriarch Benjamin I (626-665 A.D.) about the marriage in Kana. The author gives an introduction and a transcription of the complete text from various manuscripts, Coptic as well as Arabic, with translation. Added are fragments of preaches by Benjamin about Apa Shenūte and by his successor Agathon about Benjamin himself. There follows a text in Ethiopian.
Indexes, *i.a.* one of Greek loan-words, on p. 354-393.

68421 MÜLLER, H. W., Hanns Stock. 7. Oktober 1908-23. Juli 1966, *ZÄS* 95, 1 (1968), V-VI.
Obituary notice. Compare our number 68663.

68422 MÜLLER, Wolfgang, Ägyptisches Museum und Papyrussammlung, *Forschungen und Berichte* 10 (1968), 241-243.
Report on the activities of the Museum in East Berlin. Among the recent acquisitions is a so-called three-head (Amon as a ram, with the lion-heads of Shu and Tefnut) from Musawwarat es Sufra.

68423 MÜLLER-KARPE, Hermann, Handbuch der Vorgeschichte. Zweiter Band. Jungsteinzeit. Text [und] Tafeln, München, C. H. Beck'sche Verlagsbuchhandlung, 1968 (20.5 × 28.5 cm; [Text:] XIV + 612 p., 8 fig.; [Tafeln:] VI p., 6 tables, 321 pl., 5 maps; rev. *Bonner Jahrbücher* 170 (1970), 473-476 (J. Lüning); *Mitteilungen des anthropologischen Gesellschaft in Wien* 100 (1970), 436-438 (Andreas Lippert); *Mundus* 7 (1971), 38-41 (Eike Haberland).

Sequel to our number 66445.
In the text volume several sections are partly or wholly devoted to the pre- and protohistory of Egypt, altogether constituting a rather complete survey of these periods On p. 25-55 one finds a historical study of the archaeological material, from the Merimde and Heluan-el-Omari culture to the end of the IInd Dynasty, while the Nubian Nile valley in the corresponding period is studied on p. 185-189.
Short remarks on settlements on p. 262, on kingship on p. 265, and on architecture on p. 288. There are particular sections or major parts of them devoted to Egypt, dealing with: plastic arts (289-291), reliefs (302-306), paintings (310-311), drawings (320-324), writing (326-331), sanctuaries (339-345), burial (353-361), representations of animals (374-379) and man (385-392).
Particularly important is the list of major finds from the period, arranged in an alphabetical order according to the names of the finding places: Egypt on p. 396-412 and Lower Nubia on p. 412-413. Large sections are devoted to places such as Abydos and Sakkara, but there are also short ones such as that on Gebel el Arak (the flint knife). Each section also contains references to the relevant literature.
Extensive indexes on p. 557-612.
The plates volume contains except for synchronic tables and maps 321 plates representing in drawings all kinds of objects: pottery, flint implements, figurines, *etc*. Pl. 1-56 deal with Egypt, while on p. 312 there are pictures from rock-drawings in the Egyptian desert.

68424 MÜNSTER, Maria, Untersuchungen zur Göttin Isis vom Alten Reich bis zum Ende des Neuen Reiches, Berlin, Verlag Bruno Hessling, 1968 (20 × 29 cm; [12 +] IV + 239 p.) = Münchner Ägyptologische Studien herausgegeben von Hans Wolfgang Müller und Wolfhart Westendorf 11; rev. *BiOr* 27 (1970), 21-23 (Philippe Derchain); *OLZ* 66 (1971), 346-349 (E. Hornung); *Orientalia* 39 (1970), 204 (M. Heerma van Voss). Pr. DM 42

Die Arbeit umfaßt eine systematische Zusammenfassung und Interpretation der Belege für das Vorkommen dieser Göttin in dem genannten Zeitraum Die Besprechung der Isis im Osirismythos als Gattin des Osiris und Mutter des Horus bildet die Grundlage für die Ausführungen über Isis und Nephthys im Bestattungsritual und über die Rolle der Isis bei der Wiederbelebung des Toten: als Gattin des Osiris beweint sie den Toten und erweckt ihn zu neuem Leben mit Hilfe des Balsamierungsrituals; als Mutter des Horus, mit dem sich der Tote gleichsetzt, gebiert sie letzteren zu neuem Leben. Auch die meisten Verbindungen der Isis mit anderen Göttern sind von ihrer Beziehung zu Horus abhängig: sie wird Mutter aller Götter, mit denen sich Horus gleichsetzt, seien es Min, Amun, Re. der König oder andere Götter. Bei Min, Re und Amun kommt über die Kamutef-Vorstellung noch ihre Rolle als den Sohn ständig neu gebärende Gattin hinzu. Auch über ihre Funktion als Gattin des Osiris kann Isis durch Identifikation anderer Götter mit Osiris zu diesen Göttern in Verbindung treten — so als Schützerin zu Re — oder ihre Identität annehmen. Diese Identifikationen bilden wiederum die Grundlage neuer Verbindungen und Gleich-setzungen. Die Abhängigkeit der Isis von ihrem männlichen Partner spiegelt sich in der Lage ihrer Kultstätten, die — wenn der Kult nicht gemeinsam stattfindet — in engster Nachbarschaft der betreffenden Götter angesiedelt ist. Erst im Neuen Reich scheint ihre zunehmende Bedeutung als Muttergöttin und Gottesgemahlin ihr eine gewisse Selbständigkeit eingebracht zu haben.   *E. M. Wolf-Brinkmann*

68425 MUHAMMAD, Abdul-Qader Muhammad, Report on the Excavations Carried out in the Temple of Luxor. Seasons 1958-1959 & 1959-1960, *ASAE* 60 (1968), 227-279, with 106 pl., including 2 plans.

While no important discoveries were made after the removal of the ancient mudbrick houses between the western enclosure wall and the Nile, work in the area north of the 1st Pylon yielded valuable results. The paved avenue of sphinxes leading to the Karnak Temple could be followed deep into the old Mekashkesh cemetery, and turned out to be the work not of Amenophis III, but of King Nekhetnebef (XXXth Dynasty). It began directly north of the enclosure wall which was built subsequently to its completion and may be the result of Roman efforts to fortify the site. Remains of several buildings by Ekhnaton, Seti I and Psammetich, a Roman chapel and two Coptic churches were found between this wall and the 1st Pylon. In addition, statues of Amenophis III, Ramesses III, a huge head of Ramesses II, and a great number of other monuments came to light. Also cleared were the pylon gate and the corridor behind the eastern flank of the pylon adjacent to the mosque of Abul-Haggag that was found to be resting on top of very ancient walls. *Dieter Mueller*

68426 MUNRO, Peter, Altägyptische Metrik als Formprinzip und Mittel der Textinterpretationen, *OLZ* 63 (1968), 117-125.

Review article of Gerhard Fecht, *Literarische Zeugnisse zur "Persönlichen Frommigkeit" in Ägypten* (our number 65172).

68427 MUNRO, Peter, Nefertem und das Lotos-Emblem, *ZÄS* 95,1 (1968), 34-40.

Das synkretistische Wesen Nefertems erklärt sich aus seiner Bindung am Sonnengott und seiner Identität mit Osiris, Horus und dem irdischen Herrscher. *M. Heerma van Voss*

68428 MURTAGH, J., The Book of Job and the Book of the Dead, *The Irish Theological Quarterly*, Maynooth 35 (1968), 166-175.

Study of the influence of the *Book of the Dead*, particularly the "Negative Confession", on the *Book of Job*.

68429 Musée du Caire. Description sommaire des principaux monuments, Le Caire, Organisme Général des Imprimeries Gouvernementales, 1968 (13.6 × 17.9 cm; III + 261 + XXII p., 46 pl., 1 pl. in colour on cover, 2 plans). At head of title: République Arabe Unie. Ministère de la Culture. Service des Antiquités de l'Égypte.

A corrected and augmented re-edition of our number 63379. The cover bears a plate in colour and the word *Guide du*

Musée Égyptien du Caire Compare our number 68197.

68430 MUSSIES, G., Egyptianisms in a Late Ptolemaic Document, *in*: *Antidoron Martino David* oblatum. Miscellanea Papyrologica, Leiden, E. J. Brill, 1968 (= Papyrologica Lugduno-Batava, 17), 70-76.

The high degree of bilingualism in the upper class of the Egyptian population in the Greek and Roman Periods is

68431 MYŚLIWIEC, Karol, Egipskie modele rzeźbiarskie okresu ptolemejskiego, *Meander*, Warszawa 23, N° 7-8 (1968), 319-326, with 10 fig. and Latin summary.

"Modèles de sculpture égyptiens de la période ptolémaïque". L'article est consacré à des modèles de sculpture trouvés pendant les fouilles polono-françaises à Edfu et qui font actuellement partie des collections du Musée National de Varsovie. Les modèles ont été trouvés dans deux petites pièces contigues. *A. Szczudłowska*

68432 NADEL, B., Professor Piotr Jernstedt (1890-1966), *Polska Akademia Nauk, Sprawozdania z prac naukowych wydzialu nauk spolecznych* 10 (1967), fasc. 2 (45), 31-33.

Obituary notice. Compare our number 67644.

68433 NAGEL, Peter, Die Psalmoi Sarakoton des manichäischen Psalmbuches, *Probleme* 123.

Résumée de notre numéro 67416.

68434 NAVEH, Joseph, Aramaica Dubiosa, *JNES* 27 (1968) 317-325, with 7 ill.

Discussion of seven Aramaic inscriptions originating from Egypt, which the author suggests to be forgeries.
The first one, on a genuine Egyptian stela, was published by Leibovitch (our number 4719). For the next five objects cfr our number 58072. These six are now in the Michaelidis collection, while the last instance is a papyrus now in Madrid (cfr our number 64480).

68435 NEEDLER, Winifred, Egyptian Department, *Royal Ontario Museum. Annual Report*, Toronto 18 (1967-1968), 12-15, with 1 ill.

Report of the activities of the Egyptian Department.

68436 NEGENMAN, J. H., De bakermat van de Bijbel. Geschiedenis, cultuur en godsdienst van de wereld waarin de Bijbelse teksten zijn ontstaan, gegroeid en voltooid. Ingeleid door Prof. Dr. A. S. van der Woude, Met een epiloog van Luc. H. Grollenberg, Amsterdam-Brussel, Elsevier, 1968 (26.8 × 35.4 cm; 208 p., numerous ill. [partly in colour], maps [partly in colour], plans, tables, colour ill on cover); rev. *BiOr* 27

(1970), 420-421 (anonymous); *Nederlands Theologisch Tijdschrift* 23 (1968-1969), 375-377 (C. H. J. de Geus).

Pr. fl. 57.50

"The Cradle of the Bible".

Atlas containing text and maps, photographs and drawings, offering a picture of the world in which the Biblical writings were born.

For ancient Egypt cfr particularly the chapter on the alphabeth (p. 30-36) and that on Egyptian religion and history (45-49). Description and map of the battle of Kadesh on p. 52.

The English edition is entitled *New Atlas of the Bible*, edited by Harold H. Rowley. Translated by Hubert Hoskins and Richard Beckley (Collins, London, 1969; pr. £ 5.5.—.); rev. *The Expository Times* 81 (1969-1970), 152 (C. Crowther).

68437 NELSON, Dee Jay, Joseph Smith's "Eye of Ra". A Preliminary Survey and First Translation of Facsimile No. 2 in the Book of Abraham, Salt Lake City, Modern Microfilm Co., 1968 (21.5 × 26.5 cm; 31 p., 25 ill., 1 appendix).

An amateur study of the hypocephalus reproduced as "Facsimile No. 2" in the Mormon Book of Abraham. Several gross errors. *Dieter Mueller*

68438 NELSON, Dee Jay, The Joseph Smith Papyri. A Translation and Preliminary Survey of the Ta-shert-Min and Ter Papyri, Salt Lake City, Modern Microfilm Co., 1968 (14 × 21.5 cm, 45 p., many ill., 3 appendices).

An amateur description and identification of the recenty rediscovered Mormon papyri. They consist of 10 fragments of a Book of the Dead belonging to Ta-sheret-min, and 3 fragments of a Book of Breathings ("Breathing Permit") made for a certain Hor (here called Ter). The judgment scene on frg. 9-10 actually comes from another papyrus belonging to a lady Neferirnub: See our nos 68047 and 68639. *Dieter Mueller*

68439 NELSON, Dee Jay, The Joseph Smith Papyri, Part 2. Additional Translations and a Supplementary Survey of the Ta-shert-Min, Hor and Amen-Terp Papyri. Salt Lake City, Modern Microfilm Co., 1968 (21.5 × 26.5 cm; 41 p., 27 ill., 3 appendices).

A brief examination of the names and vignettes of the Mormon papyri. It seems that Joseph Smith used fragments from three different papyri belonging to Ta-sheret-min, Hor, and Amenhotep (two of the Ta-sheret-min fragments actually come from a fourth papyrus, the Book of the Dead of a lady Neferirnub: See our nos 68047 and 68639). Many typographical and other errors. *Dieter Mueller*

NELSON, Dee Jay, see also our number 68578.

68440 NEUGEBAUER, Otto, A Note on Exactly Dated Demotic Texts, *CdE* XLIII, N° 85 (1968), 93.

Compare our number 67438.

68441 NEUGEBAUER, O. and Richard A. PARKER, Two Demotic Horoscopes, *JEA* 54 (1968), 231-235, with 1 pl.; rev. *Enchoria* 1 (1971), 63 (Heinz-Josef Thissen).

The first of these is the earliest known example in Demotic being cast for May 4, 38 B.C. and is now in the Ashmolean Museum, Oxford. The second is cast for February 27, 57 A.D. in the reign of Nero and is in Berlin Museum. Translations and commentaries are included. *E. Uphill*

68442 NEYRET, Clémence, Panorama et évolution de la céramique copte d'après la collection du Musée du Louvre, *Boletín de la Asociación española de orientalistas*, Madrid 4 (1968), 145-155, with 15 pl.

Anhand der umfangreichen Sammlung des Louvre an koptischer Keramik zeigt Verfasser deren Entwicklung vom 5. bis zum 8. Jahrhundert in Form und Dekor auf, eine Entwicklung, der nach der arabischen Eroberung Ägyptens verfrüht ein Ende bereitet wird. *I. Gamer-Wallert*

68443 NIMS, Charles F., A Problem of Syntax in Demotic Documents, *Festschrift Schott* 94-98; rev. *Enchoria* 1 (1971), 63-64 (Heinz-Josef Thissen).

The author studies the use of the expression *i.ir⸗f ir* in Demotic texts from the region of Assiût, concluding that it is only a variant of the normal form of the Third Future.

68444 NIMS, Charles F., Second Tenses in Wenamūn, *JEA* 54 (1968), 161-164.

The author stresses the importance of applying Polotsky's Coptic syntactical studies on Second Tenses which emphasize an adverbial adjunct to standard Late Egyptian texts. There are twenty-six instances of the Second Present in Wenamūn, but in two recent translations the translators have not given the emphasis demanded by the text except where the adverbial adjunct is an interrogative adverbial phrase. Wenamūn himself uses the *i.sḏm.f* form of *iry* as the main verb four times, and there are two cases where Second Present follows the negative *nn*. For better understanding of the quoted passage recounting the discourse of Zakerbaʿal the change of emphasis is particularly important, Nims reading of the claims of Phoenicia being a much stronger one showing more effrontery to Amūn than those previously given by Albright and Gardiner. E. *Uphill*

NOBLE, Joseph Veach, see our number 68648.

68445 NOLTE, Birgit, Die Glasgefäße im alten Ägypten, Berlin, Verlag Bruno Hessling, 1968 (20 × 29 cm; [VIII +] 207 p., 35 pl. [2 in colours], 2 maps, many fig., frontispiece [in colours]) = Münchner Ägyptologische Studien herausgegeben von Hans Wolfgang Müller 14; rev. *BiOr* 27 (1970), 352-353 (M. Vanderhoeven); *Mundus* 7 (1971), 41-42 (Ingrid Gamer-Wallert). Pr. DM 78

Ein spezielles Wort der ägyptischen Sprache für "Glas" ist nicht bekannt; das Material, das vom Beginn des Neuen Reiches bis zur 21. Dynastie in Ägypten hergestellt wurde, wird als "künstlicher Lapislazuli" o.ä. bezeichnet, also als künstlicher Stein angesehen. Darauf deuten auch frühe Beispiele, die in Form, Farbe und Maserung zum Teil Steingefäße nachahmen.

Darstellungen von Glaswerkstätten wurden bisher nicht entdeckt. Dies und die Fundplätze einiger Werkstätten (Malkata, Tell el Amarna, Lisht und Menshiyeh) in Palastbzw. Tempelnähe legt nahe, daß die Glasherstellung jedenfalls anfangs im Dienste des Königs und unter gewisser Geheimhaltung geschah. Die Schwierigkeit der Herstellung (Sandkerntechnik), die Erfahrung und hohe Geschicklichkeit erforderte, und die Empfindlichkeit der Produkte ließen Glas auch niemals zum Gebrauchsgegenstand für breitere Volksschichten werden.

Nach einer Zusammenstellung der Formen, der Farben, der Muster und der Verwendungszwecke der Glasgefäße, folgt zunächst ein Katalog der durch Fundumstände sicher datierten Gefäße, die von Thutmosis III. bis zur 21. Dyn. (Nes-Chons) reichen. Auf dieser Grundlage ist es möglich, auch ungesicherte Exemplare zeitlich einzuordnen. Hier unterscheidet die Verfasserin auf Grund von Farbzusammenstellungen, Mustern und Formen sechs verschiedene "Werkkreise" oder "Schulen".

Zahlreiche Indices und Tafeln beschließen die umfassende Darstellung der in zahlreiche Museen und schwer zugängliche Sammlungen verstreuten Glasgefäße.

E. M. Wolf-Brinkmann

68446 O'CLERY, Helen, The Pegasus Book of Egypt, London,

Dennis Dolson, [1968] (13.3 × 20.5 cm; 185 p., numerous fig. and maps).

General description of the Egyptian history from king Narmer to President Nasser.

68447 O'CONNOR, David, Field Work in Egypt, *Expedition*, Philadelphia 11, Number 1 (Fall 1968), 27-30, with 1 map and 6 ill.

Survey of the three field expeditions of the University Museum: excavations at Abydos (together with the Yale University), the Dra' Abû el-Naga' project and the Akhenaten Temple project.

68448 ORLANDI, Tito, Un codice copto del « Monastero Bianco ». Encomii di Severo di Antiochia, Marco Evangelista, Atanasio di Alessandria, *Muséon* 81 (1968), 351-405.

Publication of a Coptic codex from the White Monastery, which the author has composed from several fragments. The printed text is given on p. 356-393, and is followed by a Latin translation (p. 393-400) and a short commentary (p. 400-405). *L. F. Kleiterp*

68449 ORLANDI, Tito, Storia della chiesa di Alessandria. Testo copto, traduzione e commento. Vol. I: da Pietro ad Atanasio, Milano-Varese, Istituto Editoriale Cisalpino, [1968] (13 × 19.7 cm; 132 p., 2 pl.) = Testi e documenti per lo studio dell' antichità 17 = Studi Copti 2; at head of title: Istituto di Papirologia dell'Università degli Studi di Milano; rev. *Muséon* 81 (1968), 570-572 (Gérard Garitte).

Pr. bound lire 2500

After the introduction (p. 9-15) follows the Coptic text, which the author has composed from several fragments (p. 17-54; text on the left hand pages, notes on the right hand pages), and a Latin translation (p. 57-69). A commentary is given on p. 73-109, after which follows a Conclusion (p. 113-121) and an index of proper names and foreign words in their Coptic form. Vol. II, da Teofilo a Timoteo II, has been published in 1970. *L. F. Kleiterp*

68450 ORLANDI, Tito, Studi Copti. 1) Un encomio di Marco Evangelista. 2) Le fonti Copte della Storia dei Patriarchi di Alessandria. 3) La leggenda di S. Mercurio, Milano-Varese, Istituto Editoriale Cisalpino, [1968] (13 × 19.7 cm; 146 p.) = Testi e documenti per lo studio dell' antichità 22 = Studi Copti 4; at head of title: Istituto di Papirologia dell'Università degli Studi di Milano; rev. *Muséon* 83 (1970), 272-274 (Gérard Garitte). Pr. bound lire 2500

Part 1) contains a publication of an Encomium of Marc by Johannes "the recluse", which once was a part of the library of the White Monastery and has been composed by the author from several fragments. Printed text on the left hand pages, a Latin translation on the right hand pages. Brief notes on p. 52. *L. F. Kleiterp*

68451 ORLANDI, Tito, Testi Copti. 1) Encomio di Atanasio. 2) Vita di Atanasio. Edizione critica, traduzione e commento, Milano-Varese, Istituto Editoriale Cisalpino, [1968] (13 × 19.7 cm; 162 p., 3 tables, 6 pl.) = Testi e documenti per lo studio dell' antichità 21 = Studi Copti 3; at head of title: Istituto de Papirologia dell'Università degli Studi di Milano; rev. *Muséon* 83 (1970), 269-272 (Gérard Garitte); *Revue de l'histoire des religions* 180 (1971), 201-202 (A. Guillaumont). Pr. bound lire 2500

1) Encomio di Atanasio. The Coptic text is published on p 17-42, and is followed by an index of proper names and foreign words in their Coptic form (p. 43-50), a concordance of fragments (p. 51-52), an Italian translation (p. 55-71) and some remarks on p. 72-77. Introduction on p. 11-14.
2) Vita di Atanasio. Introduction on p. 81-83. Coptic text on p. 87-110. Index of proper names and foreign words in their Coptic form on p. 111-118. Italian translation on p. 121-137. Commentary on p. 139-161.
Compare our number 67430. *L. F. Kleiterp*

68452 OTTO, Eberhard, Anerkennung und Ablehnung fremder Kulte in der ägyptischen Welt, *Saeculum*, Freiburg/München 19 (1968), 330-343.

Egyptian religion is an essential part of the Egyptian civilisation and could not exist outside of this civilisation. Thus it was only after the Egyptian expansion in Syria that Hathor took possession of this country.
In the Hyksos period there seems to have been no religious oppression, though later propaganda suggested it. It was only with the New Kingdom empire that foreign cults came to Egypt on equal terms, some connected with Egyptian divinities, some under the protection of the kings, and some as characters in myths and stories. Their inclusion is connected with the enrichment of the Egyptian culture, and they are particularly connected with newly developed spheres of life, but the connection was merely incidental. There also existed no religious policy in the Asian empire. Nubia, on the other hand, was definitely egyptianized also in its religion, though there is no proof of any Nubian influence on the religion of Egypt.

The author briefly discusses the egyptianisation of the Shiwa-oracle, and the rejection of Seth as god of the foreigners, particularly as symbol for the Persians.

68453 OTTO, Eberhard, Eine Darstellung der "Osiris-Mysterien" in Theben, *Festschrift Schott* 99-105, with 2 fig. and 1 ill. (on pl. IV).

Study of a relief in Room 19 of the Mortuary Temple of Sethi I representing the posthumous begetting of Horus by Osiris. This scene which appears to be unique for a mortuary temple indicates that in the room Osiris mysteries have been celebrated. Taking into account the building activities of the king in Abydos one may conclude that it was Sethi I to whose initiative the later cult-forms of the Osiris mysteries are due, by which he produced the genuine answer to the Amarna-period.

OTTO, Eberhard, see also our numbers 68202 and 68359.

68454 PARKER, Richard, The Book of Breathings, *The Joseph Smith Egyptian Papyri* 98-99.

The translation of a fragment from the "Breathing Permit" of Hor, once in the possession of Joseph Smith. For a complete rendering of this text see our number 68047.

Dieter Mueller

68455 PARKER, Richard A., The Joseph Smith Papyri: A Preliminary Report, *The Joseph Smith Egyptian Papyri* 86-88, with 2 ill.

Another description (see our number 68639) of the papyrus fragments once in the possession of Joseph Smith, founder of the Mormon church. See also our number 68047.

Dieter Mueller

PARKER, Richard A., see also our numbers 68441 and 68578.

PARR, Peter J., see our number 68647.

68456 PARROT, A., Alan Rowe (1892-1968), *Syria*, Paris 45 (1968), 432.

Obituary article.

68457 PAVLOV, V. V., Русская дореволюционная и советская наука о египетском искусстве, *ВДИ* 2 (104), 1968, 150-155.

"Russian pre-revolutionary and Sovjet-studies on Egyptian art".

An abbreviated version appeared in IV Сессия по Древнему Востоку, p. 35.

68458 PELÁEZ, Marcelino Herrero, Misión arqueológica española en Ehnasya el-Medina, *Boletín de la Asociación española de orientalistas*, Madrid 4 (1968), 183-185, with 4 pl.

Auf einen Abriss der Geschichte des alten Herakleopolis magna folgt ein kurzer Bericht der Grabungskampagnen 1966 und 1968 durch eine spanische Mission mit Illustrationen einiger Funde (Kolossalfigur Ramses' II., Scheintür des 1. Zwischenzeit, Kanopenkrüge und Uschebtis).

I. Gamer-Wallert

68459 PERC, Bernarda, Beiträge zur Verbreitung ägyptischer Kulte auf dem Balkan und in den Donauländern zu Römerzeit (mit besonderer Berücksichtigung des Quellenmaterials aus dem Gebiet des heutigen Staates Jugoslavien), München, 1968 (14.5 × 20.2 cm; [IV +] 294 p., 6 pl.).

In her thesis for a doctor's degree in Munich the Yugoslavian author discusses the archaeological material for the Egyptian cults in the Roman provinces Istria, Noricum, Pannonia, Moesia, Dalmatia and Macedonia. Each chapter, devoted to one of these provinces, consists of an introduction, a study of the monuments in their geographical and historical setting, and a summary. A short general summary on p. 112-113 stresses the importance of the cults of Isis and Serapis in this region. Bibliography on p. 116-121, index p. 122-128.

The second part of the book (129-293) contains a catalogue of the material. altogether 102 objects, statuettes, altars, stelae, *etc*. Every single object is amply discussed, while its data such as material, measurements, provenance and the relevant literature are noted.

P. 277-293 contain lists of the same monuments arranged after their provenance and the gods to whose cults they belong.

68460 PEREPELKIN, J. J., Тайна золотого гроба, Москва, Издательство "Наука". Главная редакция восточнои литературы, 1968 (13 × 20 cm; 175 p., 2 fig., 1 plan, 20 ill.). At head of title: Академия Наук СССР. Институт Народов Азии.   Pr. коп. 45

"Le mystère du cercueil en or".
L'étude porte sur Aménophis IV et certaines personnalités de son entourage, particulièrement sa femme Kija. En se fondant sur une documentation très complète, l'auteur avance des idées originales.   *G. Posener*

68461 PERNIGOTTI, Sergio, Il generale Potasimto e la sua famiglia, *Studi classici e orientali*, Pisa 17 (1968), 251-264, with 5 pl.

Potasimto was the commander of foreign troops accompanying Ptolemaeus II during his Nubian expedition in 591 B.C. (cfr our number 2558). His family has been studied in our numbers 3126 and 4749.

The present article studies three monuments of Potasimto's father Raemmaakheru: a statue (Museum of Rennes, deposited in the Louvre, E. 13109), a libation vase (Cairo J.E. 48894) and a stela (Hildesheim, Roemer-Pelizaeus Museum, Inv. No 9). These documents enable the author to draw some conclusions as to the general's family.

68462 PERNIGOTTI, Sergio, Ostraca demotici da Ossiringo, *Studi classici e orientali*, Pisa 17 (1968), 237-250, with 3 pl.

Publication of nine ostraca from Oxyrhynchus, at present in the collection in Pisa, eight of which contain grain accounts and the ninth only a name. Of each there is given a description, transliteration, translation and a photograph.

For two more ostraca of the same collection see Edda Bresciani, *Due ostraca demotici da Ossirinco*, Studi classici e orientali, Pisa 15 (1966), 269-274.

68463 PESTMAN, P. W., Eine demotische Doppelurkunde, *in*: Antidoron Martino David oblatum. Miscellanea Papyrologica, Leiden, E. J. Brill, 1968 (= Papyrologica Lugduno-Batava, 17), 100-111, with 2 pl.

Re-edition of the Demotic Pap. BM 10425, dating from the year 5 of Pharaoh Harmakhis (201 B.C.). The upper part with four lines of writing, which had been kept rolled and sealed, is now unrolled. It contains an abbreviated version of the main text, which is an IOU for 2.1 *deben* of silver.

The author presents the texts in photograph, transliteration and translation with comments.

PESTMAN, Pieter W., see also our number 68303.

68464 PETERSON, Bengt J., Archäologische Funde aus Sesebi (Sudla) in Nord-Sudan, *Orientalia Suecana*, Uppsala 16 (1967), 1968, 3-15, with 1 plan and 34 ill.

L'auteur présente un choix d'objets du Medelhavsmuseet de Stockholm, provenant de la première saison de fouilles à Sesebi (1936/37). Il les classe d'après leur provenance: région du temple, entrepôts, quartier d'habitations, endroits divers, endroits non précisés. On notera, outre une tête de granit noir, attribuée à Hatshepsout, des objets de stéatite, de céramique, de cornaline, de verre, de bronze et de terre cuite. Il y a des scarabées, de petits récipients, des amulettes, ornements et jouets, une empreinte de pied d'enfant, un fragment d'*oushebti*, une forme à *oudjat*. Le style de ces objets est bien égyptien, et les scarabées pourraient être importés. *J. Custers*

68465 PETERSON, B. J., Drei Fragmente ägyptischer Mumienkartonnagen, *Ethnos*, Stockholm 33 (1968), 134-140, with 3 ill.

Description of three fragments of mummy cartonnages, at present in the Medelhavsmuseet (MME 1961:5; 1961:6; 1961:7), the first one dated to the XXth-XXIInd Dynasties, the second to the Ptolemaic Period, and the third to the Late Period.

68466 PETERSON, Bengt J., Fragmente aus einem Totenbuch der 18. Dynastie, *Orientalia Suecana*, Uppsala 16 (1967), 1968, 16-21, with 5 ill.

Une collection particulière de Stockholm possède cinq fragments de papyrus au nom d'Amenhotep (*mr ḳdw n 'Imn* et *mr k3t n pr-Mwt*), dont sont nommés les parents, l'épouse et un fils Sennefer. Tant le nom et les titres du propriétaire que la qualité et les particularités du papyrus correspondent à ceux du papyrus British Museum 10489, dont manque en effet le début. Ce *Livre des Morts* entièrement inédit contient un texte excellent. Il est décoré d'un rang d'étoiles au dessus et au dessous du texte, ainsi que de vignettes. Au verso du rouleau court une ligne de prières. Collés sur carton, les fragments suédois portent ce qui paraît être le début du papyrus, après la scène d'adoration d'Osiris, et des textes essentiels tirés des chapitres 17B (24 et 25) et 17 (27 à 31 ainsi que 32 et 33). Enfin, un fragment de généalogie du défunt, en rouge, précède un extrait du ch. 130, avec variante additionnelle. Le papyrus daterait de l'époque des Thoutmès III-Aménophis II, et la provenance en serait Thèbes, vu la mention d'Hathor, dame d'*Išrw*. *J. Custers*

68467 PETERSON, Bengt Julius, Some Objects from the Time of Akhenaten, *JEOL* VII, 20 (1967-1968), 1968, 21-26, with 5 pl.

Il s'agit d'une plaquette et de sept études de sculpteurs conservées au Musée National de Copenhague et au Musée Victoria, d'Upsala. La plaquette en pierre dure rouge Copenhague 3606 (collection Sabatier) se présente comme une petite stèle à sommet arrondi. Les faces portent les noms d'Aton présenté comme roi, soigneusement incisés sous leurs formes d'avant et d'après le jubilé d'Akhénaton. Ce dernier est nommé sur deux tranches latérales; le cartouche de la reine est effacé .On peut fixer entre l'an 6 et l'an 8 du règne la date de ce petit monument privé ou stèle votive.

Les autres objets sont en calcaire et portent des ébauches de relief. La pièce Copenhague 11572 figure un enfant accroupi. La plupart des fragments d'Upsala portent un visage en sous-relief; l'autre face du 238 porte un relief normal. Ces ébauches, dont plusieurs sont dues à des maîtres, mettent l'accent sur la bouche lippue.

J. Custers

68468 PETROVSKI, N. S., О предельных и непредельных глаголах в египетскои языке, IV Сессия по Древнему Востоку 17-18.

"Über die terminativen und unterminativen Verben in der ägyptischen Sprache".

PHILIPPE, Robert, see our number 68572.

68469 PHILONENKO, Marc, Joseph et Aséneth, Introduction. Texte critique. Traduction et Notes, Leiden, E. J. Brill, 1968 (16 × 24.3 cm; VI + 266 p.) = Studia Post-Biblica 13. At head of title: Université de Strasbourg, Faculté de Théologie Protestante. Pr. cloth fl. 49

In this dissertation the Greek text of Joseph and Aseneth is published. After a discussion of the etymology of the name Aseneth (Sethe: *Ns.N.t.*, Spiegelberg: *ws-n-(j)t*), the author gives a description of the goddess Neith and her cult at Esna.

L. F. Kleiterp

68470 PHILONENKO, Marc, Le Testament de Job. Introduction, traduction et notes, *Semitica*, Paris 18 (1968), 7-77.

In an Additum on p. 61-63 the author calls attention to the collection of papyri of the Institut für Altertumskunde of the University of Cologne, which has many fragments of a Coptic codex dating from the 5th century. The codex, which is to be published soon, contains large parts of the Testament of Abraham and of the Testament of Job (P. Colon inv. 3221). The language is Sahidic with Bohairic influences. *L. F. Kleiterp*

68471 PIANKOFF, Alexandre, The Pyramid of Unas. Texts Translated with Commentary, [Princeton N.J.], Princeton University Press, [1968] (23.8 × 31.3 cm; XIV + 118 p., 2 plans, 7 pl. + 70 pl. with texts) = Egyptian Religious Texts and Representations, Vol. 5 = Bollingen Series 40; rev. *AJA* 73 (1969), 378-379 (Hans Goedicke); *Archaeology* 23 (1970), 351-352 (Lanny Bell); *BiOr* 26 (1969), 60-61 (Hartwig Altenmüller); *CdÉ* XLIV, N° 87 (1969), 70-72 (Philippe Derchain); *Deutsche Literaturzeitung* 90 (1969), 497-499 (Wolfgang Helck); *JARCE* 8 (1969-1970), 101 (Alan R.

Schulman); *JEA* 56 (1970), 202-203 (R. O. Faulkner); *Revue de l'Histoire des Religions* 177 (1970), 65-69 (P. Barguet).
Pr. cloth $ 10.00

Following an introduction the author offers a translation with comments of Unas' texts. These are reproduced on 69 photographic text plates.
According to Piankoff, reading should begin in the entrance corridor leading into the monument. A coherent narrative is found then, describing or alluding to the various stages of rebirth of the king.
The pyramid, its interior and its planning are shown on 7 pictorial plates and two folding plans.
After the author's sudden death, the book was seen through the press by **B.V.** Bothmer who added a finding list of utterances and spells. Obituary on p. 117-118; cfr our number 67645. *M. Heerma van Voss*

68472 PIOTROVSKI, B., Wadi Allaka — Der Weg der Alten zu den Goldminen Nubiens, *Proceedings* 12-16.

Compare our number 63414.

PIOTROVSKI, Boris, see also our number 68056.

68473 PIRENNE, Jacques, Gouvernés et gouvernants dans l'ancienne Égypte, *in*: *Gouvernés et Gouvernants*. Deuxième Partie. Antiquité et Haut Moyen Age, Bruxelles, Éditions de la Librairie Encyclopédique, 1968 (= Recueils de la Société Jean Bodin pour l'histoire comparative des institutions 23), 45-72.

The author has summarized his report in our following number, p. 13-15 and 18-20.

68474 PIRENNE, Jacques, Gouvernés et Gouvernants dans l'Antiquité Orientale. Rapport de synthèse, *in*: *Gouvernés et Gouvernants*. Deuxième Partie. Antiquité et Haut Moyen Age, Bruxelles, Éditions de la Librairie Encyclopédique, 1968 (= Recueils de la Société Jean Bodin pour l'histoire comparative des institutions, 23), 7-20.

The author summarizes a series of lectures on administration in the ancient Near East. He points out that the change from a tribal organisation, through life in cities governed by an elected council of elders, to states ruled by hereditary monarchies led to a concept of impartial law which made the ruler a representative of society protecting the weak against the powerful. The disintegration of these monarchies resulted in a partial reconstitution of local representative bodies and a more direct participation of the governed in the government.

It seems reasonable to assume that the development in Ancient Egypt (p. 13-15, see our preceding number) followed the same pattern, though no direct evidence for its first stages is available. However, there are indications that some city-states in the Delta formed a coalition which eventually became a centralized monarchy ruled by the king of Buto, and was finally conquered by Menes. The system of elected representatives never disappeared completely, and since the XXVIth Dynasty, the Delta villages were allowed to elect their own local administration.

Dieter Mueller

68475 PIRENNE, J., Storia della civiltà dell' antico Egitto. Vol. 1.2.3. Trad. di R. M. Degli Uberti Firenze, Sansoni Editore, 1968.

Translation of our numbers 61555, 62474 and 63416. Not seen.

68476 POCHAN, André P. R., Chronologie égyptienne. Les Hébreux en Égypte. Compléments, Montesson, Éditions Maât, 1968 (mimeographed; 20.7 × 26.6 cm; [IV +] 38 p. [numbered 300-331]).

Additions and corrections to our number 65389; cfr also our abstract number 62478.

68477 POLÁČEK, Vojtěch, Les magistratures dans le monde antique, *Revue Internationale de Droits de l'Antiquité*, Bruxelles série 3, tome 15 (1968), 21-38.

In this reflections on the principles according to which the Egyptian administration used to function the author rejects the idea of an ancient state-socialism. He amply discusses the role of Maat, quoting from the *Instruction of Ptahhotep* as well as from the Greek Pap. Tebtunis 703.

68478 POLLAK, Kurt, Wissen und Weisheit der alten Ärtzte. Die Heilkunst der frühen Hochkulturen, Düsseldorf-Wien, Econ-Verlag, [1968] (15.2 × 22.6 cm; 376 p., 16 pl.); rev. *Mundus* 6 (1970), 73 (Heinz Goerke).   Pr. cloth DM 20

The first part of this book on the ancient history of medicine is called *Medizin am Nil* (p. 5-98).
Proceeding from Emery's search for Imhotep's tomb the author first gives a survey of our knowledge about the cult of this sage and that of other late Egyptian gods of medicine. He then discusses the history of the present knowledge on the subject, the medical papyri, the position of the Egyptian physician, and his knowledge. He also deals with the Egyptian conception of disease and the description of

various diseases in the papyri. Special subjects are briefly discussed, as, for instance, the problem whether managers disease existed, and, of course, the physical features of Akhnaton. Other sections are devoted to surgery and dental surgery, gynaecology, and pharmacy, while there is also attention paid to magical practices and the everyday life with regard to health and hygiene. In the last section of this part one finds an attempt to summarize the significance of ancient Egypt for the development of the medical science.

68479 POLOTSKY, H. J., The 'Weak' Plural Article in Bohairic, *JEA* 54 (1968), 243-245.

Bohairic has two sets of definite articles, usually distinguished as 'strong' and 'weak'. This article discusses the use of the 'weak' plural article in two respects, when its form coincides with the prenominal 'our' and its restricted use only with a noun followed by a genitive. It has no plural article ⲛ—, but exceptions are quoted. *E. Uphill*

POMERANSEVA, N. A., see our number 68287.

68480 POMORSKA, Irena, *Uszebti w zbiorach Uniwersytetu Jagiellońskiego w Krakowie i Muzeum Narodowego (Zbiory Czartoryskich) w Krakowie*, *Rocznik Muzeum Narodowego w Warszawie*, Warszawa 11 (1967), 19-51, with 26 ill. and summaries in Russian and French on p. 50-51.

"Les *oushebti* des collections de l'Université Jagellone de Cracovie et du Musée National de Cracovie (collection des Czartoryski)".
Publication de 64 *oushebti* appartenant à deux collections cracoviennes.
A comparer notre résumé 63418.

68481 PORTEN, Bezalel, Archives from Elephantine. The Life of an Ancient Jewish Military Colony, Berkeley and Los Angeles, University of California Press, 1968 (16 × 24 cm; XXII + 421 p., 1 map, 15 fig. [including plan and tables], 16 pl.); rev. *AfO* 23 (1970), 114-115 (Johann Jakob Stamm); *BiOr* 27 (1970), 249-252 (B. Couroyer); *Booklist* 1970, 80 (R. J. C[oggins]); *Bulletin of the School of Oriental and African Studies University of London* 34 (1971), 141-142 (J. B. Segal); *JAOS* 90 (1970), 543-544 (Javier Teixidor); *Journal of Biblical Literature* 89 (1970), 92-94 (Marvin H. Pope); *Journal of Semitic Studies* 16 (1971), 240-244 (R. Yaron); *Orientalia* 39 (1970), 454-459 (Raymond A. Bowman); *Qadmoniot* 3 (1970), 145-146 (E. Stern); *Revue Biblique* 77 (1970), 463-465 (B. C[ouroyer]); *ZAW* 82 (1970), 167 ([G. Fohrer]).

Comprehensive study of the Jewish military colony at Elephantine against a background that was Israelite and Aramean, but also Babylonian, Persian, Greek and Egyptian. Part I describes the political and economic life. In chapter 1 the author deals with the settlement of Jews and Arameans in Egypt, with a particular section about Saite mercenaries and another about the Persian politics in Egypt from Cambyses to Artaxerxes I. Chapter 2 is devoted to the garrisons in Elephantine-Syene, their organisation, officials and deities; chapter 3 to the standard of living, *i. a.* prices, clothing and the Jewish quarter.

Part II discusses the religious life of the Jewish community, the worship of YHW (chapter 4) and the contacts with the pagans.

Part III is devoted to family and communal life: marriage and marriage property, letters, the history of the community with its conflicts, destruction and reconstruction of the temple, *etc.* (chapters 6-9). Throughout these chapters there are many references to Egyptian law and customs; see particularly p. 258-259 about Egyptian women. Six appendices deal with particular details, *i.a.* comparison of the schema of Aramaic and Demotic legal documents (p. 334-343). An extensive bibliography on p. 347-376, various indexes on p. 377-421.

68482 POSENER, Georges, Aménémopé, 22, 9-10 et l'infirmité du crocodile, *Festschrift Schott* 106-111.

The translation "Verily a crocodile which is void of proclaiming, inveterate is the dread of it", suggested for this passage by Griffith, cannot be correct, as the crocodile has a very distinct voice—a fact well known to the Ancient Egyptians. A much better sense can be obtained by assuming that *nis* stands for *ns*: "The crocodile which is deprived of a tongue—its prestige is old". The idea that the crocodile does not have a tongue is well attested in the Classical authors and the *Calendar of Lucky and Unlucky Days* (Pap. Sallier IV 6, 5-6). The Egyptians explained this deficiency as a punishment of Sobek's mutilation of Osiris (*CT* VII 201 k). *Dieter Mueller*

68483 POSENER, Georges, Philologie et archéologie égyptiennes, *Annuaire du Collège de France*, Paris 67 (1967-1968), 1968, 345-354.

Two subjects are dealt with: I. Investigations on the god Khonsu (sequel to our number 67452). The author concentrates on Khonsu *p3 ir shr.w*, best known from the *Bentresh Stela*, which is commented upon. This particular form of

Khonsu is textually attested from the XXth Dynasty on in Thebes, but the cult may be somewhat earlier; the god's name is a typically Late Egyptian formation. This saviour god belongs to popular religion. II. A tentative reconstruction of a Middle Kingdom Instruction: a discussion of the so-called "panégyrique royale", known *i.a.* from the stela of *Sḥtp-ib-rʿ* (Cairo 20538). The author moreover enumerates and discusses 2 papyri, 1 tablet and 26 ostraca. Both subjects are to be continued in the next year's issue.

J. F. Borghouts

68484 POSENER, Georges, Une stèle de Hatnoub, *JEA* 54 (1968), 67-70, with 3 pl.

This interesting but damaged stela dated to year 22 of Sesostris I, is the main portion of a monument of which a fragment was previously published by Grdseloff in 1951 (our number 1810), and measured about 25 cm high and 27 cm broad when complete. It represents a crudely carved figure of a man holding wands of office and had both horizontal and vertical lines of inscriptions It has the normal *ḥtp di nsw* formula and mentions the chief treasurer Sebekhotep. Grammatical notes are included. *E. Uphill*

POSENER, Georges, see also our number 68396.

68485 POSENER-KRIEGÉR (sic), Paule, Remarques sur l'ensemble funéraire de Neferirkare Kakai à Abu Sir, *Festschrift Schott* 112-120, with 1 fig. and 1 plan.

Study of one document of the Abu Sîr papyri (see our next number, pl. 31-32) recording the inspection of the temple. Following its course by the mention of doors, rooms, columns and sacred barks the author is able to explain some topographical details of the temple.

68486 POSENER-KRIÉGER, Paule and Jean Louis de CENIVAL, Hieratic Papyri in the British Museum. Fifth Series. The Abu Sir Papyri Edited, together with Complementary Texts in other collections, London, Published by the Trustees of the British Museum, 1968 (28.1 × 35.7 cm; XX + 52 p., 17 pl.+ 104 double pl.); rev. *Comptes rendus de l'Académie des Inscriptions et Belles-Lettres*. 1968, 457-459 (Jacques Vandier); *JEA* 56 (1970), 201-202 (R. O. Faulkner); *JNES* 29 (1970), 131-133 (William Kelly Simpson); *OLZ* 64 (1969), 447-448 (H. Goedicke); *RdE* 21 (1969), 174-177 (Mounir Megally); *The Times*, London, Saturday April 27, 1968, 9 (I. E. S. Edwards). Pr. bound £ 12

The fragmentary papyri published in the present volume are from the collections of the British Museum, the Louvre the Cairo Museum, the Museums of East and West Berlin, and the Petrie Museum of University College, London, and they are all that have survived of the archives of the funerary temple of Neferirkare' Kakai of the Vth Dynasty. They are concerned with the day to day administration of the temple in all its aspects and as such they include duty-tables (the daily tasks of each member of the staff) for month period and for feasts, inventories (detailed or summary), records of inspections, lists of persons, accounts, and letters. But since only a tiny fraction of all the records of the office of the temple has been preserved there may be other types of documents unrepresented.

Depending on how the dates found on the fragments are interpreted, the range of years they cover could be either 80 (year 5 of Isesi to year 12 of Teti) or 53 (year 21 of Isesi to year 1 of Teti). In any event the oldest dated document would have been written more than a half century after the death of Neferirkare'. Already there is evidence that the temple service was decaying. Deliveries were sporadic and the temple equipment damaged, sometimes beyond repair. All this poverty was carefully noted in the records.

Because this is the oldest body of hieratic texts known to date the editors have devoted seventeen plates to palaeographical forms, keyed to both Möller and Gardiner's sign lists. These precede the 104 double plates of fragments with transcription facing the original. In introductory pages every plate is described and all that is known of a fragment's physical appearance and history is recorded, as well as its general nature.

A volume of translation and commentary by the Editors is now in preparation. *R. A. Parker*

68487 POSTOVSKAJA, N. M., К вопросу о понятии „Дом", IV Сессия по Древнему Востоку 5-6.

"Zur Frage des Begriffes 'Haus' ".
Siehe unsere Nummer 67454.

68488 POULSEN, Vagn, Ägyptische Kunst. Altes und Mittleres Reich [und] Neues Reich und Spätzeit, Königstein im Taunus, Karl Robert Langewiesche Nachfolger Hans Köster, [1968] (19 × 27 cm; 88 + 92 p., map on endpapers, 86 + 83 ill. [14 + 17 in colour]); rev. *BiOr* 26 (1969), 331-332 (Winifred Needler); *CdE* XLV, N° 89 (1970), 76-77 (Herman de Meulenaere). Pr. cloth DM 17.50

Auch ohne philologische Kenntnisse kann man die Sprache, die die ägyptische Kunst redet, verstehen.
In seiner Beschreibung und seinen Bildern berührt der

Verfasser jeden Sektor der Kunst. Im ersten Teil (*Altes und Mittleren Reich*) beschäftigt er sich auch mit der Vorzeit und der Frühzeit. Der zweite Teil (*Neues Reich und Spätzeit*) schliesst beim Anfang der letzten Blüte (Kunst der Kopten). Die meisten Bilder sind rezent, die Literaturnachweise (I,4 und II,4) bis auf die Gegenwart fortgeführt.
Register: II, [86-92]. Zeittafel: I, 30.

M. Heerma van Voss

68489 POULSEN, Vagn, Ägyptische Kunst. Altes und Mittleres Reich, Königstein im Taunus, Karl Robert Langewiesche Nachfolger Hans Köster, [1968] (19 × 27 cm; 88 p., map on endpapers, 86 ill. [14 in colour]). Series: Die Blauen Bücher. Pr. cloth DM 7.80

First part of our preceding number, published separately.

68490 POULSEN, Vagn, Ägyptische Kunst. Neues Reich und Spätzeit, Königstein im Taunus, Karl Robert Langewiesche Nachfolger Hans Köster, [1968] (19 × 27 cm; 88 p., map on endpapers, 83 ill. [17 in colour]). Series: Die Blauen Bücher. Pr. cloth DM 7.80

Second part of our number 68488, published separately, without the register.

68491 [PRAUSNITZ, M.], Joseph Leibowitch, *Israel Exploration Journal*, Jerusalem 18 (1968), 133-134.

Obituary notice of our colleague, also known as Josef Leibovitch (9-VI-1898—3-IV-1968). Compare our number 68662.

PRIDEAUX, Tom, see our number 68024.

68492 PRIESE, Karl-Heinz, Nichtägyptische Namen und Wörter in den ägyptischen Inschriften der Könige von Kusch I, *MIO* 14 (1968), 165-191, with an English summary on p. 191.

L'auteur a consacré sa dissertation doctorale aux éléments de la langue de Napata notés en écriture égyptienne. Il étudie ici tout d'abord le nom de Piankhy, qui sans la finale -*y* sert aussi de titre à des rois, déjà sous Piankhy lui-même. Le signe ʿ*nḫy* prend parfois une position bizarre, et manque dans trois documents hiératiques. On peut y voir un simple idéogramme et lire le nom *Pi-ye*: *le vivant*. Cette orthographe est analogue à celle de *mlo*: *bon*, écrit avec le signe *nfr*. *Pi/e* signifierait *vivre*, comme dans le nom de lieu Abore-pi (Musawwarat). Il en serait de même dans Pi/e-ariteñ, dans trois noms d'épouses royales et dans un nom de général. La finale appartiendrait à un verbe *ye*: *être*, *exister*.
Tous les dérivés de *arike*: *engendrer* semblent composés sur

un même modèle. L'auteur lit Ark-pi/e-qo et Arike-Amnete tout comme le nom des deux Ergamène. Diodore aurait lu correctement "Ergamène" II (Ark-amni-qo). On a aussi Arki-ye, abréviation possible pour le même roi; le fils d'Arnekhamani, Ar(i)ke; enfin Arik-tekeñ (*iryg3dyd3nn*).

Aux rares exemples du titre *qore*: *roi*, on peut en ajouter trois, sur des reliefs du temple de Mout à Karnak. On y voit "Piankhy", un *gwr* qui est probablement Tanutamani, et enfin le nom ou titre *phgt3*. Qore apparaît encore dans trois formes du titre "épouse royale", sur des oushebtis de deux reines au cimetière de Nuri.   *J. Custers*

68493 PRIESE, Karl-Heinz, Zwei Wörter in den "spätäthiopischen" Inschriften, *ZÄS* 95,1 (1968), 40-47.

Die zwei Wörter sind.
1. *ikj.t* = ⲟⲕⲉ:ⲁⲕⲉ "Sesam";
2. *ip.t* "Kornmaß".   *M. Heerma van Voss*

PRIESTMAN, K. B., see our number 68245.

68494 PRITCHARD, James B., New Evidence on the Role of the Sea Peoples in Canaan at the Beginning of the Iron Age, *The Role of the Phoenicians* 99-112, with 3 fig. (on p. 105-107).

Discussion of recent discoveries of anthropoid clay coffins, pottery, tombs and metal objects, in connection with the problem of the geographical limits of the influence exercised by the Sea Peoples.

PUECH, Henri-Charles, see our number 68397.

68495 QUECKE, Hans, Ein Pachomiuszitat bei Schenute, *Probleme* 155-171.

Observations about a passage in the works of Shenute (Ch III, 35-112, 15; Am 423, 8-424, 3), where Pachomius is cited.
A translation is given on p. 160.   *L. F. Kleiterp*

QUISPEL, Gilles, see our number 68397.

68496 RACHET, Guy et Marie-Françoise, Dictionnaire de la civilisation égyptienne, Paris, Librairie Larousse, [1968] (12.1 × 17.5 cm; 256 p. containing numerous ill., colour pl. on cover); series; Dictionnaires de l'homme du XXe siècle; rev. *L'Antiquité Classique* 38 (1969), 311 (Roland Tefnin); *Archeologia* 25 (novembre-décembre 1968), 89 (R[égine] P[ernoud]); *Bulletin de l'Association G. Budé*, 1969, 290-291 (J.M.); *Bulletin critique du livre français* 24 (1969), 496 (anonymous); *Connaissance du monde*, n° 122 (février 1969), 86 (anonymous); *Les Études Classiques* 38 (1970), 269 (A. Wankenne); *Nova et Vetera*, Leuven 47 (1969-1970), 377-378 (H. Leclerq); *RdE* 21 (1969), 178 (F. Le Corsu); *Revue archéologique*, 1970, 331-332 (J. Leclant).   Pr NF 9.90

Preceded by a preface, an ample introduction and an extensive chronological table, a very detailed dictionary is offered to the general reader.   *M. Heerma van Voss*

68497 de RACHEWILTZ, Boris, Missione etnologico-archeologica tra i Bega (31 marzo-19 giugno 1967), *Africa*, Roma 23 (1968), 3-19, with 8 pl., 5 fig. (including a map) and summaries in French and English (p. 18-19).

Report of an ethnological-archaeological mission among the Bedja. The author first mentions the most significant data of their history during the Pharaonic, Meroitic and Christian Periods (p. 4-8). On p. 9 he connects the Bedja name for ancient tombs, *akratel*, with Egyptian *igrt*.
The mission excavated some of these tumuli inland of Port Sudan, suggesting that archaeological elements correlate them with the X-group. Moreover, an ancient goldmine was discovered, which the author thinks to be the "Nubian *Nwbyt*".

68498 RAINEY, A. F. Gath-Padalla, *Israel Exploration Journal*, Jerusalem 18 (1968), 1-14, with 1 map.

Study of the Palestinian town Gath-Padalla, the present day Jett, situated on the eastern edge of the Sharon plain. In Egyptian texts of the XVIIIth Dynasty it was called *Knt*, in the geographical list of Shoshenq I *dd-ptr*. The author discusses its history so far as known from the Amarna letters. Except for the Shoshenq text history is silent about it from the Amarna Age until Roman times.

68499 RATIÉ, Suzanne, Le papyrus de Neferoubenef (Louvre III 93), Le Caire, Imprimerie de l'Institut français d'Archéologie orientale, 1968 (20.5 × 28 cm; [VI +] 64 p., 20 pl.) = Bibliothèque d'étude 45; rev. *BiOr* 28 (1971), 191 (Hartwig Altenmüller).

Publication of the *Book of the Dead*, part of which is now in Montpellier and part in the Louvre (cfr our number 66492). It contains in total 69 chapters with 48 vignettes. The author describes the papyrus, its history, its outer appearance, and what is known about its original owner. She dates the text to the post-Amarna period. There are short sections concerning the orthographical characteristics, the rubrics, the style of the vignettes, and short notes to each of the chapters in the order in which they occur on the papyrus. There is no translation.

An appendix deals with chapter 1B which contains a paragraph unknown from elsewhere.

The rather small photographs (2 on one plate) depict the entire papyrus.

REGENSBURGER, Reinhold, see our number 68173.

REINEKE, Walter-Friedrich, see our number 68222.

68500 REYMOND, E. A. E., A Dispute in the Hawara Necropolis, *CdE* XLIII, N° 85 (1968), 55-77; rev. *Enchoria* 1 (1971), 66 (Heinz-Josef Thissen).

Transcription, traduction et commentaire du P. dem. Caire 50127 (Spiegelberg, *CGC* III, pl. 54) daté de l'an 20 d'un roi qui pourrait être Ptolémée Aulète (= 62/61 a.C.). Il s'agit d'une lettre écrite au scribe du temple de Hawara pour régler un litige en rapport avec le payement d'une taxe au temple, entre les embaumeurs et le clergé. L'intérêt du document provient essentiellement de ce qu'il n'appartient à aucune catégorie stéréotypée de documents administratifs ou juridiques, tout en s'intégrant par ailleurs exactement dans la tradition épistolaire figée pratiquement depuis l'époque saito-perse. On y soulignera le rôle important du scribe du temple (*sh̭ n ḥwt nṯr*) dans la gestion financière du temple, à qui une longue note est consacrée.   *Ph. Derchain*

68501 RIAD, Henri, Quelques inscriptions Grecques et Latines du temple de Louxor, *ASAE* 60 (1968), 281-295, with 5 pl.

The majority of the inscriptions published in this article comes from the entrance to the 1st pylon of Ramesses II. Many of them were written in the month of Pauni, a clear indication that they were left by pilgrims attending the famous Valley Feast. Also published is a cross-shaped Coptic epitaph found at the site of the St.-Thekla church in front of the temple.   *Dieter Mueller*

68502 RICHTER, G. M. A., Korai. Archaic Greek Maidens. A Study of the Development of the Kore Type in Greek Sculpture with 800 Illustrations, including 400 from Photographs by Alison Frantz, [London], Phaidon, [1968] (23 × 31.3 cm; XII + 327 p., many fig. 22 pl., 689 ill;); rev.*AJA* 73 (1969), 383-384 (John Griffith Pedley); *Archaeology* 22 (1969), 173-175 (Werner Fuchs); *Pantheon* 27 (1969), 432 (E. Bielefeld).

This is a companion volume to the author's *Kouroi. Archaic Greek Youths* (1960) and deals with the standing Kore type, from early to late archaic times.

On p. 4 the author demonstrates that the Kore type, like that of the Kouros, derived inspiration from Egypt (see also pl. I). From there also the type of disk earring was ultimately borrowed (p. 11).

68503 RIEFSTAHL, Elizabeth, Ancient Egyptian Glass and Glazes In The Brooklyn Museum, [New York], The Brooklyn Museum, [1968] (22.2 × 28.7 cm; XVI + 118 p., 100 ill., 12 colour pl., colour frontispiece) = Wilbour Monographs 1; rev. *AJA* 74 (1970), 210-211 (Dan Barag); *L'Antiquité Classique* 39 (1970), 319-320 (Roland Tefnin); *Apollo* Vol. XCIII, N° 108 (February, 1971), 148 (T. G. H. James); *BiOr* 26 (1969), 192-193 (Birgit Nolte); *CdE* XLV, N° 89 (1970), 79-80 (Madeleine Trokay); *Jahrbuch des Römisch-Germanischen Zentralmuseums*, Mainz 16 (1969), 199-200 (Birgit Nolte); *JEA* 56 (1970), 217-218 (Geoffrey Martin); *Rivista* 44 (1969), 327-329 (Claudio Barocas); *ВДИ* 3 (117), 1971, 153-155 (V. V. Pavlov).

The author of our number 618 presents here the best of the glass and glazed objects in the Brooklyn collection. Ninety-three pieces are shown, with descriptions and comments. Technical details are dealt with in an introduction; cfr the bibliography.
Three concordances conclude the book.
Foreword by Bernard V. Bothmer and Thomas S. Buechner. Compare our number 68445. *M. Heerma van Voss*

RINALDI, Celeste, see our number 68398.

68504 RITTER, G., Zur Entwicklungsgeschichte der Neurologie. Die altägyptischen Papyri, *Der Nervenarzt*, Heidelberg-Berlin 39 (1968), 541-546.

The author gives a survey of Egyptian texts dealing with afflictions of the nervous system and, with due caution, attempts a diagnosis of the various symptoms mentioned there. Quoting from Pap. Ebers, Med. Pap. Berlin, Med. Pap. Kahun, and Pap. Ed. Smith, he emphasizes the unique position of the latter in the history of medicine.

Dieter Mueller

68505 ROBINSON, James M., The Coptic Gnostic Library Today, *New Testament Studies*, Cambridge 14 (1967-1968), 356-401.

The author describes the history of the publication of the Nag Hammadi manuscripts with its various publication projects; the archaeology and the palaeography of the texts, and non-Christian Gnosticism in general. He adds a catalogue of the Coptic Gnostic library with a complete bibliography (p. 383-401).

68506 ROBINSON, Paul, The Three Scarabs and the Cylinder Seal from Tholos B, Platonos, *Studi micenei ed egeo-anatolici*, Roma 5 (1968), 25-29.

This is an appendix to an article by Keith Branigan about the Mesara Tholoi and the Middle Minoan Chronology. Robinson studies the three scarabs there found, all three already published by Pendlebury in his *Aegyptiaca* (Cambridge, 1930) and here dated to the XIIth or XIIIth Dynasty.

68507 ROCCATI, Alessandro, Una lettera inedita dell' Antico Regno, *JEA* 54 (1968), 14-22, with 1 table (= p. 21) and 2 pl.

This letter in Turin Museum consists of a damaged page of papyrus, measuring 21 cm × 25 cm and dates from the VIth Dynasty. In conventional official style it deals with work in the fields and mentions such figures as the Sole Companions *Šm3j* and *Sn-k3w*. The author gives translation, grammatical commentary and a table of some interesting hieratic signs. E. Uphill

ROEDER, Günther, see our number 68294.

68508 ROLLEY, Claude, Les cultes égyptiens à Thasos: à propos de quelques documents nouveaux, *Bulletin de Correspondance Hellénique*, Athènes-Paris 92 (1968), 187-219, with 36 fig. and 4 pl.

The author first studies a bronze bust of Sarapis found on Thasos, comparing it with similar pieces of sculpture and demonstrating that it has been made in Egypt. He then collects more evidence for Egyptian cults on the island, particularly by the study of three sculptured heads of children with a special coiffure.

68509 ROMANELLI, Pietro, Aristide Calderini, *Studi Romani*, Roma 16 (1968), 485-486, with a portrait.

Obituary notice.

68510 ROSENVASSER, A., Excavations of the Ramesside Temple at Aksha, Nubia, Republic of the Sudan; Their Contribution to the History of the Place and Period, *Proceedings* 17-19.

Summary of the results of the three campaigns at Aksha (cfr our numbers 62598, 63517, and 64419).

ROWLEY, Harold H., see our number 68436.

68511 RUBINSHTEIN, R. I., О природе ушебти, *ВДИ* 2 (104), 1968, 80-89, with 1 ill. and an English summary on p. 88-89.

"On the Nature of the Ushebtis".

From the study of *Coffin Texts*, Spell 472 and the *Book of the Dead*, chapter 151, the author concludes that the ushebtis neither represent the dead man himself, nor his slaves. The name written on the statuette is not its own but that of the dead man, which is invoked by the priest in pronouncing the magical formula over it in the mortuary chamber. The object of the ritual was to bring the ushebti figure to life as a magic doll which has to perform all service obligations in the Netherworld.

68512 RUDOLPH, Kurt, Der gnostische "Dialog" als literatisches Genus, *Probleme* 85-107.

The Dialogue in Coptic gnostic literature is characterized by a teacher-pupil relationship: it approaches the form of a catechism. There is no discussion with opponents.

L. F. Kleiterp

68513 SÄVE-SÖDERBERGH, Torgny, Egyptisk Egenart, Grundproblem i Gammalegyptisk Kultur, Stockholm, Wahlström & Widstrand, 1968 (11.5 × 19 cm; 124 p., 21 ill. in text, 28 ill. on 12 pl.) = W & W-serien 186.

A revised edition of a book with the same title published in 1945. The chapters contain introductions to The Prehistory of Egypt, Egyptian Theology, The Basic Problems of Art, while the final chapter contains reflections on Individual and Society. There are also a tabular summary of the Egyptian history and a short bibliography. *B. J. Peterson*

68514 SÄVE-SÖDERBERGH, Torgny, Ökenbergens Herrar, *Medeltid. Närbilder från fyra världsdelar*, Malmö (1968), 64-75.

A Swedish broadcast lecture about the Christian kingdoms in Nubia. *B. J. Peterson*

68515 SAID, Rushdi and Fouad YOUSRI, Origin and Pleistocene History of River Nile Near Cairo, Egypt, *BIE* 45 (session 1963-1964), 1968, 1-30, with 7 fig., a map and a table.

Results are given of a study on the lithology and foraminiferal content of four wells that were drilled in the River Nile flood-plain, Cairo, Egypt. Two of the wells reached the solid Middle Eocene limestone upon which the Nile sediments rest at depths 825 and 568 m. These limestones belong to the "building-stone horizon" of the Egyptian Middle Eocene which is exposed along the cliffs of the Nile in the immediate vicinity. This seems to indicate the true origin of the River hitherto taken as a feature of erosion. The date of the faulting is given as late Oligocene; this faulting was later rejuvenated in early Pliocene and Pleistocene (Sicilian) times. The Pleistocene history of the Nile is discussed and a specific table of events is attempted. *Author's own abstract*

68516 SALEH ALY, Mohammed, Een nieuw graf ontdekt in Thebe, *Spiegel Historiael*, Bussum 3 (1968), 258, with 3 ill.

A concise description of the badly damaged Theban tomb of Qenamon (number 412) discovered in 1966; period: Tuthmosis III-Amenophis II. *M. Heerma van Voss*

68517 SANKARANANDA, Swami, The Sātvatas on the Egyptian Throne (B.C. 3315-B.C. 525), *Proceedings 22*.

The author suggests the presence of an Indian tribe in Egypt.

68518 SARIANIDI, V. I., О великом лазуритовом пути на древнем Востоке, Краткие сообщения о докладах и полевых исследованиях Института археологии. 114. Древности Сибири, Дальнего Востока и Средней Азии (at head of title: Академия наук СССР. Институт археологии), Москва, 1968, 3-9.

"Über dem großen Lasursteinweg im alten Orient".

68519 SATZINGER, Helmut, Äthiopische Parallelen zum ägyptischen s$\underline{d}$m.f, *MDAIK* 23 (1968), 163-166.

Den verschiedenen s$\underline{d}$m.f— Bildungen können nur teilweise passivische Partizipien zugrunde liegen. Für die übrigen möchten die beiden hier besprochenen Parallelen eine Erklärung bieten. *M. Heerma van Voss*

68520 SATZINGER, Helmut, Koptische Urkunden. III. Band, 2. Heft, Berlin, Bruno Hessling, 1968, (18.4 × 23.3 cm; [II +]142 p. [= p. 87 — 228], 4 pl. [= pl. V-VIII]); at head of title: Ägyptische Urkunden aus den Staatlichen Museen Berlin; rev. *Orientalia* 40 (1971), 128-129 (E. des Places). Pr. DM 52

Sequel to our number 67486.
This second part contains 170 documents (nos 375-544), of which the nos 437 to 544 are small fragments. Six of the larger texts are biblical, eight magical, three contain records of debts, eleven of them are letters, while the remainder is of various nature, literary as well as legal and economic. Apart from a description there is given of every document a transcription and a translation with notes to both.
A concordance to the inventory numbers for both fascicles on p. 195-196; complete indexes to Coptic and Greek words, names, *etc.*, on p. 197-224; additions and corrections on p. 225-228.

68521 SATZINGER, Helmut, Die negativen Konstruktionen im Alt- und Mittelägyptischen, Berlin, Bruno Hessling, 1968 (17 × 24 cm; XIV + 77 p.) = Münchner Ägyptologische Studien herausgegeben von Hans Wolfgang Müller und Wolfhart Westendorf 12; rev. *BiOr* 26 (1969), 202-203 (Alessandro Roccati); *CdE* XLIV, N° 88 (1969), 286-288 (J. Quaegebeur); *JEA* 56 (1970), 205-214 (Mordechai Gilula); *Mundus* 5 (1919), 36-37 (Hellmut Brunner). Pr. DM 24

Die Negationspartikel *n*, die prädikative Negation *nn*, die Negationsverben *tm* und *jm*, das Relativadjektiv *jwtj* und *jwt*, die Negationen *w*, *nfr pw* und *nfr n* werden nach Funktion, Stellung im Satz und Bedeutung dargestellt. Zahlreiche Beispiele erläutern die Gebrauchsweisen.
Register S. 69-72; Stellenverzeichnes S. 73-77.
E. M. Wolf-Brinkmann

68522 SATZINGER, Helmut, Der Opferstein des *Šmswj* aus dem Mittleren Reich, *MDAIK* 23 (1968), 160-162, with 1 pl.

Re-publication of an offering table; cfr *ASAE* 16 (1916), 95-96. This time, translation, commentary and photograph have been added.
The object (early Dyn. XII ?) was acquired by the museum in Berlin-Charlottenburg in 1966; Inv. N° 30/66.
M. Heerma van Voss

68523 SAUNERON, Serge, Les désillusions de la guerre asiatique (Pap. Deir el-Médinêh 35), *Kêmi* 18 (1968), 17-27, with 1 pl. and 1 p. with hieroglyphic text.

Le feuillet de papyrus hiératique étudié ici, ramessé à Deir el-Médinêh, mesure 11 × 18 cm. A part le petit texte du verso, qui forme un document indépendant, il porte une page incomplète de sept lignes en noir sans rubrique. On y trouve un texte littéraire dont le thème est la satire du métier des armes. L'auteur donne la photographie, la copie en hiéroglyphes, une traduction française et un commentaire. Des détails caractéristiques font la valeur du texte, témoin de la rivalité entre civils et militaires au Nouvel Empire; il évoque toutes les misères humaines que peut comporter une victoire. *J. Custers*

68524 SAUNERON, Serge, L'Égyptologie, Paris, Presses Universitaires de France, 1968 (11.5 × 17.7 cm; 128 p.) = "Que sais-je?". Le point des connaissances actuelles. N° 1312; rev. *BiOr* 26 (1969), 325-326 (Claudia Dolzani); *CdE* XLIV, N° 88 (1969), 263-265 (Michel Malaise); *OLZ* 66 (1971), 239-241 (E. Staehelin); *RdE* 21 (1969), 179 (F. Le Corsu).

Chapter I deals with the origins and history of Egyptology. In chapter II the author explains what seem to him to be the tasks of the science: protection and restoration of the monuments, scientific exploitation of the available sources, extension of the field of researches, publication of the results of studies.

Chapter III discusses the present state of Egyptology: institutions, handbooks and periodicals, university chairs, *etc.*, while in Chapter IV the author sketches his views on its future.

Bibliographical notes on p. 127.

68525 SAUNERON, Serge, Les Inscriptions Ptolemaïques du Temple de Mout à Karnak, *BIE* 45 (session 1963-1964), 1968, 45-52.

Quatre séries de textes aident à comprendre mieux les rites.
1. Mout et Sekhmet sont les deux fonctions d'une même déesse, qui répartit les génies de mort, mais protège qui lui plaît.
2. La musique écarte les mauvais génies; la danse, à laquelle participiaient des étrangers, célèbre et assure le retour périodique de la déesse lointaine.
3. Outre les cycles de la lionne vengeresse qui s'endort, et du lac en demi-lune *išrw*, on entrevoit celui du saule, qui revient (!) à Thèbes deux fois l'an, "pourvu de tous ses ornements".
4. La barque sacrée se rendait normalement au temple d'Amon, mais pouvait aussi naviguer plusieurs jours de suite sur l'*išrw*. *J. Custers*

68526 SAUNERON, Serge, Liminaire, *Kêmi* 18 (1968), 7-8.

The author sketches his programm for *Kêmi* of which he is the new editor.

68527 SAUNERON, Serge, Pierre Montet (1885-1966), *Kêmi* 18 (1968), 9-15, with a photograph.

Obituary notice. Compare our number 66651.

68528 SAUNERON, Serge, Quelques monuments de Soumenou au Musée de Brooklyn, *Kêmi* 18 (1968), 57-78, with 6 pl.

La stèle trouvée récemment, parmi les restes d'un temple du Nouvel Empire, au village de Dahamcha permet d'identifier cet endroit, et non Gebelein, qui est un peu au sud, avec *Swmnw*, lieu de culte de Sobek. Ces dernières années, le Musée de Brooklyn a acquis plusieurs monuments qui évoquent les cultes de Soumenou et datent de la XVIIIe dynastie. L'auteur en publie ici les inscriptions. La stèle

66.174.2 représente le fantassin Amenemhat devant Sobek-Rê, *nb* et *ḥry-ib* de Soumenou. Le joli groupe 40.523 montre le couple Nebsen — Nebet-ta; des divinités de Thèbes et de Soumenou s'y trouvent associées. Le propriétaire de la statue-bloc 66.174.1, datée par un cartouche d'Aÿ, porte le même nom que le roi; pour la clarté, l'auteur rend le nom sous la forme Iÿ. Dans l'épigraphie, on relève plusieurs épithètes de Sobek-Rê et de Thot. Le dernier est dit notamment "dans l'arbre *im3*", désignation que le Papyrus de Strasbourg attribue à Sobek. Les deux dieux devaient partager une même chapelle à Dahamcha. Iÿ était "second prophète d'Amon, premier prophète de Mout, intendant de la maison de la reine Tiyi dans la maison d'Amon". Sa mère Moutemnebou fut favorite royale, et sœur d'une reine, probablement Tiyi ou peut-être Nefertity. La fonction occupée par un allié de la dynastie porte à voir le retour des rois à Thèbes, après Amarna, dans une atmosphère rassérénée.

J. Custers

68529 SAUNERON, Serge, La statue d'Ahmosé, dit Rourou au Musée de Brooklyn, *Kêmi* 18 (1968), 45-50, with 3 pl.

Cette jolie petite statue de grès sombre, à peine poli, porte au Musée de Brooklyn le n° 61.196. L'attitude du personnage assis évoque l'art du Moyen Empire, mais les noms de personnes et le lieu de trouvaille indiquent les règnes de Hatshepsout et de Thoutmès III. L'auteur traduit les textes, qui décorent le long manteau collant, les faces latérales du siège et le pilier dorsal. Ahmosé surnommé Rourou, *wʿb* et premier fils royal d'Amon (c.-à-d. porteur de barque) en avant d'Amon, y rappelle des cadeaux royaux. Pour la famille de Rourou, voir notre n° 68256. La mention d'Anubis *nb T3-ḥḏ* pourrait s'expliquer par la présence d'une chapelle à proximité de Gebelein.

J. Custers

68530 SAUNERON, Serge, Le Temple d'Esna, Le Caire, 1968 (21.9 × 28 cm; XXXVIII + 394 p., numerous [unnumbered] fig., 3 pl.) = Publications de l'Institut français d'Archéologie orientale. Esna III; rev. *BiOr* 28 (1971), 318-320 (E. A. E. Reymond); *JEA* 57 (1971), 229-230 (J. Gwyn Griffiths).

Sequel to our number 63449.

The present volume contains the texts on the 18 columns of the hypostyle hall. Compare also our number 62514, where most of them have been translated.

The introduction describes the columns, the disposition of the signs, and the use of cryptography, and discusses the date of the texts (between A.D. 81 and 161), the mutilations of some signs, as well as the problems encountered in publishing the present volume.

There follow copies of all texts in printed hieroglyphs, while the exact shape of individual signs frequently has been indicated in the notes. Moreover the scenes on the columns are reproduced in line drawings. At the head of each of the 205 sections three drawings indicate the exact place of the text.

Various indexes on p. 387-392.

68531 SAUNERON, Serge, Villes et légendes d'Égypte (§ XV-XXIV), *BIFAO* 66 (1968), 11-35, with 2 pl. and 4 ill. including 3 maps.

Suite de notre n° 67491.

L'auteur s'occupe du camp de Toëto-Psinaula dans le Panopolite, de Pakerkê du Panopolite, du village d'Edfa (voir notre n° 64428, V), de Thkabat, près de Tabenêsé, de Tafnîs, de *Pr-ḥf* (nouveau temple ptolemaïque en Moyenne Égypte; à comparer aussi notre no 63282), de la prémière identification du site de Memphis, de Mechellat Chais chez Léon l'Africain, de Mesia dans l'*Itinéraire Éthiopien* de Zorzi, enfin de Beni 'Ady: l'arrivée des caravanes du Soudan.

M. Heerma van Voss

SAUNERON, Serge, see also our numbers 68364 and 68365.

68532 SAVAGE, George, A Concise History of Bronzes, London, Thames and Hudson, [1968] (14.8 × 20.9 cm; 264 p., 209 ill. [16 in colour], colour ill. on cover).

Ancient Egypt is mentioned in the Introduction (p. 11-12, with ill. 3 and 8), and particularly in chapter one (p. 36-42, with ill. 17-23).

68533 SCHAEFERS, Rolf, Die Goettermärchen auf dem Granitschrein von Ismailia, *Armant*, Köln 1, 1968, 10-19.

Traduction partielle précédée d'une courte introduction mais non commentée des inscriptions du naos 2248 du musée d'Ismailia, publié en dernier lieu par G. Goyon (et non Gordon comme l'imprime l'auteur) "les travaux de Chou et les tribulations de Geb" dans *Kêmi* 6 (1936), 1-42.

Ph. Derchain

68534 SCHENKE, Hans-Martin, Exegetische Probleme der zweiten Jakobusapokalypse in Nag-Hammadi-Codex V, *Probleme* 109-114.

Codex V of the Nag-Hammadi papyri, pp. 46/47: the author disputes the suggestions of Böhlig (A. Böhlig/P. Labib, *Koptisch-gnostische Apokalypsen aus Codex V von Nag-*

Hammadi im Koptischen Museum zu Alt-Kairo, Wiss. Z. Halle 1963 Sonderband) and Kasser (*Museon* 78 [1965] 85-91; 302-304) and gives his own emendation and translation. *L. F Kleiterp*

68535 SCHENKEL, Wolfgang, Beiträge zur mittelägyptischen Syntax V. Sätze mit (festem) Verbum in der Suffixkonjugation oder im Imperativ, *ZÄS* 95,1 (1968), 47-54.

The article lists sentence patterns where the "finite" verb is followed by one or two nouns that can, but need not be, expressed. *Dieter Mueller*

68536 SCHENKEL, Wolfgang, Syntagmen mit infiniten Verbalformen als Transformate von Sätzen, *MDAIK* 23 (1968), 167-181.

The author points out that syntagms with an infinite verb form (infinitive, participles, *etc.*) as predicate are closely related to ordinary sentences, and gives a survey of the various sentence patterns from which such syntagms may be derived through transformation. *Dieter Mueller*

68537 SCHENKEL, W., Wortakzent und Silbenstruktur im Ägyptischen, *OLZ* 63 (1968), 533-541.

Review article of Gerhard Fecht, *Wortakzent und Silbenstruktur* (our number 60232).

SCHILD, Romuald, see our number 68630.

68538 SCHILLER, A. Arthur, The Budge Papyrus of Columbia University, *JARCE* 7 (1968), 79-118, with 8 folding pl.

Editio princeps of the manuscript described in our abstracts 64436 and 64437.
The author offers a printed text with *apparatus criticus*, and a parallel translation with notes, as well as photographic plates. He discusses palaeography, philology, prosopography, geography, and the events described in the hearings. *M. Heerma van Voss*

68539 SCHIPPERGES, Heinrich, 5000 Jahre Chirurgie. Magie. Handwerk. Wissenschaft. Die Geschichte der Wundarzneikunst seit den vor- und frühgeschichtlichen Anfängen, Stuttgart, Kosmos-Verlag, Franckh'sche Verlagshandlung, 1967 (13.2 × 19.1 cm; 96 p., 16 pl. and 8 fig.); rev. *Mundus* 4 (1968), 272-273 (W. Hoffmann-Axthelm). Pr. DM 3.80

This survey of the history of surgery by the director of the Institute for the History of Medicine at Heidelberg contains a chapter on the *Papyrus Edwin Smith* (p. 13-22), with translations after Breasted.

68540 SCHMID, Hans Heinrich, Gerechtigkeit als Weltordnung. Hintergrund und Geschichte des alttestamentlichen Gerechtigkeitsbegriffes, Tübingen, J. C. B. Mohr, 1968 (16 × 23.5 cm; VIII + 203 p.) = Beiträge zur historischen Theologie herausgegeben von Gerhard Ebeling 40; rev. *BiOr* 28 (1971), 153-154 (anonymous); *Booklist* 1969, 51 (A. R. J[ohnson]); *Journal of Biblical Literature* 88 (1969), 484-486 (Burke O. Long); *Nederlands Theologisch Tijdschrift* 24 (1969-1970), 130-133 (C. J. Labuschagne). Pr. paper DM 32 cloth DM 37

In a particular section (p. 46-61) the author deals extensively with Maat. There are the following subsections: kingship, wisdom, law, nature and fertility, war and victory, cult and offering, and common parlance. Several texts are cited in translation.

68541 SCHOTT, Siegfried, Falke, Geier und Ibis als Krönungsboten, *ZÄS* 95, 1 (1968), 54-65, with 1 pl.

Verfasser bearbeitet ein Bild, das sich — verschieden beschriftet — im Chonstempel von Karnak und im Horustempel von Edfu findet. Cfr unsere Nummer 57178, Nr. 99a-99k. Er erläutert das Thema fast ausschließlich an Hand ptolemäisches Materials. *M. Heerma van Voss*

68542 SCHOTT, Siegfried, Schreiber und Schreibgerät im Jenseits, *JEA* 54 (1968), 45-50.

The writer discusses the role of scribes and the use of scribes tools in the hereafter as conceived by the Egyptians. Next to the group of Spells on Embalming, the Offering Feast, comes another rite in which the *Pyramid Texts* deal with the ascent of the dead king to Heaven. When the king goes through a great gate guarded by two gods he invokes a scribe, calling on him to break up his writing materials and tear up his papyrus roll (*P T.* 952-5). In the office of the Sun god boxes ($hn.w$) stand ready, as depicted in the tomb scenes for the writer of documents, and the office overseer opens his enactment ($wḏ.w.f$). "Letters" ($mḏ3.wt$) are also mentioned in *P.T.* 491.

Connections with magic and demons found in the next world are also discussed and the evidence supplied by the *Coffin Texts* on the part played by Thoth and the scribe of Osiris in this context. *E. Uphill*

68543 SCHULMAN, Alan R., A Private Triumph in Brooklyn, Hildesheim and Berlin, *JARCE* 7 (1968), 27-35, with 5 ill. on 2 pl.

The Brooklyn relief 48.112 was published *i.a.* by Cooney in

our number 2302, fig. 39 and p. [46]. He accepted Capart's identification of the fragments Hildesheim 2370 and Berlin 12964 as parts of the same scene.
Schulman agrees so far as the Hildesheim piece is concerned. He substitutes, however, Berlin 24025 for 12964 (the former with reservations).
The author dates the scene to the reign of Horemheb.

M. Heerma van Voss

68544 SEDKI, Kamâl, Ptolemaic Baths of Kôm Ganâdy, *ASAE* 60 (1968), 221-225, with 6 pl.

In 1962, several baths with bath-tubs and numerous footbaths were excavated at a *kôm* 10 km west of Abû-Ḥommos. They resemble those found at Kôm El Aḥmar and Edfou.

Dieter Mueller

68545 SEIDL, Erwin, Ägyptische Rechtsgeschichte der Saiten- und Perserzeit. 2. neubearbeitete Auflage, Glückstadt, Verlag J.J. Augustin, 1968 (21 × 29.6 cm; 99 p.) = Ägyptologische Forschungen begründet von Alexander Scharff†, herausgegeben von Hans-Wolfgang Müller. Heft 20; rev. *Enchoria* 1 (1971), 66 (Heinz-Jozef Thissen); *Studia et Documenta Historiae et Iuris* 35 (1969), 497-499 (Edda Bresciani).

Second, revised and enlarged edition of our number 4858.
Although this second edition deals with the same subjects in the same order as the first one there are several new paragraphs, and what have been paragraphs have become now complete sections. The total length has been enlarged from 78 to 99 pages.
There is a completely new introduction, and three indexes, a general one, one of Greek and one of Egyptian terms (p. 95-99).

68546 SEIDL, Erwin, Der Prozeß Chrateanch gegen Tefhape im Jahre 170 v. Chr., *Zeitschrift für vergleichende Rechtswissenschaft*, Stuttgart 69 (1968), 96-117.

New translation of the Demotic Pap. Brit. Mus. 10591 containing the lawsuit of a lady Khrateankh, the only case from the ancient world of which all documents have been preserved. The case concerns the rights of inheritance of sons born in two successive marriages of their father.

68547 SEIDL, Erwin, Eine Ptolemäische Eheurkunde der Kölner Sammlung, *in*: *Antidoron Martino David oblatum. Miscellanea Papyrologica*, Leiden, E. J. Brill, 1968 (= Papyrologica Lugduno Batava, 17), 122-125, with 1 pl.

Publication of the Demotic Pap. Köln inv. 1864 of the years 207-205 B.C. concerning matrimonial property. The author presents the texts in photograph, transliteration and translation, with some comments.

68548 SEIDLER, G. L., The Emergence of the Eastern World. Seven Essays on Political Ideas. With a Foreword by Sir Isaiah Berlin, Oxford-London-Edinburgh-New York-Toronto-Sydney-Paris-Braunschweig, Pergamon Press, [1968] (15.3 × 23.5 cm; XII + 260 p.); rev. *American Historical Review* 74 (1968-1969), 1244-1245 (Hayden V. White).

In the first essay *The Political Thought of the Ancient East* a section is devoted to "The Egyptian Theocracy" (p. 46-50). The Polish author not being an Egyptologist there are numerous mistakes and misinterpretations of the sources.

SELHEIM, Rudolf, see our number 68198.

68549 SEMPER, N. E., Элементы содержания двух амарнских гимнов Солнцу, IV Сессия по древнему Востоку 40-41.

"Elemente der Komposition der zwei Amarnahymnen an der Sonne".
Vergleichende Untersuchung der grossen und der kleinen Hymne. Es wird versucht die religiös-politische Konzeption Akhnaton's zu formulieren. *E. S. Bogoslovsky*

SETTGAST, Jürgen, see our number 68038.

68550 SEWELL, Barbara, Egypt under the Pharaohs, London, Evans Brothers Limited, [1968] (18.5 × 25.2 cm; 144 p., 2 maps, 88 ill., 16 colour pl., ill. on endpapers); series: Life in Ancient Lands. Edited by Edward Bacon; rev. *BiOr* 26 (1969), 53-54 (Birgit Nolte). Pr. bound 42 s.

Description of the Egyptian civilisation for the general public.

SHINER, Joel L., see our number 68630.

68551 SHORE, A. F., The Sale of the House of Senkhonsis Daughter of Phibis, *JEA* 54 (1968), 193-198, with 1 pl.; rev. *Enchoria* 1 (1971), 67 (Heinz-Jozef Thissen).

This interesting legal document is one of a series of demotic papyri dealing with property on the east bank of the Nile at Thebes in a quarter known as The-House-of-the-Cow, which lay in the angle formed by the north side of the temenos wall of the temple of Amūn at Karnak and the west side of the wall of the temple of Monthu. Two pieces of papyrus in the British Museum, dated to Year 5 of King Ptolemy Soter supply details of the sale of a house, the vendor being the husband of Senkhonsis who was a pastophoros of Amūn apparently, the reason for the transaction being the funeral expenses of the wife, which as usual in ancient Egypt seem to have been considerable. *E. Uphill*

68552 SKEAT, T. C., and E. G. TURNER, An Oracle of Hermes Trismegistos at Saqqâra, *JEA* 54 (1968), 199-208, with 2 pl.; rev. *Enchoria* 1 (1971), 67 (Heinz-Josef Thissen).

Study of two Greek ostraca found during Emery's excavations at Saqqara in 1966. One of them (C. G. 7-42), also contains four lines written in Demotic, which are here transliterated and translated by H. S. Smith (p. 201).

68553 ŚLIWA, Joachim, Menat-égide du Musée National de Cracovie, *Études et Travaux* II 33-37, with 3 ill.

The author describes an aegis from the National Museum in Cracov (Inv. N° XI-879, formerly in the collection of Czartoryski). After a detailed description of the object, he pays attention to its destination. *A. Szczudłowska*

SLOW, Dorothy, see our number 68245.

68554 SMITH, H. S., A Note on Amnesty, *JEA* 54 (1968), 209-214.

The Ptolemies followed Hellenic practice in the use of amnesty at times of national peril or after civil war, which is exemplified by the Rosetta Decree of Ptolemy V Epiphanes following the revolts of 197 B.C. Prisoners were released and property restored to combatants. But these Ptolemaic amnesties unlike the Greek ones were not emergency measures but royal boons granted at the beginning of new reigns or periods thus following an older oriental custom, as for example when the Hebrews released slaves in the sabbatical fallow year or in the jubilee year. The release of the Jewish King Jehoiachin by Amel-Marduk King of Babylon and the 'release to the provinces' by the King of Persia at Esther's feast, are both of a different order, but Pharaonic Egypt provides similar examples in the *Instruction of 'Onkhsheshonqy* and much earlier under Ramesses IV, which although described in poetical form is comparable as is another case mentioned in the Israel stela hymn of Merneptah. *E. Uphill*

SMITH, H. S., see also our number 68552.

68555 SÖDERBERG, Bertil, The Sistrum. A Musicological Study, *Ethnos*, Stockholm 1-4, 1968, 90-133, with 20 fig.

It is possible that sistra with closed frames had their origin in Egypt.

In Ethiopia the sistrum is still used, and it can be assumed that it is based on a Jewish tradition.

From a physiological point of view, the sistrum is an instrument which effects the musician's bodily rhythm as he plays. *M. Heerma van Voss*

68556 SOLLE, Gerhard, Die Katarakte des Nils, *Natur und Museum*, Frankfurt 98 (1968), 211-216; 269-274; 341-348; 449-460.

Der Aufsatz bringt eine geologisch hervorragend fundierte Übersicht über den Nillauf von Sennar-Damm bis Assuan, wobei besonders die Katarakte gründlich auf ihr Gestein, aber auch auf ihre Funktion bei Niedrig- und Hochwasser hin untersucht werden. Die ältere Literatur wird berücksichtigt und behutsam, aber einleuchtend berichtigt (so besonders die grundlegende Untersuchung von Fairbridge, unsere Nummer 63159). Manche Ergebnisse über geschichtliche Wandlungen der Flußhöhe haben für Ägyptologen Bedeutung; die Rätsel der rund 20 m über dem heutigen Höchststand liegenden Wassermarken der 12./13. Dynastie von Semna-Kumma bleiben trotz eingehender Diskussion bestehen, wenn man nicht den Ausdruck "Mund des Nils" als Wasserstandsmarke, sondern als Bezeichnung der Südgrenze des ägyptischen Reiches ansehen will, wie Solle als Ausweg aus dem Dilemma erwägt. Eine Erklärung der Höhendifferenz scheint den Geographen nicht möglich zu sein. *H. Brunner*

SOLLER, Karl, see our number 68570.

68557 SPAULL, C. H. S., Bibliography of Jaroslav Černý, *JEA* 54 (1968), 3-8.

68558 STADELMANN, Rainer, Die Abwehr der Seevölker unter Ramses III, *Saeculum*, Freiburg/München 19 (1968), 156-171.

The author gives a survey of the present knowledge concerning the Sea-Peoples, among others dealing with the following subjects: the difference between the peoples mentioned under Merenptah and those of the attack in year 8 of Ramses III; the origin of the Sea-Peoples; the place of Ramses' battles; the settlement of the Philistines in Palestine and the subsequent loss of their Asian empire by the Egyptians.

68559 STÄGER, Lorenz, Jean-Jacques Hess-von Wyss. 11. Januar 1866 bis 29. April 1949, *Asiatische Studien*, Bern 22 (1968), 137-145.

Short biography of J. J. Hess, between 1889 and 1908 professor of Egyptology and Assyriology at Freiburg (Switzerland). He is known by his publication of the Story of Setne: *Der demotische Roman von Stne Ḥa-m-us*, Leipzig, 1888.

68560 STARK, Kurt, Arbeitsbericht über Untersuchungen zu Kompositionsgesetz und Maßordnung am Löwentempel von Musawwarat es Sufra, *Wissenschaftliche Zeitschrift der Humboldt-Universität zu Berlin*, Gesellschafts-Sprachwissenschaftliche Reihe 17 (1968), 685-687, with 1 fig.

An examination of the dimensions of the pylon showed that its proportions are based on medial section. The measurements, probably based on the Meroitic cubit of 51 cm, follow an arithmetic progression where the sum of the two preceding numbers yields the third. *Dieter Mueller*

68561 STETTLER, Michael, Die Abegg-Stiftung Bern in Riggisberg, *Du. Kulturelle Monatsschrift*, Zürich 28 (1968), 312-370, with 49 pl. (one on cover; 13 in colour) and summary in English on p. [I].   Pr. of separate copy Sw. fr. 5

The May issue of this periodical is devoted to the art collection of Werner Abegg in the Swiss village Riggisberg.
Among the pieces published here two originate from pharaonic Egypt. 4 is a relief fragment (40 × 22 cm) showing a male head and ascribed to the reign of Amenophis III (p. 314 and 318). A bronze Horus falcon (height 19 cm) is given the number 5; p. 314 and 319 (in colour); XXVIth Dynasty.
Out of four Coptic objects we mention Nr. 20 (p. 335 and 338) to be compared with our numbers 60511, 61143 and 63108, 1. *M. Heerma van Voss*

68562 STEWART, H. M., A Monument with Amarna Traits, *Bulletin of the Institute of Archaeology*, London 7 (1967), 1968, 85-87, with 1 pl.

Study of the stelophorous statue of the scribe Nakhtmin (B.M. No 1222); cfr I. E. S. Edwards, *Hieroglyphic Texts from Egyptian Stelae, etc.*, part VIII (1939), pl. 44.
In the arch of the stela the owner and his wife are represented kneeling in front of the solar bark with the sun-disk. On account of its technique and representations the author ascribes the statue to the early Amarna Period, when the traditional religion was not yet proscribed. The text, a short hymn and a funerary prayer, is in the traditional style. The author gives a translation of this text.

68563 STILLFRIED, Bernhard, Arbeit der Österreichischen Kulturinstituten im Nahen und Mittleren Osten, *Bustan*, Wien 9, Heft 3-4 (1968), 17-20.

The author refers to the Austrian excavations in Sayala and Tell el Dab'a (p. 18).

68564 STRECKER, Johannes, Restaurierungsmethoden an ägyptischen Denkmälern, *Raggi*, Zürich 8 (1968), 127-145, with 24 ill. and an English summary (p. 145).

The author, member of the staff of the Roemer-Pelizaeus Museum in Hildesheim, discusses different methods for preserving Egyptian limestone monuments with salt content. He decidedly prefers the method of leaching the stone in water, by which also restorations with gypsum, old as well as modern, will disappear, showing in some instances particularities of the sculptor's methods. Strecker also defends judicious restorations, particularly of the paint.
The article is well illustrated by various examples from the museum in Hildesheim, the treatment of which is amply described.

68565 STRICKER, B. H., De geboorte van Horus II, Leiden, E. J. Brill, 1968 (19.4 × 26.6 cm; 122 p. [numbered 87-207], 13 fig. [numbered 14-26]) = Mededelingen en Verhandelingen van het Vooraziatisch-Egyptisch Genootschap "Ex Oriente Lux" (Mémoires de la Société d'Études Orientales "Ex Oriente Lux") XVII.

Sequel to our number 63491.
As in the first volume the author, annotating the texts in the burial chamber of Ramses VI, adduces passages from the Egyptian, classical and Jewish literatures.
The present volume deals with the semen, its origin and structure (p. 87-121); the function and origin of the female secretions (121-147); the share of men and woman in the fruit.
Notes on p. 180-207.

68566 STRICKER, B. H., De praehelleense ascese, § 3-5, *OMRO* 49 (1968), 18-39.

Suite de notre numéro 67532.
L'auteur aborde les textes d'ascèse égyptiens et hébraïques. Il envisage successivement l'hygiène, la sobriété et le tabou.
I. L'excès d'aliments, altérant la santé, demandait un traitement mensuel de trois jours. L'usage des lavements, saignées et jeûnes prenait exemple sur différentes espèces d'animaux. L'ibis règle en outre son régime alimentaire sur les phases de la lune. La plante *soum*, "sang d'ibis", était censée favoriser la chasteté.
II. Les diverses pratiques étudiées déjà chez Pythagore le sont ici pour les prêtres, le roi, le peuple égyptien, ainsi que

pour les Hébreux. Ces derniers paraissent moins rigoristes. Des parallèles carthaginois figurent à propos du vin, cas difficile à débrouiller: le culte solaire devait entraîner l'interdiction, au moins de jour.

III. Le culte avait fixé des tabous, tirés des antipathies du dieu. Tels ceux liés à l'étranger: son couteau, des aliments importés et, chez les Juifs, le mariage avec une femme étrangère. L'Hébreu obligé de séjourner hors de son pays ne pouvait consommer que des plantes. Ces conceptions, déjà vieillies au moment où nos documents les attestent, s'orientaient vers le plan moral. *J. Custers*

68567 STRICKER, B. H., Tijd, *OMRO* 49 (1968), 40-56, with 2 pl. and 6 fig.

"Temps".

L'Égypte s'est interrogée sur la nature du temps, qui semble fuir; deux thèmes mythologiques au moins, étudiés ici, en font foi. *Les deux oiseaux* du dieu-soleil se retrouvent ailleurs dans l'Antiquité, et 56 textes en sont rappelés ici. En Égypte même en témoignent la rencontre Osiris-Rê à Mendès, et la paire héliopolitaine Isis-Nephtys, qui reparaît dans l'Amdouat, protégeant un monticule appelé "Nuit". (L'omphalos de Delphes est représenté de manière quasi identique. L'auteur en rapproche aussi les "Cherubim" hébraïques ailés qui abritent l'Arche, et que Philon explique notamment comme symboles des hémisphères.) Coptos et Létopolis vénéraient aussi deux oiseaux. Ce premier motif est figuré sur les suaires, de chaque côté de la tête du défunt; près des pieds veillent *les deux chacals ou chiens*. (Les Eddas germaniques connaissent les deux motifs disposés de même). Les "chacals", guides des Enfers selon Hérodote, images des hémisphères ou des solstices selon Clément d'Alexandrie, interviennent dans 14 textes. Ils symbolisent parfois le jour et la nuit, mais surtout la mort. Une peinture du Ramesseum les figure comme deux mois placés aux extrémités de l'année, le mois de Thot occupant le milieu. *J. Custers*

68568 STROUHAL, E., Contribution à la question du caractère de la population préhistorique de la Haute-Égypte, *Anthropologie*, Brno 6 (1968), 19-22.

Evalution of the nasal measurements of a Badarian population sample from the point of view of Negroid admixture.
M. Verner

68569 STROUHAL, Eugen, Czechoslovak research in Nubia, 1961-67, *Current Anthropology*, Chicago 9 (1968), 539-541; rev. *African Abstracts* 21 (1970), 50 (L. R. Sobel).

Survey of the archaeological and physical anthropological research by the Czechoslovak Institute of Egyptology in Egypt.

68570 STROUHAL, Eugen, Über die Längenmaße der langen Gliedmaßenknochen der Bevölkerung der nubischen Gruppe X, *in*: *Anthropologie und Humangenetik*. Festschrift zum 65. Geburtstag von Professor Dr. Dr.h.c. Karl Soller, Stuttgart, Gustav Fischer Verlag, 1968, 84-92, with 3 tables.

Analysis of the long bones dimensions of the X-group people in comparison with other Egyptian data. *M. Verner*

68571 STRUVE, V. V., Этюды по истории Северного Причерноморья, Кавказа и Средней Азии, Ленинград, Издательство "Наука", Ленинградское отделение, 1968 (17 × 26 cm; 356p.). At head of title: Академия наук СССР. Институт истории. Ленинградское отделение. Pr. 2 P. 32 коп

"Studien zur Geschichte des nördlichen Schwarzseeufers, Kaukasus, und Mittelasiens".
Sehe S. 269-346: *Beilage. Stelen der Eremitage.*
Diese Beilage enthält eine kurze Beschreibung mit den Text und Angaben über Herkunft, Datum und Veröffentlichungen von 55 Stelen und 4 Opfertafeln aus der Eremitage-Sammlung. Struve's Manuskript war verloren und erst nach seinem Tode gefunden worden. *E. S. Bogoslovsky*

68572 SUSSEL, Philippe and Robert PHILIPPE, Les pyramides. Les rois-prêtres, *in*: *3000 av. J.C./600 av. J.C. La naissance de l'histoire* (collection: Les métamorphoses de l'humanité. Une histoire de l'art et du monde sous la direction de Robert Philippe), Paris, Éditions Planète, 1968.

Not seen.

68573 SWAN HALL, Emma, Some Ancient Egyptian Sculpture in American Museums, *Apollo*, London 88, N° 77 (July 1968), 4-17, with 21 ill. (2 in colour).

Article for the general reader on Egyptian sculpture in various American collections. We mention the less known statue of Cleopatra VII in the Rosicrucian Egyptian Museum, San Jose (fig. 21).

68574 SWAN HALL, Emma, Some Ancient Egyptian Sculpture in British Collections, *Apollo*, London 87, N° 73 (March 1968), 160-169, with 15 ill.

Article for the general reader on Egyptian statues in the British Museum and various other British museums.

68575 SZCZUDŁOWSKA, Albertyna, Egiptologiczna konferencja w Lipsku, *Przegląd Orientalistyczny*, Warszawa 4 (68), 1968, 360-361.

"La conférence égyptologique à Leipzig".

68576 SZCZUDŁOWSKA, Albertyna, Faras—Wystawa w Muzeum Narodowym, *Przegląd Orientalistyczny*, Warszawa 2 (66), 1968, 168-171.

"Faras. An exhibition in the National Museum".

68577 TADMOR, Miriam, Egyptian Art of the Amarna Period. Norbert Schimmel Collection, Summer, 1967, *The Israel Museum News*, Jerusalem 3 (1968), 16-20, with 5 ill.

Note to the exhibition of the Norbert Schimmel Collection. Compare our number 67546.

68578 TANNER, Jerald and Sandra, The Case Against Mormonism. Volume two, Salt Lake City, Utah, Modern Microfilm Company, 1968 (21.5 × 26.5 cm; [VI +]182 p., 17 ill.).

A polemical survey of early Mormonism and its writings. Egyptian matters are touched upon p. 73 (etymology of the name Nephi), and p. 112 ff. (the history of the Egyptian papyri purported to be the source of the Books of Abraham and Joseph). Photos of the 11 (13) fragments are found on p. 114-19, translations of the Book of Breathings by Richard Parker and Dee Jay Nelson on p. 175-176. *Dieter Mueller*

68579 TANNER, Jerald and Sandra, The Case Against Mormonism. Volume three, Salt Lake City, Utah, Modern Microfilm Company, no date (21.5 × 26.5 cm; 86 p., many ill.).

A comparison of Egyptian funerary texts with the recently rediscovered Mormon papyri, and the controversy surrounding them. *Dieter Mueller*

68580 TANNER, Jerald and Sandra, Is the Book of Abraham True?, Salt Lake City, Utah, Modern Microfilm Company, 1968 (14 × 21.5 cm; 23 p., many ill.).

A confrontation of Joseph Smith's "Egyptian Alphabet and Grammar" with the papyrus fragment from which he translated the Book of Abraham. It contains the beginning of the Book of Breathings ("Breathing Permit") and is reproduced on p. 3-4. *Dieter Mueller*

68581 TANNER, Jerald and Sandra, The Mormon Papyri Question, Salt Lake City, Utah, Modern Microfilm Company, 1968 (14 × 21.5 cm; 32 p., many ill.).

A brief survey on the controversy surrounding the Egyptian

papyri on which the Mormon prophet Joseph Smith based his doctrine, with many excerpts from letters by renowned Egyptologists. *Dieter Mueller*

TANNER, Jerald, see also our number 68283.

68582 TAVERNA, Donatella, Sull'origine del nome Νεῖλος, *Aegyptus* 48 (1968), 31-35.

Les Égyptiens appelaient le Nil soit Hâpy, soit *itrw*, "fleuve". Les Grecs l'ont d'abord nommé comme le pays: *Aigyptos*, terme qui désigna d'abord Memphis et passa par Ugarit sous la forme *Ḥikuptaḥ*. Le nom actuel Nil apparaît en Grèce au VIe siècle, sans étymologie connue. Vycichl, dans notre n° 57512, a pensé au berbère *lil-*. Mais le terme est-sémitique *nâru*, "fleuve, cours d'eau", satisfait mieux aux exigences historiques et phonétiques. Cette traduction de l'égyptien ne laisse en Égypte aucune trace. La conquête assyrienne précède d'un bon siècle l'apparition du nom en Grèce. Le *â* très long devenait en néo-babylonien *e* ultra-long, voyelle que note en grec le *ei*, et le passage est aisé du *r* à *l*. Le mot chemina sans doute par la Crète et peut-être par Chypre. *J. Custers*

68583 TERRACE, Edward L. B., The Age of Empire and Rebellion: the New Kingdom in Boston, *The Connoisseur*, London Vol. 169, No 679 (September 1968), 49-56, with 21 ill. including 4 in colour, colour pl. on cover.

Third article (compare our numbers 68587 and 68584) devoted to the art of the New Kingdom.
After indicating the way in which objects of this period came to the collection the author describes examples of various kinds, such as an ebony statuette of a dwarf holding an unguent jar and a relief showing the palace of Amarna, together with other reliefs and fragments from this palace.

68584 TERRACE, Edward L. B., An Age of Reflection: the Egyptian Middle Kingdom in Boston, *The Connoisseur*, London Vol. 168, No 678 (August 1968), 265-272, with 23 ill. including 4 in colour.

Second article of the series (compare our number 68587), dealing with the art of the Middle Kingdom. We mention the description of a painted relief from Gebelên (fig. 1), a typical example of the style of the First Intermediate Period, and some fragmentary faience tiles (fig. 16) and ivory inlays (fig. 17) from Kerma.

68585 TERRACE, Edward L. B., Egyptian Paintings of the Middle Kingdom. The Tomb of Djehuty-nekht, New York, George

Braziller, [no year] (30 × 31.8 cm; 172 p., 2 maps, 2 plans, 1 fig., 13 ill., 51 colour pl,, 2 colour ill. on cover [= pl. XXXII and XXXVII]); rev. *The Antiquaries Journal* 50 (1970), 113-114 (Peter A. Clayton); *Apollo* Vol. XCIII, N° 108 (February 1971), 147 (T. G. H. James); *Arts Magazine*, May 1969, 12 (Henry G. Fischer); *JEA* 56 (1970), 214-215 (C. H. S. Spaull). Pr. cloth $ 25.00

Notwithstanding the title the book is mainly devoted to the study of Djehuty-nekht's coffin, found by Reisner at Bersheh in 1915 and now in the Boston Museum of Fine Arts.

In the first chapter the author briefly deals with the history of Bersheh, the excavations, the tomb of Djehuty-nekht and the offices of the owner and his wife. He then discusses Egyptian tomb decoration and its purpose in general and presents a detailed description of the two coffins of Djehuty-nekht and his wife, their construction and their decoration. He particularly demonstrates the impressionistic character of the painting of the former.

The last chapter (p. 42-52) contains a thorough study of painting from the Old Kingdom to the end of the Middle Kingdom. The author stresses the experimentation with the use of colour during the First Intermediate Period which proves to be of so much consequence to painting during the Middle Kingdom. He discusses in detail on the basis of choice examples the development of the tomb-decoration during the period resulting in the work of three masters under Sesostris III, one of whom responsable for Djehuty-nekht's coffin. This artist is provisionally related to the painter of Wah-ka's tomb at Qau el Kebir, who worked during the reign of Amenemhat III.

All 51 splendid colour plates are accompanied with a commentary on the opposite page. A bibliography on p. 160-162, notes on p. 163-166. Some technical appendices containing an analysis of pigments by William J. Young and Florence E. Whitmore on p. 167-169, and an index on p. 170-172.

An English edition was published by George Allen & Unwin Ltd (Pr. bound £ 10/10 s.).

68586 TERRACE, Edward L. B., The Entourage of an Egyptian Governor, *Bulletin of the Museum of Fine Arts*, Boston Vol. 66 (1968), No. 343, 5-27, with 27 ill. and colour ill. on cover.
Discussion of wooden figures found during the excavations in Bersheh in 1915 (cfr our preceding number), particularly the "procession" of four servants (Boston No 21.326), probably painted, but not carved, by the master who also decorated the coffin from Djehuty-nekth's tomb.

The author also studies four wooden objects from another tomb at Bersheh: two so-called "concubines" (Nos 20.1120 and 20.1121), a female head with a tall crown, probably representing a foreigner (No 20.1125) and a model censer (No 20.1124).

The article gives a survey of the two different styles in the art of the Middle Kingdom, publishing as illustrations a recently acquired black granite bust of a queen (Boston, Eg. Curator's Fund 67.9) and a relief fragment from the tomb of Djehuty-hetep at Bersheh (No 47. 1658) representing attendants, here published in photograph for the first time.

68587 TERRACE, Edward L. B., Masterpieces of the Pyramid Age in Boston, *The Connoisseur*, London Vol. 168, No 677 (July 1968), 197-204, with 17 ill. including 2 in colour.

First article of a series devoted to the Egyptian collection in the Museum of Fine Arts, Boston (compare our numbers 68584, 68583 and 68588).

After a few remarks on the history of the collection and on Reisner's excavations on behalf of the museum the author deals with statues and reliefs of the Old Kingdom.

68588 TERRACE, Edward L. B., Urbanity and Verism: the Late Period in Boston, *The Connoisseur*, London Vol. 169, No 680 (October 1968), 117-123, with 24 ill. including 9 in colour.

Fourth and last article of the series (compare our preceding number), describing some works of art from the Late Period, among which a detail of an altar erected by Atlanersa at Gebel Barkal, statues and statue heads, jewellery, *etc*. The last object is a headless granite statue of King Haker, an ephemeral ruler in the Persian Period.

68589 THÉODORIDÈS, Aristide, Procès relatif à une vente qui devait être acquittée par la livraison d'un travail servile (Papyrus Berlin 9785), *Revue internationale des droits de l'antiquité*, Bruxelles 15 (1968), 39-104.

Study of Pap. Berlin 9785 formerly edited by Gardiner together with Pap. Berlin 9784 and Pap. Gurob II,1 and II,2 (*ZÄS* 43 [1906], 27-47).

After giving a French version of Gardiner's translation the author first studies the term *snḫ*, "to bind" or "to be bound" (p. 44-55), which may also have been the juridical meaning "to be under obligation", for which the author quotes O. Chicago 12073 (cfr *Hieratic Ostraca* 77). Théodoridès also translates with comments the three other documents of the dossier (55-74), particularly discussing the word *šmm*, "to be hot", which here means "to be prevented from working".

Then he translates and comments upon Pap. Berlin 9785 itself (74-85), concluding that it is a document about a complete and real lawsuit, though an incomplete procès-verbal of the session, in contrast to the other documents which contain contracts.

In a discussion of the characteristics of Pap. Berlin 9785 (85-102) the author demonstrates that the female slave remained the property of the lender. She may have been a specialized artisan, like the slaves of the other documents, though they seem to have been property of the community. In the appendix (102-104) the author deals with the dates of the four documents, rejecting the arguments for a high chronology (cfr our number 67465) derived from them by Redford, though without committing himself on either a long or a short coregency of Amenophis IV.

68590 THÉODORIDÈS. Ar., Le testament d'Imenkhâou, *JEA* 54 (1968), 149-154.

This papyrus, Turin 2021, was originally edited by Černý and Peet in *JEA* 13, and deals with a marriage settlement of the XXth Dynasty, a new examination confirming that it is a contract for the second marriage of the 'divine father' Imenkhâou. The formal swearing is made before the court (*knbt*) of Medinet Habu presided over by the Vizier and the rights of the wife and children of the first marriage set out. Sections of the text are quoted in translation and points of meaning that are obscure are discussed. *E. Uphill*

THÉODORIDÈS, Aristide, see also our number 68377.

68591 THIBAULT, Jean, Le masque d'or de Toutankhamon radiographié, *Photo-ciné-revue*, Paris (Mai 1968), 216-217, with 2 radiophotographies.

Considérations techniques: utilisation d'un émetteur gamma, deux heures de pose. *J. Custers*

THIMME, Jürgen, see our number 68046.

68592 THOMAS, Homer L., Archaeological Implications of Near Eastern Historical Chronology, *Opuscula Atheniensia*, Lund 8 (1968), 11-22.

Reconsideration of the implications of either a high or a low Egyptian and Near Eastern chronology. For Egypt the controversy centres upon the dating of the Ist Dynasty and the regnal dates of the pharaohs of the XVIIIth and XIXth Dynasties. For the former, carbon-14 dates from the Aegean and Europe as well as recent excavations at Tell Gat and Tell Arad may point to a high chronology.

The author further deals with the date of Neferhotep I of the XIIIth Dynasty, contemporary with Zimrilim and Hammurabi; with the date of the Hyksos; with some certain dates, *e.g.* those of the Middle Kingdom and the Amarna Age; and the difficult choice between 1304 or 1290 B.C. for the accession of Ramses II.

TILL †, Walter, see our number 68397.

68593 TRIGGER, Bruce G., Beyond History: The Methods of Prehistory, New York, Holt, Rinehart and Winston, [1968] (16.3 × 23.6 cm; XVI + 105 p., 2 fig.). Series: Studies in Anthropological Method.

The aim of this study is to provide a discussion of the methodology of prehistory as distinguished from archaeology. After an introduction in which prehistory and its methods are roughly described the author discusses in 4 chapters the various concepts and techniques that prehistorians use in their studies of particular areas.

Although these chapters, written by a trained ethnologist, are to be read with much profit by Egyptologists, their attention is particularly drawn to chapter 6 in which the methods discussed are applied to Predynastic Egypt. After a short summary of the Badarian, Amratian and Gerzean cultures and of Predynastic Lower Egypt Trigger discusses the validity of the archaeological evidence, raising, for example, the question whether the Badarian culture indeed has been as primitive as it is assumed to be.

Special sections are devoted to geological evidence, language and physical anthropology, in which the problems are indicated which may be solved by specialized research. There is also a section on oral traditions, in which Trigger rejects for reasons of method the use made by various scholars such as Sethe of the later myths in order to interpret predynastic history.

In a section about migration and diffusion the author criticizes various migration theories by which scholars have attempted to explain the origin of the predynastic cultures and of the dynastic civilisation. They all are based on insufficient data, demonstrating their author's lack of theoretical knowledge of the subject as it is developed by modern ethnologists. On the other hand, Trigger sees several indications of cultural contacts between Egypt and Palestine, and even with Mesopotamia, so that diffusion seems to be the most important characteristic of the growth of these predynastic cultures.

In the last section concerning social and political development, the author studies the origin of the Pharaonic state, which he conceives to be a conquest state that acquired exceptional stability through rapid development of foreign trade, occupational specialisation and bureaucratic administration. The Egyptian society thus has been unilateral in origin, quickly assuming the feature of an organic state. In an epilogue the conclusions of the book are summarized. There follows a selected bibliography of methodological studies, intended to be a guide to important readings, and a very extensive general bibliography.

68594 TRIGGER, Bruce G., Two Notes on Meroitic Grammar, *Meroitic Newsletter. Bulletin d'Informations Méroïtiques*, Paris 1 (Oct. 1968), 4-8.

Es wird die Äquivalenz von *ḫ* und *k* untersucht. Die Wörter *terikelêwi* ("gezeugt von") und *tedḫelêwi* ("geboren von") lassen möglicherweise eine Morphemanalyse von *teri-ke-lê-wi* und *ted-*ke-lê-wi* zu. Deshalb sollte eine Wurzelverwandtschaft des meroitischen *teri* mit dem nubischen *teri* "Samen" nochmals überprüft werden (vgl. Trigger, unsere Nummer 64497). Einer *-bk-* Pluralpartikel in Deskriptionssätzen steht eine *-bḫ-*Partikel in den Opferformeln gegenüber. Es ist möglich, daß *bk* und *bḫ* nur zwei Varianten derselben Partikel sind. Somit scheint es lediglich zwei Formen der Pluralbildung zu geben: *-b* oder *-eb* als Suffix bei Nomina und Verbalausdrücken der Schlußformel und *-bḫ-* oder *-bk-* als Infix bei Verbalausdrücken.   *Inge Hofmann*

68595 TRIGGER, Bruce, G., Jean LECLANT, André HEYLER, *Meroitic Newsletter. Bulletin d'Informations Méroïtiques*, Paris 1 (Oct. 1968), 1-3.

Auf dem XXVII. Internationalen Orientalistenkongress im August 1967 in Ann Arbor ist der Meroitistik eine eigene Sektion zuerteilt worden. Ein wachsender regelmäßiger Informationsaustausch der Herausgeber der vorliegenden Zeitschrift mit anderen Wissenschaftlern macht es deshalb sinnvoll, ein eigenes meroitistisches Organ zu schaffen, um in einer furchtbaren Zusammenarbeit Probleme oder Teilforschungsergebnisse öffentlich zu diskutieren.

Inge Hofmann

68596 TROKAY, Madeleine, Les origines du décor à granulations dans l'orfèvrerie égyptienne, *CdE* XLIII, N° 86 (1968), 271-280, with 2 ill.

Étudiant les objets égyptiens du Moyen Empire dont le décor est composé d'une granulation d'or, l'auteur propose de voir dans cette technique un emprunt fait par les Égyptiens aux orfèvres mésopotamiens, car elle paraît avoir été inventée en Asie et de là s'être répandue dans tout le bassin oriental de la Méditerranée. *Ph. Derchain*

68597 TRÜMPY, Hans, Die Göttin Isis in schweizerischen Sagen, *in*: *Provincialia*. Festschrift für Rudolf Laur-Belart. Herausgegeben von der Stiftung Pro Augusta Raurica, Basel/Stuttgart, Schwabe & Co Verlag, [1968], 470-486, with a map.

The author discusses the occurrence of Isis temples in northern Switzerland in 16th century and later scientific works, connected with names such as Islisberg and Isenberg. He argues that legendary tales mentioning Isis and pagan churches are no genuine reminiscences of an original Isis cult in the country.

68598 TURCAN, Robert, Littérature astrologique et astrologie littéraire dans l'Antiquité classique, *Latomus*, Bruxelles 27 (1968), 392-405.

Egyptian influences on the astrology of the classical antiquity are mentioned throughout the article.

TURNER, E. G., see our number 68552.

68599 TURSKA, Krystyna, Próba odczytania konstrukcji szat egipskich z okresu Nowego Państwa, *Odzież*, Łódź n° 6, 1968, 186-188.

"Attempts at Reading the Construction of the Egyptian Clothes from the New Kingdom".
The article contains some suggestions concerning the drape of the fabric and the ways by which the attire used to be maintained on the figure. *A. Szczudłowska*

68600 TUTUNDŽIĆ, Sava P., The Rendering of Animal Skin on Two White Cross-lined Vases with Dancing Scenes, Зборника философског факултета, Београд X, 1, 1968, 41-46, with 2 ill. on one pl.

The author studies the representations on two prehistoric vases, one now in Brussels, the other in University College, London. On the former there is shown a trapezoid object filled in with two zigzag lines, on the other the space between the legs of the dancers is filled in by a zigzag line. Both are here suggested to represent animal skins.

68601 UCKO, Peter J., Anthropomorphic Figurines of Predynastic Egypt and Neolithic Crete with Comparative Material from the Prehistoric Near East and Mainland Greece, London, Andrew Szmidla, [1968] (20.5 × 29 cm; XVI + 532 p., 195 fig., 39 tables, 77 ill. on 56 pl.) = Royal Anthropological Institute Occasional Papers No. 24; rev. *American Anthro-*

pologist 72 (1970), 1181-1182 (William Kelly Simpson); *Anthropos* 65 (1970), 1022-1023 (Johannes Maringer); *Antiquity* 44 (1970), 68-69 (C. C. Lamberg-Karlovsky); *BiOr* 27 (1970), 187-188 (Ingrid Gamer-Wallert); *Bulletin of the School of Oriental and African Studies* 33 (1970), 603-604 (John Oates); *JEA* 56 (1970), 198-201 (Elise J. Baumgartel); *Man* 4 (1969), 297-298 (Colin Renfrew); *Mitteilungen des anthropologischen Gesellschaft in Wien* 100 (1970), 436 (Andreas Lippert). Pr. bound £ 6.6 s.

Part 1, dealing with ancient Egypt, is confined to the figurines proper, excluding those attached to vessel-rims, decoration of combs, *etc*. After 64 pages illustrating 70 pieces in drawing (36 more are illustrated on pl. I-XXXVI at the end) there follows a catalogue of 226 items (p. 65-164), each of which is technically described. Chapter 2 discusses points arising from the catalogue, such as the dating and the steatopygious nature of some figurines, while chapter 3 analyses part of the material (95 pieces) after sex, posture, arm position, material, facial features, clothing and anatomical details.

Part 2 and 3 deal with Crete, the Near East and Greece. Part 4 discusses the Inter-Cultural Relations, p. 403-406 particularly the possibility of such relations between Egypt and other areas. In Part 5, "Interpretations", the author presents tentative proposals for the interpretation of the function of various types (427-434).

Bibliography on p. 501-508; indexes on p. 509-530.

68602 UPHILL, E. P., Pithom and Raamses: Their Location and Significance, *JNES* 27 (1968), 291-316, with 1 map and 4 plans.

The old views of Gardiner and other scholars writing a generation ago on this subject are no longer tenable in the light of present archaeological evidence from the E. Delta. The first part of this article deals with the question of the whereabouts of the two cities mentioned in the Bible and the claims of Tell el Maskhutah to be Per Atum are discussed. Instead of this site a new claimant is put forward in the immense site of Tell Hisn, or the old sun temple of Iunu or Heliopolis. The evidence for and against equating four different sites with Per Ramesses is presented in great detail and at length, before ruling them out as possibilities, Tell er-Retabeh, Pelusium, Tanis and Tchel, each having had its own supporters. A fifth site, Qantîr, has now of recent years produced such an overwhelming mass of archaeological evidence in the form of the remains of palaces, temples, great statues and other vestiges of a great city that it must be taken very seriously as the possible site chosen by the XIXth Dynasty kings for their Delta Residence. This coupled with the parallels it shows to the literary descriptions suggests that here may be the Raamses mentioned in the Exodus narrative. *E. Uphill*

68603 VANDERSLEYEN, Claude, Deux nouveaux fragments de la stèle d'Amosis relatant une tempête, *RdE* 20 (1968), 127-134.

A la stèle publiée par l'auteur dans *RdE* 19 (notre numéro 67567) sont venus s'ajouter deux fragments qui permettent de compléter les quatre premières lignes du texte et fournissent des indications sur la décoration du cintre.

Ph. Derchain

68604 VANDERSLEYEN, Claude, Un titre du vice-roi Mérimose à Silsila, *CdE* XLIII, N° 86 (1968), 234-258.

Dans la titulature de Mérimose, vice-roi de Nubie sous le règne d'Aménophis III, apparaît le titre de *ḥrp nsty*, rarement attesté après l'Ancien Empire, en dehors du domaine hermopolitain. L'auteur a réuni toutes les attestations du titre, qui semblerait avoir désigné originairement le préposé aux deux trônes du roi, jouant un rôle important dans la célébration du *heb sed*, auquel il aurait été réservé à partir d'une certaine époque, pour ne plus être, tardivement, qu'un titre sacerdotal hermopolitain. L'auteur discute également à cette occasion le problème de la célébration d'un *heb sed* d'Aménophis III à Soleb, dont Mérimose aurait été l'organisateur. *Ph. Derchain*

68605 VANDIER, Jacques, Deux textes religieux du Moyen Empire, *Festschrift Schott* 121-124, with 2 fig.

Publication, without translation or commentary, of two texts occurring on a monument recently acquired by the Louvre Museum (cfr *La Revue du Louvre et des Musées de France*, Paris 13 [1963], 1-10). The texts are entitled "The Chapter of the Bouquet offered in the Tomb" and "The Chapter of Repelling the Serpent *rkk*".

68606 VANDIER, Jacques, La donation L. de Clerq — H. de Boisgelin. Antiquités égyptiennes, *La Revue du Louvre et des Musées de France*, Paris 18 (1968), 309-320, with 31 ill.

The author describes the objects from the collection de Clerq which have entered into the Egyptian Department of the Louvre Museum.

They consist *i.a.* of a large group of scarabs; several bronze statuettes of divinities, among which we mention that of Neferhotep (E 25954) crowned with the *pshent* and that of Osiris (E 25951) with rings attached to the back pillar and the right side of the base; a bronze statuette of a naked woman of a rare type (E 25959); a bronze situla decorated with religious representations (E 25956); a faience kohl vessel in the form of a hedge-hog dominated by a human head (E 25962); a fine shawabti of Kenamon (E 25960), the owner of Theban tomb N° 93; and a head of the 1st century A.D.

68607 VANDIER, Jacques, Éloge de Sir Harold Idriss Bell, correspondant de l'Académie, *Comptes rendus de l'Académie des Inscriptions et Belles-lettres*. 1968, Paris, 289-293.

Obituary notice. See our number 67639.

68608 VANDIER, Jacques, Iousâas et (Hathor)-Nébet-Hétépet. Quatrième article (additions), *RdE* 20 (1968), 135-148.

Depuis la publication du dernier article (notre numéro 66593), quatorze documents nouveaux sont venus s'ajouter à la riche documentation rassemblée autrefois par l'auteur.

La discussion la plus importante concerne le toponyme 〈hieroglyphs〉 où se trouve un sanctuaire de Nebet Hetepet (Caire JE 26427). Il s'agirait d'une localité sébennytique, différente de Takhbéti et de Bout, dont les orthographes sont proches.

Ph. Derchain

68609 VANDIER, Jacques, Nouvelles acquisitions. Musée du Louvre. Département des antiquités égyptiennes, *La Revue du Louvre et des Musées de France*, Paris 18 (1968), 95-108, with 35 ill.

The author enumerates the acquisitions of the year 1967, of which we mention the following objects: a group of Middle Kingdom vases and funerary masks from Mirgissa (E 25707-25725 and 25691-25706); a peculiar vase with a lid shaped as a human head, probably from the Nagâda culture (E 25727); a fragmentary kneeling statue of Maia (E 25984), the Chief of the Treasury, whose famous statues are in the Leiden Museum; the lower part of a squatting statue of Pehsukher (E 25965), the owner of Theban tomb N° 88; a granite stelophorous statue of vizier Paser (E 25980), with on the stela representations of the deities Neith, Ptah, Sekhmet and Urethekau and an important inscription; a late Ptolemaic or early Roman stela (E 25981) of a standing man with a small naos in his hands; a small alabaster box containing three cylinder seals of King Mentuhotep the Great (E 25685-25688).

Two other important acquisitions will later on be published, namely a large Greco-Roman stela from the Faiyûm and a IIIrd Dynasty stela with representations of Horus and a king called Kahedjet, who may be either Nebka or Nisutekh. See also the acquisitions mentioned on p. 162 and p. 475.

68610 VANDIER, Jacques, La statue d'un grand prêtre de Mendès, *JEA* 54 (1968), 89-94, with 1 ill. and 2 pl.

This granite statue was given to the Louvre in 1958 (E. 25429) and is 52 cm. high. It represents Ibeba the first prophet of Banebdjed as a kneeling figure with a table of offerings before him. The inscriptions are on the base and back pillar and date it to the reign of Eye. The *ḥtp dỉ nsw* formula invokes Hathor-Nebet-Hetepet. E. Uphill

68611 VANDIER, Jacques, Une stèle égyptienne portant un nouveau nom royal de la troisième dynastie, *Comptes rendus de l'Académie des Inscriptions et Belles-Lettres*. 1968, Paris, 16-22, with 2 ill.

Publication of a stela recently acquired by the Louvre Museum (E. 25982) and representing a king with the white crown, embraced by Horus. The style is the same as that of Djeser's stelae in his tombs. According to the inscription, the Horus is the sun-god of Heliopolis (*ỉmi ḥwt-ʿ3t*), so that this is the earliest known indication of a relationship between the king and the sun-god. The king himself is called Kahedjet, an unknown Horus-name which Vandier suggests to be either that of Nisutekh-Huni or, perhaps, of his predecessor Nebka (?).

68612 VANTINI, Giovanni, con introduzione di Sergio DONADONI, Gli scavi nel diff di Sonqi Tino (Nubia sudanese), *Rendiconti della Pontifica Accademia Romana di Archeologia*, serie III, 40 (1967-1968), 1968, 247-273, with 2 plans (one folded), 9 ill. and 3 fig.

Report of the excavations by the archaeological mission of the University of Rome at Sonqi Tino, near the northern end of the second cataract, where a Nubian church has been found.

For the wall paintings, compare our number 68182.

68613 VARGA, Edith, Le fragment d'un hypocéphale égyptien, *Bulletin du Musée Hongrois des Beaux-Arts*, Budapest, N° 31, 1968, 3-15, with 7 fig.

Als Deposit aus einer Privatsammlung bewahrt das Museum der Bildenden Künste in Budapest ein Bruchstück von einem magischen Hypokephal. Von diesen sind bisher 86 Exemplare in den verschiedenen Sammlungen der Welt bekannt (vgl. unsere Nummer 61692). Die Verfasserin rekonstruiert die fehlenden Teile des Bruchstückes. Die auf die Hypokephalen dargestellten Bilder sind alle Beweise der Idee der Wiedergeburt aus dem Tode, des über dem Tode siegreichen Lebens. Der Budapester Hypokephal ist in dem Anfang der Ptolemäerzeit zu datieren und ist wahrscheinlich aus einem thebanischen Grab in die Antiquitätenhandlung gelangt.

The same article in Hungarian is to be found on p. 95-103.

Vilmos Wessetzky

68614 VARILLE, Alexandre, Inscriptions concernant l'architecte Amenhotep fils de Hapou, Le Caire, Imprimerie de l'Institut français d'Archéologie orientale, 1968 (20.6 × 27.8 cm; XIV +164 p., 14 pl. [2 folding], frontispiece, 1 plan., 7 ill., 24 fig.) = Institut français d'Archéologie orientale. Bibliothèque d'étude, T. 44.

On the first pages Jean Vercoutter relates that the present study was ready in 1939, but for several reasons has only been published in 1968. Although on certain points obsolete it was considered to be sufficiently valuable to publish it as the author had written it. Varille's life is briefly described by Marthe and Jean Varille in the introduction. For a portrait, see frontispiece, for a bibliography of the author composed by Maurice Alliot and Louis A. Christophe, see p. 153-157.

The first chapter discusses the seven statues of Amenophis son of Hapu erected at Karnak, one during his lifetime, the others after his death in year 31 of Amenophis III. The text of each statue is given in printed hieroglyphs, with a description, bibliography, translation and commentary. We mention particularly the note about 'Iwnw Šm', which according to Varille is Thebes, not Hermonthis (p. 28-31). Chapter II deals in the same way with Amenhotep's inscriptions on Bigeh and in Soleb.

Chapter III is devoted to his funerary temple excavated by the author (cfr C. Robichon and A. Varille, *Le temple du scribe royal Amenhotep fils de Hapou I*, Le Caire, 1936 = Fouilles de l'Institut français d'Archéologie orientale, tome 11). This chapter contains i.a. a study of the famous decree concerning the temple personnel in hieratic writing (Brit. Mus. N° 138), which the author suggests to have been composed during the XXIst Dynasty with the help of genuine documents; further several fragmentary inscriptions from the temple, and the funerary cones.

Chapter IV deals with the coffins of Amenhotep, parts of which are at present in the Louvre Museum, Cairo, Brussels, Grenoble and University College, London. In chapter V Amenhotep's representation in the tomb of the vizier Ramose is discussed, the only instance where he is accompanied by a woman.

On account of the material Varille sketches in chapter VI the biography of the great architect, favourite of Amenophis III.

In an appendix there is given a bibliography of the cult of Amenhotep during the Greco-Roman period, mentioning temple reliefs, statues and hieroglyphic, Demotic and Greek texts. There follows a list of Amenhotep's titles.

68615 de VAUX, R., Le pays de Canaan, *JAOS* 88 (1968), 23-30.

Study of the names of the land of Canaan in various Semitic languages, including also Egyptian $Kn'n$ and $Ḫuru$.

68616 de VAUX, R., Le problème des Hapiru après quinze années, *JNES* 27 (1968), 221-228.

Survey of the results of the discussion concerning the Ḫapiru-$'prw$ since the 4e Rencontre Assyriologique in 1953 (see our number 3493). For the $'prw$ one may consult p. 227.

68617 te VELDE, H., The Egyptian God Seth as a Trickster, *JARCE* 7 (1968), 37-40.

Seth appears to have five characteristics in common with the very complex phenomenon of the Trickster known in other cultures. He is disorderly and uncivilised, a murderer, a homosexual and a slayer-of-the-monster.
Compare our number 67575. *M. Heerma van Voss*

68618 VERCOUTER, Jean, Six années de fouilles à Mirgissa, *BSFE* N° 52 (Juillet 1968), 7-14, with 2 pl.

Suite de notre n° 67576.
Les fouilles actuelles, commencées en 1962, devaient être achevées en décembre 1968. L'exploration de la citadelle, mieux à l'abri de l'eau, a été réservée pour la fin: un exposé ultérieur complet l'étudiera. Dans la ville fortifiée, le type d'habitation est plus grand que dans la ville ouverte. Pour cette dernière, les huttes de pierres sèches ont livré beaucoup de poteries et d'ustensiles, mais aucun document écrit. La petite nécropole au nord pourrait remonter à la fondation de l'établissement, tandis que le dépôt de textes d'envoûtement daterait de la fin même de son existence. Parmi les travaux défensifs éloignés figurent un petit fortin sur plan

carré et la longue "glissière" pour aider le passage à sec des bateaux. La grande nécropole occidentale a donné une ample moisson de mobilier funéraire. *J. Custers*

VERCOUTTER, Jean, see also our numbers 68396 and 68614.

68619 VERMEERSCH, Pierre, Quelques industries lithiques d'El Kab et environs, *CdE* XLIII, N° 85 (1968), 13-21, with 1 map and 4 pl.

L'auteur décrit ses trouvailles de silex faites en surface, au cours de la prospection du district d'El Kab. Six concentrations de silex ont été ainsi repérées dans la grande enceinte de la ville et dans l'ouady Hellal jusqu'à une distance de six kilomètres de la première, s'étendant depuis le paléolithique inférieur et moyen, jusqu'au sébilien et aux industries microlithiques du paléolithique final ou du néolithique. Quatre planches au trait présentent les types les plus caractéristiques de chaque site. Dans une note additionnelle, l'auteur annonce que sa fouille de 1968, exécutée à l'emplacement de la concentration N° 2 à l'ouest de la porte orientale de la grande enceinte, a fait connaître une industrie microlithique sur lamelles, d'un type jusqu'a présent inconnu en Égypte. *Ph. Derchain*

68620 VERNER, Miroslav, Ancient Egyptian Monuments as seen by a Bohemian Missionary V. R. Prutký in the 18th century, *Archiv Orientální*, Praha 36 (1968), 371-380, with 3 pl.

Cfr our number 67578.
The Franciscan monk Václav Remedius Prutký, who was a missionary in Egypt and Abyssinia in the middle of the 18th century, kept a diary, a copy of which is preserved in the University Library in Prague. The author deals with three of its chapters: ch. XIX (De Pyramidibus), ch. XX (De Sphinge Idolo) and ch. XXI (De Mumiis), the first containing a description of Prutký's visit to the great pyramid, the second a description of other pyramids as well as of the great sphinx. The information corresponds to what we would expect from that time.
The plates reproduce three steel engravings bound to the manuscript, but, as it is apparrent from their usual 18th century style, not made by Prutký himself.

68621 VOLBACH, Wolfgang Fritz, Ägypten, *in*: Wolfgang Fritz Volbach und Jacqueline Lafontaine-Dosogne, *Byzanz und der christliche Osten* (= Propyläen Kunstgeschichte, Band 3), Berlin, Propyläen Verlag, 1968, 354-360, with 16 ill. (= nos. 397-407b) and 1 colour pl. (= no. L).

Short study of the Coptic art, followed by an extensive description of the illustrations.

VOORHOEVE, J., see our number 68403.

68622 VOS, Clarence J., Woman in Old Testament Worship, Delft, N.V. Verenigde Drukkerijen Judels & Brinkman, [1968] (15.5 × 24.4 cm; X + 219 p.) rev. *Biblische Zeitschrift* 13 (1969), 274-276 ([Josef Scharbert]); *ZAW* 80 (1968), 445 ([G. Fohrer]).

Thesis for a doctor's degree at the Free University, Amsterdam.
Excursus II (p. 51-59) deals with the possible Egyptian influence on circumcision in Israel, presenting a survey of what is known about the custom in Egypt (53-56). The author suggests that male circumcision was administered only to elite groups and for a religious reason, marking off the man for special service to the deity.

68623 van de WALLE, Baudouin, La princesse Isis, fille et épouse d'Aménophis III, *CdE* XLIII, N° 85 (1968), 36-54, with 5 ill. and 1 fig.

L'auteur rouvre et complète le dossier des monuments des filles d'Aménophis III et de Tiy. Grâce en particulier à un fragment de groupe conjugal conservé dans une collection privée néerlandaise ayant représenté Aménophis III et sa fille et épouse Isis, qu'il publie, il montre que l'illustre pharaon n'avait pas seulement fait épouse royale sa fille aînée Satamon, mais aussi certainement la seconde Isis. Si l'identification tentante de la troisième, *Ḥnwt-t3w-nbw*, avec la conjointe d'Horus (*sm3yt Ḥr*) *Ḥnwt* peut être acceptée, il faudrait donc compter que trois des filles d'Aménophis III auraient été épousées par leur père. Divers indices permettent de suggérer que ces mariages auraient été célébrés à l'occasion des *heb sed* successifs du roi.
L'auteur attire finalement l'attention sur les incidences que ces diverses unions pourraient avoir sur notre connaissance de la généalogie de la fin de la XVIIIe dynastie.
A comparer *CdE* XLIV, N° 87 (1969), 25-26.

Ph. Derchain

68624 WÅNGSTEDT, Sten V., Demotische Steuerquittungen nebst Texten andersartigen Inhalts, *Orientalia Suecana*, Uppsala 16 (1967), 1968, 22-56, with 9 ill. and 15 fig.; rev. *Enchoria* 1 (1971), 68 (Heinz-Josef Thissen).

Des 24 documents publiés, 16 sont conservés au Musée Britannique, 5 à Oxford, 3 dans la collection de l'auteur. Ils comprennent, outre des ostraca, une bandelette de momie d'époque romaine (n° 24), semblant provenir de Deir el-Médineh et portant des formules habituelles sur les étiquettes, ainsi qu'une planchette thébaine (n° 18), écrite des deux côtés et datant probablement de 253/2 av. J.-C. Cette dernière et la quittance n° 1 sont les documents les plus anciens de la série. Le plus récent est sans doute l'ostracon thébain (n° 15) portant reconnaissance d'une livraison de vin, et qui date de 144 de notre ère. Tous ces documents proviennent de Haute Égypte, la plupart de Thèbes, le n° 12 (quittance de ricin) vient de Gebelein, le n° 16 (collecte) d'Hermonthis. Il est ailleurs question de bains, de blé, de comptes, d'enterrement, d'impôts, de paiement en espèces, de paille, de teinture à la garance, et de fourneaux. Pour ces derniers on note les dates d'emploi.   *J. Custers*

68625 WARD, William A., The Four-winged Serpent on Hebrew Seals, *Rivista* 43 (1968), 135-143, with 7 fig.

En Égypte, le motif de l'uraeus ne porte que deux ailes. On ne l'y trouve qu'une fois avec quatre ailes avant le VIIIe siècle, et même par la suite, cette forme demeure extrêmement rare. Il doit s'agir d'un emprunt, en retour, aux sceaux hébreux. Le scarabée à double paire d'ailes n'est pas plus fréquent. Les composés panthées peuvent avoir eu un développement indépendant.   *J. Custers*

68626 WARD, William A., Humor from the Tombs, *Aramco World Magazine*, May-June 1968, 31-33, with 7 fig.

The author mentions some instances of humor, *i.a.* the queen of Punt at Deir el Bahri and her donkey, a scene of a sleeping storekeeper from a Theban tomb, and some scenes with animals in the role of human beings, which Ward compares with modern cartoons.

68627 WARD, William A., Notes on Some Egypto-Semitic Roots, *ZÄS* 95, 1 (1968), 65-72.

The author examines the Egyptian roots $wḏ'$, bn, $'wn$, mdw, pds, $'ḏ$, $šm$,*df, and their various derivations. The Semitic equivalents, which are noted in each case, often help to shed new light on the meaning of hitherto difficult Egyptian words. Of special interest is the relation between Sem. $ḥm$ "parent-in-law", and Eg. $šm$, attested in Demotic, but found only twice in Hieroglyphic so far. The two examples come from a M.K. funerary stela in Cairo, and the XVIIIth Dyn. tomb of Tati in Thebes.   *Dieter Mueller*

WEBER, Manfred, see our numbers 68162 and 68259.

68628 WEIGANDT, Peter, Koptologische Arbeitsvorhaben des Instituts für neutestamentliche Textforschung der Universität Münster/W. und der Arbeitsstelle Münster/W. der Patristischen Kommission der Akademien der Wissenschaften zu Göttingen, Heidelberg, Mainz, München, *Probleme* 233-235.

A survey of activities undertaken or planned by
I. The Institut für neutestamentliche Textforschung: (*e.g.*)
A collection of microfilms or photo's of all Coptic manuscripts of the New Testament;
A list of all Coptic fragments and manuscripts of the New Testament;
A new edition of the sahidic New Testament;
A publication of all Greek-Coptic bilingual manuscripts.
II. The Patristische Arbeitsstelle: (*e.g.*)
Publication of Nag-Hammadi manuscripts;
Publication of documents from the Apa-Apollon monastery.
L. F. Kleiterp

68629 WEISS, Hans-Friedrich, Beobachtungen zur Frage der griechischen Komponente in der Sprache des Schenute, *Probleme* 173-185.
The writings of Shenute contain relatively many Greek words. The author discerns no puristic tendency in Shenute's language, but observes on the other hand that many of the Greek words were either christian "termini technici" or not commonly understood to be foreign. *L. F. Kleiterp*

68630 WENDORF, Fred, The Prehistory of Nubia. Papers Assembled and Edited, 2 volumes and atlas, Fort Burgwin Research Center and Dallas, Southern Methodist University Press, 1968 (22 × 28.5 cm; XI + 1084 p., 623 fig., 136 tables, 27 pl., 10 maps) = Southern Methodist University Contributions in Anthropology, 2 = Fort Burgwin Research Center Publications, 5; at head of title: Combined Prehistoric Expedition to Egyptian and Sudanese Nubia; rev. *Antiquity* 44 (1970), 158-160 (William Y. Adams); *AJA* 73 (1969), 380-381 (Hans Goedicke); *Journal of African History* 10 (1969), 487-489 (A. J. Arkell); *Man* 4 (1968), 142-143 (F. A. Evans); *Mitteilungen der anthropologischen Gesellschaft in Wien* 100 (1970), 460-461 (Andreas Lippert). Pr. $ 37.50

In Einzelbeiträgen werden die Forschungsergebnisse der Combined Prehistoric Expedition in den Jahren zwischen 1962 und 1966 vorgelegt. Nach einer Einführung von Fred Wendorf folgen: Jean de Heinzelin, *Geological History of the Nile Valley in Nubia*; Francine Martin, *Pleistocene Mollusks from Sudanese Nubia*; A. Gautier, *Mammalian Remains of the Northern Sudan and Southern Egypt*; P. H. Greenwood, *Fish Remains*; Waldemar Chmielewski, *Early and Middle*

Paleolithic Sites near Arkin, Sudan; Jean and Geneviève Guichard, *Contributions to the Study of the Early and Middle Paleolithic of Nubia*; Anthony E. Marks, *The Mousterian Industries of Nubia*; ders., *The Khormusan: An Upper Pleistocene Industry in Sudanese-Nubia*; ders., *The Halfan Industry*; ders., *The Sebilian Industry of the Second Cataract*. Der 2. Band beinhaltet: Joel L. Shiner, *The Cataract Tradition*; ders., *Miscellaneous Sites*; Romuald Schild, Maria Chmielewska, and Hanna Więckowska, *The Arkinian and Shamarkian Industries*; Joel L. Shiner, *The Khartoum Variant Industry*; Fred Wendorf, *Late Paleolithic Sites in Egyptian Nubia*; ders., *Site 117: A Nubian Final Paleolithic Graveyard near Jebel Sahaba, Sudan*; J. E. Anderson, *Late Paleolithic Skeletal Remains from Nubia*; Fred Wendorf, *Summary of Nubian Prehistory*.

Eine Bibliographie, ein Index und ein Atlasband mit 38 losen Tafeln, die in der Hauptsache zu dem Artikel von de Heinzelin gehören, vervollständigen das Werk.

Inge Hofmann

68631 WENIG, Steffen, Eine Grabkammer des Mittleren Reiches aus Kom Ombo, *Forschungen und Berichte* 10 (1968), 71-94, with 7 fig., 7 pl. (2 in colour) and 2 pl. on loose sheets.

Publication of a tomb from Kom Ombo formerly in the Berlin Museum but destroyed during the last war. The tomb, which has never been published, is reconstructed from the diary of the excavation and some photographs and colour drawings. Its scenes and inscriptions are carefully described and translated.

The tomb may date from the Middle Kingdom, and its original owner was called *Sbk-ḥtp*. It has been usurped, probably in the XXIst Dynasty, by a certain *Wnn-t3-w3t*, who added some paintings and texts, one of them dated in a year 49 (of Shoshenq III ?). In the tomb there have been found remains of three coffins of the second burial, which appears to be in fact a re-burial.

68632 WESSETZKY, Vilmos, A Würzburgi Orientalista Konferencia egyiptológiai elödásai, *Archaeologiai Értesítő*, Budapest 95 (1968), 264-265.

"Die ägyptologischen Vorträge der Orientalisten-Konferenz in Würzburg".

Kurze Zusammenfassung der ägyptologischen Vorträge des XVII. Deutschen Orientalistentages in Würzburg vom 21. bis 27. Juli 1968. *Vilmos Wessetzky*

68633 WESTENDORF, Wolfhart, Das Alte Ägypten, Baden-Baden, Holle Verlag, [1968] (19.2 × 22.6 cm; [IV +] 260 p., containing numerous ill. and drawings [many in colour], 9 fig. including plans, 1 table, 1 map, 2 ill. on endpapers); series: Kunst im Bild. Der neue Weg zum Verständnis der Weltkunst; rev. *Mundus* 6 (1970), 36-37 (Wolfgang Helck); *OLZ* 65 (1970), 545-550 (Dietrich Wildung).

Pr. cloth DM 29

Dies Bilderbuch beschäftigt sich mit der Kunst, mit Inbegriff der koptischen Zeit. In einer umfassenden Einführung und in ausführlichen Unterschriften erörtertert der Verfasser auch religiöse Vorstellungen.

Am Ende rubrizierte Bibliographie und Register.

Es gibt auch eine holländische Ausgabe, *Het oude Egypte*, Amsterdam, Elsevier, 1968=Kunst in Beeld 4; rev. *BiOr* 26 (1969), 329 (R. Dusoir); *Phoenix* 15 (1969), 239-240 (anonymous) (Pr. fl. 26,50) und eine englische, *Painting, Sculpture and Architecture of Ancient Egypt*, New York/London, Harry N. Abrams, Inc., 1968; series: Panorama of World Art.

M. Heerma van Voss

68634 WESTENDORF, Wolfhart, Die Pantherkatze Mafdet, *ZDMG* 118 (1968), 248-256.

Study about the cat-goddess Mafdet, probably a hunting-leopard or cheetah, called "the runner" (m-$i/3fd$), which seems to have been a central figure in the early religion. She was mistress of the king's life, but also of his death, and related to the Sun-god and the Horus-eye. Though expelled from her central position at the beginning of the Ist Dynasty her memory remained vivid in various religious conceptions.

68635 WESTENDORF, Wolfhart, Sinuhe B 160, *Festschrift Schott* 125-131.

The author discusses the difficult passage Sinuhe B 160. Proceeding from his interpretation of the hymn in B 149-156 he suggests to translate either: "Come to help me! What when 'the good event' (*i.e.* the death) occurs?", or "what (does it mean), that a good event has happened?", which would point to Sinuhe's present condition.

WHITMORE, Florence E., see our number 68585.

68636 WHYBRAY, R. N., The Succession Narrative. A Study of II Sam. 9-20; I Kings 1 and 2, London, SCM Press Ltd, [1968] (14 × 21.5 cm; X + 118 p.) = Studies in Biblical Theology. Second Series, 9; rev. *Booklist* 1969, 44-45 (W. Mck[ane]); *The Expository Times* 80 (1968-1969), 56 (J. W. Rogerson).

The author, conceiving the so-called Succession Narrative

in the Old Testament as a combination of propagandist polititical novel and wisdom instruction in narrative form, draws the attention to the correspondences with these kinds of literature in ancient Egypt.

In the fourth chapter (p. 96-116) he deals with the 'royal novel' in Egypt, the *Story of Sinuhe* and other Egyptian stories, the *Prophecy of Neferty*, the *Instruction of Amenemhat*, *etc*. He concludes that, although the Sucession Narrative is of the purest Hebrew style, it shows strong influences of the Egyptian literary tradition.

66837 WIDMER, Werner, Ein Gefäß der späten Negadezeit, *MIO* 14 (1968), 365-371, with 4 fig., 3 pl., and an English summary on p. 371.

Ce vase à "anses" plates et ondulées, à décoration brun-orangé, sans indication d'origine, est datable de Nagada II. La décoration couvre plus de la moitié supérieure; différents groupes de traits ondulés la bordent et la divisent en deux registres. On y rencontre un cas unique de stylisation de végétaux, deux bateaux à personnages, et des flamants, répartis en trois groupes homogènes. Les motifs permettent de dater l'objet d'une période relativement tardive du gerzéen.   *J. Custers*

WIĘCKOWSKA, Hanna, see our number 68630.

68638 WILSON, John A., A Century of Near Eastern Archaeology and the Future, *The Role of the Phoenicians* 113-123.

In this lecture the author, proceeding from the beginning of Renan's Mission de Phénicie in 1860, summarizes the history of archaeological research in the Near East, with emphasis on the development of attitudes and techniques, from cavalier pillage of ancient sites to modern specialized science. He also sketches the present shift of interests to social problems.

68639 WILSON, John A., A Summary Report, *The Joseph Smith Egyptian Papyri* 67-85, with 9 ill.

The papyrus fragments that were once in the possession of Joseph Smith, founder of the Mormon Church, come from six or eight different documents. Those from the *Book of the Dead* belonging to Ta sheret-min (photos 2-4 and 7-9) are subsequently translated and annotated.   *Dieter Mueller*

WILSON, R. Mcl., see our number 68397.

68640 WINTER, E., Die Hieroglyphe △ als *imj-* „befindlich in", *RdE* 20 (1968), 175-176.

Dans le nom d'une des Touéris du temple d'Opet le signe △ doit se lire *imi* "qui se trouve dans" par variante graphique de △ dont la valeur *imi* est connue comme impératif du verbe *rdy* "donner". *Ph. Derchain*

68641 WINTER, Erich, Untersuchungen zu den ägyptischen Tempelreliefs der Griechisch-Römischen Zeit, Graz-Wien-Köln, Hermann Böhlaus Nachfolger/Wien, Kommissionsverlag der Österreichischen Akademie der Wissenschaften in Wien, 1968 (21.2 × 29.8 cm; 105 p., 6 ill., 16 pl.) = Österreichische Akademie der Wissenschaften. Philosophisch-Historische Klasse. Denkschriften, 98. Band; rev. *AfO* 23 (1970), 118-120 (Hellmut Brunner); *Archaeologiai Értesítő* 97 (1970), 143) Vilmos (Wessetzky; *CdE* XLV, N° 89 (1970), 98-102 (Jean-Claude Goyon); *JEA* 56 (1970), 228-230 (J. Gwyn Griffiths); *OLZ* 66 (1971), 458-459 (V. Wessetzky); *Oriens Antiquus* 10 (1971), 173-174 (S[ergio] D[onadoni]); *Orientalia* 39 (1970), 184-185 (Constant de Wit); *RdE* 22 (1970), 242-243 (Ph. Derchain); *ZDMG* 121 (1971), 1972, 118-121 (Dietrich Wildung). Pr. ö. S. 160

Die literarische Form der seitlichen Randzeilen der Tempelszenen war strengen Gesetzen unterworfen, deren Entwicklung sich von Ptolemaios II. Philadelphos an verfolgen läßt. Nicht nur die Beischriften, die gesamte Ausschmückung der Tempelwände wurde nach einem genauesten Programm neu gestaltet. Dabei beherrschten die Ägypter das theologische Traditionsgut völlig.

Im zweiten Teil seiner Arbeit untersucht der Verfasser die ʿnḫ ḏd wȝś-Szenen, eine Neuschöpfung der Ptolemäerzeit. Diese Symbole werden nicht nur dem König überwiesen, er bringt sie auch dar. Gleichzeitig vollzieht sich eine neue Mythologisierung: ʿnḫ und wȝś werden Schu und Tefnut und zugleich Eltern des Osiris(= ḏd). *M. Heerma van Voss*

68672 de WIT, Constant, Les inscriptions du temple d'Opet, à Karnak. III. Traduction intégrale des textes rituels — Essai d'interprétation, Bruxelles, Édition de la Fondation égyptologique Reine Élisabeth, 1968 (22 × 28 cm; XXII + 196 p.) = Bibliotheca aegyptiaca 13; rev. *BiOr* 28 (1970), 41-42 (Eberhard Otto); *JEA* 57 (1971), 228-229 (J. Gwyn Griffiths). Pr. b.fr. 1100

Sequel to our numbers 58653 and 62640.
In the Introduction the author briefly deals with the history of the temple. Then follows an extensive bibliography.
The main part of the book consists of a translation of all texts in the temple in the order in which they occur in volume I, with a complete transliteration at the foot of the

pages, and followed by notes to the translation. Excepted are, however, the purely geographical texts to the representation of the processions of the Nile-gods, which will be dealt with in a separate volume.
There follows a chapter about myths and rites represented in the texts and scenes, which particularly concern the conception of Amon in his Osirian form. Summaries are given in a "General Synthesis" and a very brief "Conclusion".
Indexes of words discussed and of divinities and their epithets on p. 179-194.

68643 de WIT, Constant, Some Remarks concerning the so-called "Isis" in the Museum Vleeshuis — Antwerp, *Proceedings* 6-7.

The so-called "Isis" in the Vleeshuis at Antwerp, found around 1750 in the ruins of a house in that city, is in fact the statue of a private individual on which at an unknown date a head belonging to a Ptolemaic king has been adjusted. The author enumerates seven statues from the Ptolemaic period with which the torso may be compared.

68644 WOLF-BRINKMANN, Elske Marie, Versuch einer Deutung des Begriffes '*b3*' anhand der Überlieferung der Frühzeit und des Alten Reiches, Freiburg i. Br., 1968 (14.6 × 20.5 cm; 128 p.); rev. *BiOr* 27 (1970), 343-344 (Dieter Mueller).

Thesis for a doctor's degree in Basel.
The first chapter deals with the concept *b3* or *b3w* on the basis of names of the Old Kingdom, the only period in which such names seem to occur. The author discusses names of kings, pyramids, private persons, ships and domains, giving for each the name in hieroglyphs, transcription and translation. The second chapter is devoted to the *b3* in the *Pyramid Texts*, a particular section (p. 57-60) dealing with its relations to similar concepts such as *3ḥ* and *šm*. The third chapter discusses the *b3w-P*, *b3w-Nḫn* and *b3w-'Iwnw*, in the *Pyr. Texts* and elsewhere.
The main conclusion is that in the Old Kingdom *b3* points to the ability and will of a divinity to reveal himself in a form, either human, animal, vegetable or astral ("Gestaltfähigkeit"). In the concluding chapter the author indicates how already during this period the first traces are to be found of a development by which *b3* points more to the ability to convert thoughts and plans into reality ("Gestaltungsvermogen"). This development is briefly followed through the Middle and New Kingdom.
Notes on p. 92-111, indexes on p. 117-124, bibliography on p. 125-126.
Compare our number 68557.

68645 WORTHAM, John David, Uraeus: A History of British Interest in the Antiquities of Egypt in the Sixteenth, Seventeenth, Eighteenth, and Nineteenth Centuries, *A Dissertation Abstracts*, Ann Arbor, Michigan 28, Number 10 (1968), 4075.

Abstract of a thesis (The University of Texas, 1967), obtainable in microfilm and xerography (500 p.).
Study of the development of Egyptology in England during the period 1586-1906. The author's abstract amply criticizes all earlier histories of this kind, stating that his study is a more realistic and comprehensive account aiming at correcting the distortions in the history of Egyptology.
The thesis itself has been published in 1971 (Newton Abbot, David & Charles).

68646 WORTMANN, D., Das Blut des Seth (P. Colon. inv. 3323), *Zeitschrift für Papyrologie und Epigraphik*, Bonn 2 (1968), 227-230.

The author demonstrates that the sentence "I conjure the blood, that the great god Iothath took" (Pap. Col. inv. 3323) points at the blood that Seth drank, which is the wine and the water of the Nile flood.

van der WOUDE, A. S., see our number 68436.

68647 WRIGHT, G. R. H., Tell el-Yehūdīyah and the Glacis, *Zeitschrift des Deutschen Palästina-Vereins*, Wiesbaden 84 (1968), 1-17, with 4 plans [2 folding], a folding fig. and 8 pl.

The author discusses nature and purpose of the so-called "glacis", in fact a sloping rampart, of Tell el-Yahudiyeh. He first summarizes its description and its explanation by various authors such as Brugsch, Naville, Griffith, Petrie and du Mesnil du Buisson. Petrie's interpretation as a work of fortification of "a great camp" was associated by him, and afterwards by Albright, with the Hyksos. Albright even tried to connect it with "charioteers and archers of the Eurasian steppes", and such has been the usual explanation also for what were assumed to be similar fortifications in Syria and Palestine.
Ricke, however, explained in 1935 a similar structure at Heliopolis as a cult place ("the High Sand"), and this was generally accepted by the Egyptologists.
Wright demonstrates that for Tell el-Yahudiyeh and Heliopolis the latter explanation is correct, pointing at another example of such an enclosure in the northern extremity of the excavation area of Mendes (cfr our numbers 65227 and 67247). The plastering over of earthwork constitutes a protec-

tive revetment against weathering, having no military significance at all. For the "glacis" in Palestine and Syria one may compare the article by Peter J. Parr, *Zeitschrift des Deutschen Palästina-Vereins*, Wiesbaden 84.

68648 WULFF, Hans E., Hildegard S. WULFF and Leo KOCH, Egyptian Faïence. A Possible Survival in Iran, *Archaeology* 21 (1968), 98-107, with 15 ill.

In search of the old process of making so-called "Egyptian faïence" the first authors gained access to a workshop in Qom (Iran), where they were able to study the technique. The process is carefully described and analysed, while the last author provides a chemical analysis.
See also Joseph Veach Noble, *An Archaeological Coincidence*, *Archaeology* 21 (1968), 220 and *The Technique of Egyptian Faience*, *AJA* 73 (1969), 435-439.

68649 YEIVIN, Sh., Additional Notes on the Early Relations between Canaan and Egypt, *JNES* 27 (1968), 37-50, with 6 fig. including 1 map, and 1 pl.

An ostracon found on the mound at Tel 'Erany, although the work of a local potter, had a design incised on it depicting horns with looped lines across representing stars, obviously imitating Egyptian Hathor patterns. The saw-blade found in the Kefar Monash cache has a pointillé decoration that appears to represent a scorpion adorned with stars, a symbol of the divine king Scorpion, and may therefore be compared with his mace-head from Hierakonpolis. From this set of objects examples are cited with Egyptian connections. Metal plaques found here and at Tel 'Erany where they were discovered in a stratum immediately below the one with (Merynar) Narmer pottery, belonged to leather jackets used for armour, and represented an advance on those illustrated on the Ur standard of later date, but were probably given up afterwards on account of their weight. Curved knives not of the *khepesh* type also date from this age and one is shown in the Sinai relief dated by the writer to Semerkhet and not Sekhemkhet as Černý has suggested. Kefar Monash items thus constitute the equipment of an Egyptian army unit.
E. Uphill

YOUNG, William J., see our number 68585.

YOUSRI, Fouad, see our number 68515.

YOUSSEF, Abdel Hamid, see our number 68060.

68650 YOYOTTE, Jean, La date supposée du couronnement d'Hatshepsout, *Kêmi* 18 (1968), 85-91.

En préparant l'édition de la "chapelle rouge", à Karnak, l'auteur a revu le bloc 287, où se trouve la date de "l'an II". La technique des pierres permet de rétablir le contexte, discontinu mais cohérent. Une première partie fait mention des oracles et évoque le couronnement d'Hatshepsout, mais le bloc 287 prend place dans une seconde partie, contenant un discours de la reine, à épisodes autobiographiques. L'auteur copie et traduit l'inscription. Le couronnement proprement dit n'y est pas relaté, mais il y est prédit en l'an II d'un roi dont le bloc précédent, perdu, portait le nom. Chacun des trois premiers Thoutmès peut être envisagé ici; Yoyotte opte pour le père de la reine, Thoutmès Ier.

J. Custers

68651 YOYOTTE, Jean, Religion de l'Égypte ancienne, *École Pratique des Hautes Études. V^e section — Sciences religieuses. Annuaire.* Paris 76 (1968-1969), 1968, 108-121.

I. Suite de notre n° 67630, I;
II. Suite de notre n° 67630, II;
III. Exercices XXIV-XXIX de Gardiner, *Egyptian Grammar*;
IV. Rapports divers.

68652 YOYOTTE, Jean, Religion de l'Égypte ancienne, *in*: *Problèmes et méthodes d'histoire des religions.* Mélanges publiés par la Section des Sciences religieuses à l'occasion du centenaire de l'École Pratique des Hautes Études, Paris, Presses Universitaires, 1968, 79-85.

Report on the activities of the "étude de Religion de l'Égypte" by the E.P.H.E., in which the author stresses the fundamental unity of the Egyptian religion, the preference for the study of limited subjects above high speculations, and the importance of the study of the Greco-Roman temples.

68653 YOYOTTE, Jean, Religion de l'Égypte (Études pharaoniques). "Centre Wladimir Golénischeff", *École Pratique des Hautes Études. V^e section — Sciences religieuses. Annuaire*, Paris 76 (1968-1969), 1968, 267-269.

Suite de notre n° 67631.

68654 YOYOTTE, Jean, Une théorie étiologique des médecins égyptiens, *Kêmi* 18 (1968), 79-84.

Article compte rendu de notre n° 59572.
L'origine du *sèpton perittôma* ne serait donc pas dans la surabondance des aliments, mais dans la phase finale de la digestion (*sèpsis*). Une traduction nouvelle est donnée du Pap. Berlin 3038, 13 (3-7, cfr 11-14), passage important sur l'expansion des matières fécales dans le corps, à partir d'un

foyer d'infection. Quant aux *iadet* (ou *idw*), entités néfastes liées au temps, leurs contextes ne sont pas médicaux mais magiques; les *wḥdw* en diffèrent radicalement. M. Yoyotte estime le rôle des communications entre médecins égyptiens et étrangers, intenses aux temps présocratiques, spécialement en Asie Mineure, bien plus déterminant que dans la civilisation hellénistique, coloniale. *J. Custers*

68655 YOYOTTE, Jean, Les trésors des Pharaons. Les Hautes Époques. Le Nouvel Empire. Les Basses Époques. Introduction de Christiane Desroches Noblecourt, [Genève, Éditions d'Art Albert] Skira, [1968] (26.8 × 33.5 cm; XII + 260 p., 3 maps, 120 ill. [85 in colour]); rev. *BiOr* 26 (1969), 327-328 (H. de Meulenaere); *Bulletin critique du livre français* 24 (1969), 184 (anonymous); *Phoenix* 15 (1969), 238-239 (K. R. V[eenhof]).

The illustrations have been selected by John R. Harris, while the text is written by Jean Yoyotte.
Apart from an introduction the book is divided into three parts: Old and Middle Kingdom, New Kingdom, and the Later Periods, up to the Roman Empire.
The text, though throughout in connection with the illustrations, constitutes a description of the Egyptian cultural history. The author pays special attention to the later periods.
Index on p. 246-252, list of illustrations (with measures and museum numbers) on p. 253-258.
There are also published a Spanish version, an English: rev. *Arts Magazine*, May 1969, 12 (Henry G. Fischer); and a German: rev. *Universitas* 24 (1969), 1107-1108 (Hellmut Brunner).

68656 ŽÁBA, Z., Tesáno do kamene, psáno na papyrus, Praha, Nakladatelství Svoboda, 1968 (17 × 20 cm; 198 p., 40 ill. [16 in colours]).

"Carved in Stone, Written on Paper".
The author demonstrates in this book on ancient Egyptian literature its richness in genres presenting many specimens of original translations. New ideas and interpretations are advanced, *e.g.* where the author takes the so-called commemorative scarabs for actual beginnings of journalism, or where he compares one of the Siusirēʿ stories with Dante's division of the Netherworld in his *Inferno*, etc. *M. Verner*

68557 ŽABKAR, Louis V., A Study of the Ba Concept in Ancient Egyptian Texts, Chicago, Illinois, The University of Chicago Press, [1968] (17 × 24 cm; XIV + 163 p., 6 pl.) = The

Oriental Institute of the University of Chicago. Studies in Ancient Oriental Civilisation No 34; rev. *Acta orientalia academiae scientiarum hungaricae* 23 (1970), 248-249 (L. Kákosy); *BiOr* 27 (1970), 20-21 (Erik Hornung); *CdE* XLV, N° 89 (1970), 87-91 (A. Barucq); *JARCE* 8 (1969-1970), 86-87 (David Lorton); *JEA* 56 (1970), 227-228 (J. Gwyn Griffiths); *OLZ* 66 (1971), 132-135 (E. M. Wolf-Brinkmann).
Pr. $ 8

After summarizing in the introduction the opinions concerning the Ba of various scholars the author discusses in chapter I the relationship between the Ba and the gods in early as well as late sources. Chapter II deals with the king and the Ba, mainly though not exclusively, in the *Pyramid Texts*. Chapter III is devoted to the Ba in the *Coffin Texts*, chapter IV to the didactic literature and chapter V to the New Kingdom and the later periods.

In the summary (p. 160-163) the author states that the Ba originally denoted the manifestation of a deceased king or god, or, alternatively, the king or god himself in a state in which his power is manifest. In non-mortuary texts of the Middle and New Kingdom the Ba is found to apply primarily to the living king and the gods, while in the mortuary texts of these periods its meaning is predominantly that of the alter ego of the deceased. The Ba signifies a "Ganzheitsbegriff" rather than a "Teilbegriff", and does not belong exclusively to the "Diesseitsbegriffen". The translation "soul" is rejected; since there is no equivalent in our languages Žabkar suggests to leave Ba untranslated.

For another study of the same subject, though restricted to the older periods of the Egyptian history, see our number 68644.

ZANDEE, Jan, see our number 68397.

68658 ZAUZICH, Karl-Theodor, Die ägyptische Schreibertradition in Aufbau, Sprache und Schrift der demotischen Kaufverträge aus ptolemäischer Zeit, Band I. Text; Band II. Anmerkungen, Indices, Tabellen der Anlage, Wiesbaden, Otto Harrassowitz, 1968 (21 × 29.9 cm; Band I: [VII +] 241 p.; Band II: [II +] 96 p. [= p. 242-337], 4 loose tables) = Ägyptologische Abhandlungen herausgegeben von Wolfgang Helck und Eberhard Otto, Band 19; rev. *CdE* XLV, N° 89 (1970), 84-86 (Herman de Meulenaere); *Enchoria* 1 (1971), 69 (Heinz-Josef Thissen); *JEA* 56 (1970), 226-227 (G. R. Biggs); *Mundus* 6 (1970), 138-140 (Schafik Allam); *OLZ* 66 (1971), 350-351 (H. Brunner); *RdE* 21 (1969), 192-198 (Bernadette Menu); *ZDMG* 120 (1970), 1971, 329-332 (Dietrich Wildung).

The author studies the traditions of the Egyptian scribe in the Ptolemaic Period, particularly that of the *sh-knbt* (μονογράφος), the scribe responsible for drawing up the documents concerning sales and cessions.

To this purpose he closely examines (p. 9-128) 159 documents, 95 of which relating to sales and 64 to cessions. 112 of these documents come from Thebes, 26 from Edfu, 19 from Hermopolis, while smaller numbers come from a few other places. They include several papyri from the Louvre published long ago by Revillout. If no modern publication is available the author presents transliteration and translation. From these documents he draws up a list of the various types of formulation. A summary of this part on p. 125-128.

Zauzich further discusses the tradition in the language (129-156) and the writing (157-228) of the documents, illustrating the latter by 37 pages of tables containing facsimiles of representative words and names in Demotic script.

A general summary of the study on p. 229-230. In all three fields, construction, language and writing, there appear to have been characteristics differing in the various places, the clearest being those of Edfu. On account of the results it may be possible to suggest a place of origin for those papyri of which the provenance is unknown.

The second volume contains over 925 notes to the text, various extensive indexes, and four large tables.

68659 ZAYED, Abd el Hamid, Painted Wooden Stelae in the Cairo Museum, *RdE* 20 (1968), 149-170, with 10 pl.

Publication de quinze stèles en bois stuqué provenant de la nécropole thébaine, datables des XXIe-XXXe dynasties et ayant appartenu pour la plupart à des prêtres de Montou. De chacune est donnée une brève description comprenant la traduction des textes (hymnes) ainsi que de bonnes photographies, qui permettent à l'auteur de s'épargner la peine de les transcrire, car elles sont inscrites en hiéroglyphes linéaires facilement lisibles. *Ph. Derchain*

NECROLOGIES

68660 BLOK, Henri Peter: *Jaarboek der Leidse Universiteit 1968/1969*, 1968, 268-269, with portrait (A. E. Meeussen — J. Voorhoeve).

68661 BOTTI, Giuseppe: *CdE* XLIV, N° 88 (1969), 298-299 (B. van de Walle); *Rivista* 43 (1968), 379-382 (Sergio Donadoni); *ZÄS* 96,2 (1970), VI-VII, with portrait (Silvio Curto).

68662 LEIBOVITCH, Joseph: *CdE* XLIV, N° 88 (1969), 299-300 (Jacques Schwartz): *Israel Exploration Journal* 18 (1968), 133-134 (M. Prausnitz); *Sefunim* 2 (1968), 16 (R. Giveon).

68663 STOCK, Hanns: *AfO* 22 (1968/69), 219-220 (Wolfgang Helck); *MDAIK* 24 (1969), V-VIII, with portrait (W. Kaiser); *ZÄS* 95, 1 (1968), V-VI (H. W. Müller).